Talking

the

Winner's
Way

**92 LITTLE TRICKS
FOR BIG SUCCESS
IN BUSINESS AND PERSONAL
RELATIONSHIPS**

LEIL LOWNDES

MJF BOOKS
NEW YORK

Published by MJF Books
Fine Communications
322 Eighth Avenue
New York, NY 10001

Talking the Winner's Way
ISBN 1-56731-431-7
LC Control Number 00-136511

This edition published by arrangement with Contemporary Books, an
imprint of NTC/Contemporary Publishing Group, Inc.

Manufactured in the United States of America on acid-free paper
MJF Books and the MJF colophon are trademarks of Fine Creative Media,
Inc.

BG   11   10   9   8   7   6   5   4   3   2

⭐ Contents

⭐Having It *All*

HAVE YOU EVER ADMIRED those successful people who seem to have it all? You see them chatting confidently at business meetings, comfortably at social parties. They're the ones with the best jobs, the nicest spouses, the finest friends, the biggest bank accounts, the most fashionable zip codes.

But wait a minute! A lot of them aren't smarter than you. They're not more educated than you. They're not even better looking! So what is it? (Some people suspect they inherited it. Others say they married it, or were just plain lucky. Tell them to think again.) What it boils down to is their more skillful way of dealing with fellow human beings.

You see, nobody gets to the top alone. Over the years, people who seem to "have it all" have captured the hearts and conquered the minds of hundreds of others who helped boost them, rung by rung, to the top of whatever corporate or social ladder they chose.

Wanna-bes wandering around at the foot of the ladder often gaze up and grouse that the Big Boys and Big Girls at the top are snobs. When Big Players don't give them their friendship, love, or business, they call them "cliquish" or accuse them of belonging to an "old-boy network." Some grumble they hit their heads against a "glass ceiling."

The complaining Little Leaguers never realize the rejection was their own fault. They'll never know they blew the affair, the friendship, or the deal due to their *own* communications fumbles. Why don't they see it? Because some of the moves Big Winners make are so smooth, so subtle, it takes another Big Winner to recognize them.

The old boys—in the days when top management was, unfortunately, mainly old boys—complimented each other by saying, "Buddy, you ain't no accident." They bestowed this slang tribute with a tinge of jealousy when one old boy saw some sensitive act the other had executed.

Indeed, today the old (and not so old) boys and girls who run our country, our corporations, and our arts "ain't no accident." Each has a bag of tricks, a magic, a Midas touch that turns everything they do into success.

What's in their bag of tricks? You'll find a lot of things: There's a substance that solidifies friendships, a wizardry that wins minds, and a magic that makes people fall in love with them. There's also a quality that makes bosses hire and then promote, a characteristic that keeps clients coming back, and an asset that makes customers buy from them and not the competition. We all have a few of those tricks in our bags, some more than others. Those with a whole lot of them are Big Winners in life. *Talking the Winner's Way* gives you ninety-two of these little tricks used by Big Winners so you, too, can play the game to perfection and get whatever you want in life.

How the Techniques Were Developed

Many years ago, a drama teacher, exasperated at my bad acting in a college play, shouted, "No! No! Your body is belying your words. Every tiny movement, every body position," he howled, "divulges your private thoughts. Your face can make seven thousand different expressions, and each exposes precisely who you are and what you are thinking at any particular moment." Then he said something I'll never forget: "And your body! The way you *move* is your autobiography in motion."

How right he was! On the stage of real life, every physical move you make subliminally tells everyone in eyeshot the story of your life. Dogs hear sounds our ears can't detect. Bats see shapes in the darkness that elude our eyes. And people make moves that are beneath human consciousness but have tremendous power to attract or repel. Every smile, every frown, every syllable you utter, every arbitrary choice of word that passes between your lips, can draw others toward you, or make them want to run away.

Men, did your gut feeling ever tell you to jump ship on a deal? Women, did your women's intuition make you accept or reject an offer? On a conscious level, we may not be aware of what the hunch is. But like the ear of the dog or the eye of the bat, the elements that make up subliminal sentiments are very real.

Imagine, please, two humans in a complex box wired with circuits to record all the signals flowing between the two. As many as 10,000 units of information flow per second. "Probably the lifetime efforts of roughly half the adult population of the United States would be required to sort the units in one hour's interaction between two subjects," a University of Pennsylvania communications authority estimates.[1]

With the zillions of subtle actions and reactions zapping back and forth between two human beings, can we come up with concrete techniques to make our every communication clear, confident, credible, and charismatic?

Determined to find the answer, I read practically every book written on communications skills, charisma, and chemistry between people. I explored hundreds of studies conducted around the world on what qualities made up leadership and credibility. Intrepid social scientists left no stone unturned in their quest to find the formula. For example, optimistic Chinese researchers, hoping charisma might be in the diet, went so far as to compare the relationship of personality type to the catecholamine level in subjects' urine.[2] Needless to say, their thesis was soon shelved!

Most of the studies simply confirmed Dale Carnegie's 1936 classic, *How to Win Friends and Influence People*.[3] His wisdom for the ages said success lay in smiling, showing interest in other people, and making them feel good about themselves. "That's no surprise," I thought. It's as true today as it was over sixty years ago.

So if Dale Carnegie and hundreds of others since offer the same astute advice, why do any of us lack the right stuff to win friends and influence people?

Suppose a sage told you, "When in China, speak Chinese"—but gave you no language lessons? Dale Carnegie and many communications experts are like that sage. They tell us *what* to do, but not *how* to do it. In today's sophisticated world, it's not enough to say "smile" or "give sincere compliments." Cynical business people today see more subtleties in your smile, more complexities in your compliment. Accomplished or attractive people are surrounded by smiling sycophants feigning interest and fawning all over them. Prospects are tired of salespeople who say, "The suit looks great on you," when their fingers are caressing cash register keys. Women are wary of suitors who say, "You are beautiful," when the bedroom door is in view.

The world is a very different place than it was in 1936, and we need a new formula for success. To find it, I observed the superstars of today. I explored techniques used by top salespeople to close the sale, speakers to convince, clergy to convert, performers to engross, sex symbols to seduce, and athletes to win.

I found concrete building blocks to the elusive qualities that lead to their success.

Then I broke them down into easily digestible, news-you-can-use techniques. I gave each a name that will quickly come to mind when you find yourself in a communications conundrum. As I developed the techniques, I began sharing them with audiences around the country. Participants in my communications seminars gave me their ideas. My clients, many of them CEOs of Fortune 500 companies, enthusiastically offered their observations.

When I was in the presence of the most successful and beloved leaders, I analyzed their body language, their facial expressions. I listened carefully to their casual conversations, their timing, and their choice of words. I watched as they dealt with their families, their friends, their associates, and their adversaries. Every time I detected a little nip of magic in their communicating, I asked them to pluck it out with tweezers and expose it to the bright light of consciousness. We analyzed it together, and I then turned it into a technique others could duplicate and profit from.

In this book are my findings and the strokes of some of those very effective folks. Some are subtle. Some are surprising. But all are achievable. When you master them, everyone from new acquaintances to family, friends, and business associates will happily open their hearts, their homes, their companies, even their wallets to give you whatever they can.

There's a bonus. As you sail through life with your new communications skills, you'll look back and see some very happy givers smiling in your wake.

There are two kinds of people in this life:
Those who walk into a room and say,
"Well, here I am!"
And those who walk in and say,
"Ahh, there you are."

PART ONE

You Only Have Ten Seconds to Show You're a Somebody

The Incredible, Inescapable, Unique Essence of You

The moment two humans lay eyes on each other has awesome potency. The first sight of you is a brilliant holograph. It burns its way into your new acquaintance's eyes and can stay emblazoned in his or her memory forever.

Artists are sometimes able to capture this quicksilver, fleeting emotional response. I have a friend, Robert Grossman, an accomplished caricature artist who draws regularly for *Forbes*, *Newsweek*, *Sports Illustrated*, *Rolling Stone*, and other popular publications. Bob has a unique gift for capturing not only the physical appearance of his subjects, but zeroing in on the essence of their personalities. The bodies and souls of hundreds of luminaries radiate from his sketch pad. One glance at his caricatures of famous people and you can see, for instance, the insecure arrogance of Madonna, the imperiousness of Newt Gingrich, the bitchiness of Leona Helmsley.

Sometimes at a party, Bob will do a quick sketch on a cocktail napkin of a guest. Hovering over Bob's shoulder, the onlookers gasp as they watch their friend's image and essence materialize before their eyes. When he's finished drawing, he puts his pen down and hands the napkin to the subject. Often a puzzled look comes over the subject's face. He or she usually mumbles some politeness like, "Well, er, that's great. But it really isn't me."

The crowd's convincing crescendo of *"Oh yes it is!"* drowns the subject out and squelches any lingering doubt. The confused subject is left to stare back at the world's view of himself or herself in the napkin.

Once when I was visiting Bob's studio, I asked him how he could capture people's personalities so well. He said, "It's simple. I just look at them."

"No," I asked, "How do you capture their *personalities*? Don't you have to do a lot of research about their lifestyle, their history?"

"No, I told you, Leil, I just look at them."

"Huh?"

He went on to explain, "Almost every facet of people's personalities is evident from their appearance, their posture, the way they move. For instance . . ." he said, calling me over to a file where he kept his caricatures of political figures.

"See," Bob said, pointing to angles on various presidential body parts, "here's the boyishness of Clinton," showing me his half smile; "the awkwardness of George Bush," pointing to his shoulder angle; "the charm of Reagan," putting his finger on the ex-president's smiling eyes; "the shiftiness of Nixon," pointing to the furtive tilt of his head. Digging a little deeper into his file, he pulled out Franklin Delano Roosevelt and, pointing to the nose high in the air, "Here's the pride of FDR." It's all in the face and the body.

First impressions are indelible. Why? Because in our fast-paced information-overload world of multiple stimuli bombarding us every second, people's heads are spinning. They must form quick judgments to make sense of the world and get on with what they have to do. So, whenever people meet you, they take an instant mental snapshot. That image of you becomes the data they deal with for a very long time.

Your Body Shrieks Before Your Lips Can Speak

Is their data accurate? Amazingly enough, yes. Even before your lips part and the first syllable escapes, the essence of YOU has already axed its way into their brains. The way you look and the way you move is more than 80 percent of someone's first impression of you. Not one word need be spoken.

I've lived and worked in countries where I didn't speak the native language. Yet, without one understandable syllable spoken between us, the years proved my first impressions were on target. Whenever I met new colleagues, I could tell instantly how friendly they felt toward me, how confident they were, and approximately how much stature they had in the company. I could sense, just from seeing them move, which were the heavyweights and which were the welterweights.

I have no extrasensory skill. You'd know, too. How? Because before you have had time to process a rational thought, you get a sixth sense about someone. Studies have shown emotional reactions occur even *before* the brain has had time to register what's causing that reaction.[4] Thus the moment someone looks at you, he or she experiences a massive hit, the impact of which lays the groundwork for the entire relationship. Bob told me he captures that first hit in creating his caricatures.

Deciding to pursue my own agenda for *Talking the Winner's Way*, I asked, "Bob, if you wanted to portray somebody really cool—you know, intelligent, strong, charismatic, principled, fascinating, caring, interested in other people . . ."

"Easy," Bob interrupted. He knew precisely what I was getting at. "Just give 'em great posture, a heads-up look, a confident smile, and a direct gaze." It's the ideal image for somebody who's a Somebody.

How to Look Like a Somebody

A friend of mine, Karen, is a highly respected professional in the home-furnishings business. Her husband is an equally big name in the communications field. They have two small sons.

Whenever Karen is at a home-furnishings industry event, everyone pays deference to her. She's a Very Important Person in that world. Her colleagues at conventions jostle for position just to be seen casually chatting with her and, they hope, be photographed rubbing elbows with her for industry bibles like *Home Furnishings Executive* and *Furniture World*.

Yet, Karen complains, when she accompanies her husband to communications functions, she might as well be a nobody. When she takes her kids to school functions, she's just another mom. She once asked me, "Leil, how can I stand out from the crowd so people who don't know me will approach me and at least *assume* I'm an interesting person?" The techniques in this section accomplish precisely that. When you use the next nine techniques, you will come across as a special person to everyone you meet. You will stand out as a Somebody in whatever crowd you find yourself in, even if it's not your crowd.

Let's start with your smile.

⭐ 1 ⭐ The Flooding Smile

Smile Quick? Or Smile *Special*?

In 1936, one of Dale Carnegie's six musts in *How to Win Friends and Influence People* was SMILE! His edict has been echoed each decade by practically every communications guru who ever put pen to paper or mouth to microphone. However, at the turn of the millennium, it's high time we reexamine the role of the smile in high-level human relations. When you dig deeper into Dale's dictum, you'll find a 1936 quick smile doesn't always work. Especially nowadays.

The old-fashioned instant grin carries no weight with today's sophisticated crowd. Look at world leaders, negotiators, and corporate giants. Not a smiling sycophant among them. Key Players in all walks of life enrich their smile so, when it does erupt, it has more potency and the world smiles with them.

Researchers have catalogued dozens of different types of smiles. They range from the tight rubber band of a trapped liar to the soft squishy smile of a tickled infant. There are warm smiles and cold smiles. There are real smiles and fake smiles. (You've seen plenty of those plastered on the faces of friends who say they're "delighted you decided to drop by," and presidential candidates visiting your city who say they're "thrilled to be in, uh . . .

uh . . .") Big Winners know their smile is one of their most powerful weapons, so they've fine-tuned it for maximum impact.

How to Fine-Tune Your Smile

I have an old college friend named Missy who, just last year, took
over her family business, a Midwestern company supplying corrugated boxes to manufacturers. One day she called saying she
was coming to New York to court new clients and she invited me
to dinner with several of her prospects. I was looking forward to
once again seeing my friend's quicksilver smile and hearing her
contagious laugh. Missy was an incurable giggler, and that was
part of her charm.

When her Dad passed away last year, she told me she was
taking over the business. I thought Missy's personality was a little bubbly to be a CEO in a tough business. But, hey, what do I
know about the corrugated box biz?

She, I, and three of her potential clients met in the cocktail
lounge of a midtown restaurant and, as we led them into the dining room, Missy whispered in my ear, "Please call me Melissa
tonight."

"Of course," I winked back, "not many company presidents
are called Missy!" Soon after the maitre d' seated us, I began noticing Melissa was a very different woman from the giggling girl I'd
known in college. She was just as charming. She smiled as much
as ever. Yet something was different. I couldn't quite put my finger
on it.

Although she was still effervescent, I had the distinct impression everything Melissa said was more insightful and sincere. She
was responding with genuine warmth to her prospective clients,
and I could tell they liked her, too. I was thrilled because my
friend was scoring a knockout that night. By the end of the
evening, Melissa had three big new clients.

Afterward, alone with her in the cab, I said, "Missy, you've
really come a long way since you took over the company. Your
whole personality has developed, well, a really cool, sharp
corporate edge."

"Uh uh, only one thing has changed," she said.

"What's that?"

"My smile," she said.

"Your *what?*" I asked incredulously.

"My smile," she repeated as though I hadn't heard her. "You see," she said, with a distant look coming into her eyes, "when Dad got sick and knew in a few years I'd have to take over the business, he sat me down and had a life-changing conversation with me. I'll never forget his words. Dad said, 'Missy, Honey, remember that old song, 'I Loves Ya, Honey, But Yer Feet's Too Big?' Well, if you're going to make it big in the box business, let me say, 'I loves ya, Honey, but your smile's too quick.'

"He then brought out a yellowed newspaper article quoting a study he'd been saving to show me when the time was right. It concerned women in business. The study showed women who were slower to smile in corporate life were perceived as more credible."

As Missy talked, I began to think about women like Margaret Thatcher, Indira Gandhi, Golda Meir, Madeleine Albright, and other powerful women of their ilk. True, they were not known for their quick smiles.

Missy continued, "The study went on to say a big, warm smile is an asset. But *only* when it comes a little slower, because then it has more credibility." From that moment on, Missy explained, she gave clients and business associates her big smile. However, she trained her lips to erupt more slowly. Thus her smile appeared more sincere and personalized for the recipient.

That was it! Missy's slower smile gave her personality a richer, deeper, more sincere cachet. Though the delay was less than a second, the recipients of her beautiful big smile felt it was special, and just for them.

I decided to do more research on the smile. When you're in the market for shoes, you begin to look at everyone's feet. When you decide to change your hairstyle, you look at everyone's haircut. Well, for several months, I became a steady smile watcher. I watched smiles on the street. I watched smiles on TV. I watched the smiles of politicians, the clergy, corporate giants, and world

leaders. My findings? Amidst the sea of flashing teeth and part-
ing lips, I discovered the people perceived to have the most credibility and integrity were just ever so slower to smile. Then, when
they did, their smiles seemed to seep into every crevice of their
faces and envelop them like a slow flood. Thus I call the following technique *The Flooding Smile.*

TECHNIQUE #1:
THE FLOODING SMILE

Don't flash an immediate smile when you greet
someone, as though anyone who walked into your line
of sight would be the beneficiary. Instead, look at the
other person's face for a second. Pause. Soak in their
persona. Then let a big, warm, responsive smile flood
over your face and overflow into your eyes. It will
engulf the recipient like a warm wave. The split-second
delay convinces people your flooding smile is genuine
and only for them.

Let us now travel but a few inches north to two of the most
powerful communications tools you possess, your eyes.

2 Sticky Eyes

How to Detonate Those Grenades Resting on Your Nose

It's only a slight exaggeration to say Helen of Troy could sink ships with her eyes and Davy Crockett could stare down a bear. Your eyes are personal grenades that have the power to detonate people's emotions. Just as martial arts masters register their fists as lethal weapons, you can register your eyes as psychological lethal weapons when you master the following eye-contact techniques.

Big Players in the game of life look beyond the conventional wisdom that teaches "Keep good eye contact." For one, they understand that to certain suspicious or insecure people, intense eye contact can be a virulent intrusion.

When I was growing up, my family had a Haitian housekeeper whose fantasies were filled with witches, warlocks, and black magic. Zola refused to be left alone in a room with Louie, my Siamese cat. "Louie looks right through me—sees my soul," she'd whisper to me fearfully.

In some cultures, intense eye contact is sorcery. In others, staring at someone can be threatening or disrespectful. Realizing this, Big Players in the international scene prefer to pack a book on cultural body-language differences in their carry-on rather than a Berlitz phrase book. In our culture, however, Big Winners know exaggerated eye contact can be extremely advantageous, especially between the sexes. In business, even when romance is not in the picture, strong eye contact packs a powerful wallop between men and women.

A Boston center conducted a study to learn the precise effect.[5] The researchers asked opposite-sex individuals to have a two-minute casual conversation. They tricked half their subjects into maintaining intense eye contact by directing them to count the number of times their partner blinked. They gave the other half of the subjects no special eye-contact directions for the chat.

When they questioned the subjects afterward, the unsuspecting blinkers reported significantly higher feelings of respect and fondness for their colleagues who, unbeknownst to them, had simply been counting their blinks.

I've experienced the closeness intense eye contact engenders with a stranger firsthand. Once, when giving a seminar to several hundred people, one woman's face in the crowd caught my attention. The participant's appearance was not particularly unique. Yet she became the focus of my attention throughout my talk. Why? Because not for one moment did she take her eyes off my face. Even when I finished making a point and was silent, her eyes stayed hungrily on my face. I sensed she couldn't wait to savor the next insight to spout from my lips. I loved it! Her concentration and obvious fascination inspired me to remember stories and make important points I'd long forgotten.

Right after my talk, I resolved to seek out this new friend who was so enthralled by my speech. As people were leaving the hall, I quickly sidled up behind my big fan. "Excuse me," I said. My fan kept walking. "Excuse me," I repeated a tad louder. My admirer didn't vary her pace as she continued out the door. I followed her into the corridor and tapped her shoulder gently. This time she whirled around with a surprised look on her face. I mumbled some excuse about my appreciating her concentration on my talk and wanting to ask her a few questions.

"Did you, uh, get much out of the seminar?" I ventured.

"Well, not really," she answered candidly. "I had difficulty understanding what you were saying because you were walking around on the platform facing different directions."

In a heartbeat, I understood. The woman was hearing impaired. I did not captivate her as I had suspected. She was not intrigued by my talk as I had hoped. The only reason she kept her eyes glued on my face was because she was struggling to read my lips!

Nevertheless, her eye contact had given me such pleasure and inspiration during my talk that, tired as I was, I asked her to join me for coffee. I spent the next hour recapping my entire seminar just for her. Powerful stuff this eye contact.

Sticky Eyes Also Means Intelligent Eyes

There is yet another argument for intense eye contact. In addition to awakening feelings of respect and affection, maintaining strong eye contact gives you the impression of being an intelligent and abstract thinker. Because abstract thinkers integrate incoming data more easily than concrete thinkers, they can continue looking into someone's eyes even during the silences. Their thought processes are not distracted by peering into their partner's peepers.[6]

Back to our valiant psychologists. Yale researchers, thinking they had the unswerving truth about eye contact, conducted another study which, they assumed, would confirm "the more eye contact, the more positive feelings." This time, they directed subjects to deliver a personally revealing monologue. They asked the listeners to react with a sliding scale of eye contact while their partners talked.

The results? All went as expected when women told their personal stories to women. Increased eye contact encouraged feelings of intimacy. But, whoops, it wasn't so with the men. Some men felt hostile when stared at too long by another man. Other men felt threatened. Some few even suspected their partner was more interested than he should be and wanted to slug him.

Your partner's emotional reaction to your profound gaze has a biological base. When you look intently at someone, it increases their heartbeat and shoots an adrenalinelike substance gushing through their veins.[7] This is the same physical reaction people have when they start to fall in love. And when you consciously increase your eye contact, even during normal business or social interaction, people will feel they have captivated you.

Men talking to women and women talking to men or women: use the following technique, which I call *Sticky Eyes*, for the joy of the recipient—and for your own advantage. (Guys, I'll have a man-to-man modification of this technique for you in a moment.)

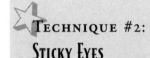

TECHNIQUE #2:
STICKY EYES

Pretend your eyes are glued to your Conversation Partner's with sticky warm taffy. Don't break eye contact *even after* he or she has finished speaking. When you must look away, do it ever so slowly, reluctantly, stretching the gooey taffy until the tiny string finally breaks.

What About Guys' Eyes?

Now gentlemen: when talking to men, you, too, can use *Sticky Eyes*. Just make them a little *less* sticky when discussing personal matters with other men, lest your listener feel threatened or misinterpret your intentions. But do increase your eye contact slightly more than normal with men on day-to-day communications—and *a lot* more when talking to women. It broadcasts a visceral message of comprehension and respect.

I have a friend, Sammy, a salesman who unwittingly comes across as an arrogant chap. He doesn't mean to, but sometimes his brusque manner makes it look like he's running roughshod over people's feelings.

Once while we were having dinner together in a restaurant, I told him about the *Sticky Eyes* technique. I guess he took it to heart. When the waiter came over, Sammy, uncharacteristically, instead of bluntly blurting out his order with his nose in the menu, looked at the waiter. He smiled, gave his order for the appetizer, and kept his eyes on the waiter's for an extra second before looking down again at the menu to choose the main dish. I can't tell you how different Sammy seemed to me just then! He came across as a sensitive and caring man, and all it took was two extra seconds of eye contact. I saw the effect it had on the waiter, too. We received exceptionally gracious service the rest of the evening.

A week later Sammy called me and said, "Leil, *Sticky Eyes* has changed my life. I've been following it to a T. With women, I make my eyes *real* sticky, and with men slightly sticky. And now everybody's treating me with such deference. I think it's part of the reason I've made more sales this week than all last month!"

If you deal with customers or clients in your professional life, *Sticky Eyes* is a definite boon to your bottom line. To most people in our culture, profound eye contact signals trust, knowledge, an "I'm here for you" attitude.

Let's carry *Sticky Eyes* one step further. Like a potent medicine that has the power to kill or cure, the next eye-contact technique has the potential to captivate or annihilate.

3 Epoxy Eyes

Bring on the Big Guns

Now we haul in the heavy eyeball artillery: *very* sticky eyes or superglue eyes. Let's call them *Epoxy Eyes*. Big Bosses use Epoxy Eyes to evaluate employees. Police investigators use *Epoxy Eyes* to intimidate suspected criminals. And clever Romeos use *Epoxy Eyes* to make women fall in love with them. (If romance is your goal, *Epoxy Eyes* is a proven aphrodisiac.)

The *Epoxy Eyes* technique takes at least three people to pull off—you, your target, and one other person. Here's how it works: Usually, when you're chatting with two or more people, you gaze at the person who is speaking. However, the *Epoxy Eyes* technique suggests you concentrate on the listener—your target—rather than the speaker. This slightly disorients Target and he or she silently asks, "Why is this person looking at *me* instead of the speaker?" Target senses you are extremely interested in his or her reactions. This can be beneficial in certain business situations when it is appropriate that you judge the listener.

Human resources professionals often use *Epoxy Eyes*, not as a technique, but because they are sincerely interested in a prospective employee's reaction to certain ideas being presented. Attorneys, bosses, police investigators, psychologists, and others who must examine subjects' reactions also use *Epoxy Eyes* for analytical purposes.

When you use *Epoxy Eyes*, it sends out signals of interest blended with complete confidence in yourself. But because Epoxy Eyes puts you in a position of evaluating or judging someone else, you must be careful. Don't overdo it or you could come across as arrogant and brazen.

TECHNIQUE #3:
EPOXY EYES

This brazen technique packs a powerful punch. Watch your target person even when someone else is talking. No matter who is speaking, keep looking at the man or woman you want to impact.

Sometimes using full *Epoxy Eyes* is too potent, so here is a gentler, yet effective, form: Watch the speaker but let your glance bounce to your target each time the speaker finishes a point. This way Mr. or Ms. Target still feels you are intrigued by his or her reactions, yet there is relief from the intensity.

When Love Is on Your Mind

If romance is on the horizon, *Epoxy Eyes* transmits yet another message. It says, "I can't take my eyes off you" or "I only have eyes for you." Anthropologists have dubbed eyes "the initial organ of romance" because studies show intense eye contact plays havoc with our heartbeat.[8] It also releases a druglike substance into our nervous system called *phenylethylamine*. Since this is the hormone detected in the human body during erotic excitement, intense eye contact can be a turn-on.

Men, *Epoxy Eyes* is extremely effective on women—*if* they find you attractive. The lady interprets her nervous reaction to your untoward gaze as budding infatuation. If she does *not* like you, however, your *Epoxy Eyes* are downright obnoxious. (Never use *Epoxy Eyes* on strangers in public settings or you could get arrested!)

Do you remember the lyrics to the old Shirley Bassey song?

> The minute you walked in the joint, I could see
> you were a man of distinction—a real big spender.
> Good looking, so refined. Say wouldn't you
> like to know what's going on in my mind?

The goal of this first section is not to make you look like a real big spender. Rather it is to give you the cachet of a real big Somebody the moment people lay eyes on you. To that end, we now explore the most important technique to make you look like a Very Important Person.

4 ⭐ Hang by Your Teeth

"The Minute You Walked in the Joint, I Knew You Were a Real Big Winner"

When the doctor smacks your knee with that nasty little hammer, your foot jerks forward. Thus the phrase *knee-jerk reaction*. Your body has another instinctive reaction. When a big jolt of happiness hits your heart and you feel like a Winner, your head jerks up automatically and you throw your shoulders back. A smile frames your lips and softens your eyes.

This is the look Winners have constantly. They stand with assurance. They move with confidence. They smile softly with pride. No doubt about it! Good posture symbolizes you are a man or woman who is used to being on top.

Obviously millions of mothers sticking their knuckles between their kids' shoulder blades, and trillions of teachers telling students, "Stand up straight!" hasn't done the trick. We are a nation of slouchers. We need a technique more stern than teachers, more persuasive than parents, to make us stand like a Somebody.

In one profession, perfect posture, perfect equilibrium, perfect balance is not only desirable—it's a matter of life and death.

One false move, one slump of the shoulders, one hangdog look, can mean curtains for the high-wire acrobat.

I'll never forget the first time Mama took me to the circus. When seven men and women raced into the center ring, the crowd rose as though they were all joined at the hips. They cheered with one thunderous voice. Mama pressed her lips against my ear and reverently whispered these were the Great Wallendas, the only troupe in the world to perform the seven-person pyramid without a net.

In an instant, the crowd became hushed. Not a cough or a Coke slurp was heard in the big top as Karl and Herman Wallenda shouted cues in German to their trusting relatives. The family meticulously and majestically ascended into the position of a human pyramid. They then balanced precariously on a thin wire hundreds of feet above the hard dirt with no net between them and sudden death. The vision was unforgettable.

To me, equally unforgettable was the beauty and grace of the seven Wallendas racing into the center of the big top to take their bows. Each perfectly aligned—head high, shoulders back—standing so tall it still didn't seem like their feet were touching the ground. Every muscle in their bodies defined pride, success, and their joy of being alive. (Still!) Here is a visualization technique to get your body looking like a Winner who is in the habit of feeling that pride, success, and joy of being alive.

Your Posture Is Your Biggest Success Barometer

Imagine you are a world-renowned acrobat, master of the iron-jaw act waiting in the wings of the Ringling Bros. and Barnum & Bailey circus. Soon you will dart into the center ring to captivate the crowd with the precision and balance of your body.

Before walking through any door—the door to your office, a party, a meeting, even your kitchen—picture a leather bit hanging by a cable from the frame. It is swinging just an inch higher than your head. As you pass through the door, throw your head back and chomp on the imaginary dental grip which first pulls your cheeks back into a smile, and then lifts you up. As you ascend high above the gasping crowd, your body is stretched into perfect alignment—head high, shoulders back, torso out of hips, feet weightless. At the zenith of the tent, you spin like a graceful top to the amazement and admiration of the crowd craning their necks to watch you. Now you look like a Somebody.

One day, to test *Hang by Your Teeth*, I decided to count how many times I walked through a doorway. Sixty times, even at home. You calculate: twice out your front door, twice in, six times to the bathroom, eight times to the kitchen, and through countless doors at your office. It adds up. Visualize anything sixty times a day and it becomes a habit! Habitual good posture is the first mark of a Big Winner.

TECHNIQUE #4:
HANG BY YOUR TEETH

Visualize a circus iron-jaw bit hanging from the frame of every door you walk through. Take a bite and, with it firmly between your teeth, let it swoop you to the peak of the big top. When you *Hang by Your Teeth*, every muscle is stretched into perfect posture position.

You are now ready to float into the room to captivate the crowd or close the sale (or maybe just settle for looking like the most important Somebody in the room).

You now have all the basics Bob the artist needs to portray you as a Big Winner. Like he said, "great posture, a heads-up look, a confident smile, and a direct gaze." The ideal image for somebody who's a Somebody.

Now lets put the whole act into motion. It's time to turn your attention outward to your Conversation Partner. Use the next two techniques to make him or her feel like a million.

⭐5 The Big-Baby Pivot

"Well, How Do You Like Me So Far?"

Remember the old joke? The comic comes onstage and the first words out of his mouth are, "Well, how do you like me so far?" The audience always cracks up. Why? Because we all silently ask that question. Whenever we meet someone, we know, consciously or subconsciously, how they're reacting to us.

Do they look at us? Do they smile? Do they lean toward us? Do they somehow recognize how wonderful and special we are? We *like* those people. They have good taste. Or do they turn away, obviously unimpressed by our magnificence. The cretins!

Two people getting to know each other are like little puppies sniffing each other out. We don't have tails that wag or hair that bristles. But we do have eyes that narrow or widen. And hands that flash knuckles or subconsciously soften in the palms-up "I submit" position. We have dozens of other involuntary reactions that take place in the first few moments of togetherness.

Attorneys conducting voir dire are exquisitely aware of this. They pay close attention to your instinctive body reactions. They watch to see how fully you are facing them and just how far forward or back you're leaning while answering their questions. They check out your hands. Are they softly open, palms up, signifying acceptance of the ideas they're expressing? Or are you making a slight fist, knuckles out, signaling rejection? They scrutinize your face for the split seconds you break eye contact when discussing relevant subjects like your feelings on big awards for damages, or the death penalty. Sometimes attorneys bring along a legal assistant whose sole job is to sit on the sidelines and take precise note of your every fidget.

An interesting aside: trial lawyers often choose women to do this twitch-and-turn spying job because, traditionally, females are sharper observers of subtle body cues than males. Women, more sensitive to emotions than men, often ask their husbands, "Is something bothering you, Honey?" (These supersensitive women accuse their husbands of being so insensitive to emotions that they wouldn't notice anything is wrong until their neckties are drenched in her tears.)

The attorney and the assistant then review your "score" on the dozens of subconscious signals you flashed. Depending on their tally, you could find yourself on jury duty or twiddling your thumbs back in the juror's waiting room.

Trial lawyers are so conscious of body language that, in the 1960s during the famous trial of the Chicago Seven, defense attorney William Kuntsler actually made a legal objection to Judge Julius Hoffman's posture. During the summation by the prosecution, Judge Hoffman leaned forward which, accused Kuntsler, sent a message to the jury of attention and interest. During his defense summation, complained Kuntsler, Judge Hoffman leaned back, sending the jury a subliminal message of disinterest.

You're on Trial—and You Only Have Ten Seconds!

Like attorneys deciding whether they want you on their case, everybody you meet makes a subconscious judgment on whether they want you in their lives. They base their verdict greatly on the same signals, your body-language answer to their unspoken question, "Well, how do you like me so far?"

The first few moments of your reactions set the stage upon which the entire relationship will be played out. If you ever want anything from the new acquaintance, your unspoken answer to their unspoken question, "How do you like me so far?" must be, "Wow! I *really* like you."

When a little four-year-old feels bashful, he slumps, puts his arms up in front of his chest, steps back, and hides behind mommy's skirt. However, when little Johnny sees daddy come home, he runs up to him, he smiles, his eyes get wide, and he opens his arms for a hug. A loving child's body is like a tiny flower bud unfolding to the sunshine.

Twenty, thirty, forty, fifty years of life on earth make little difference. When forty-year-old Johnny is feeling timid, he slumps and folds his arms in front of his chest. When he wants to reject a salesman or business colleague, he turns away and closes him off with a myriad of body signals. However, when welcoming his loved one home after an absence, big Johnny opens his body to her like a giant daffodil spreading its petals to the sun after a rainstorm.

Respond to the Hidden Infant

Once I was at a corporate star-studded party with an attractive recently divorced friend of mine. Carla had been a copywriter with one of the leading advertising agencies which, like so many companies then, had downsized. My girlfriend was both out of work and out of a relationship.

At this particular party, the pickings for Carla were good, both personally and professionally. Several times as Carla and I stood talking, one good-looking corporate male beast or another would find himself within a few feet of us. More often than not, one of these desirable males would flash his teeth at Carla. She sometimes graced the tentatively courting male with a quick smile over her shoulder. But then she'd turn back to our mundane conversation as though she were hanging on my every word. I knew she was trying not to look anxious, but inside Carla was crying out, "Why doesn't he come speak to us?"

Right after one prize corporate Big Cat smiled but, due to Carla's minimal reaction, wandered back into the social jungle, I had to say, "Carla, do you know who that was? He's the head of the Young & Rubicam in Paris. They're looking for copywriters willing to relocate. *And* he's single!" Carla moaned.

Just then we heard a little voice down by Carla's left knee. "Hello!" We looked down simultaneously. Little five-year-old Willie, the hostess's adorable young son, was tugging on Carla's skirt, obviously craving attention.

"Well, well, well," Carla cried out, a big smile erupting all over her face. Carla turned toward him. Carla kneeled down. Carla touched little Willie's elbow. And Carla crooned, "Well, hello there, Willie. How are you enjoying mommy's nice party?"

Little Willie beamed.

When little Willie finally trundled off to tug on the garments of the next group of potential attention givers, Carla and I returned to our grown-up conversing. During our chat, corporate beasts continued to stalk Carla with their eyes. And Carla continued casting half smiles at them. She was obviously disappointed none of them were making a further approach. I had to bite my tongue. Finally, when I felt it was going to bleed from the pressure of my teeth, I said, "Carla, have you been noticing that four or five men have come over and smiled at you."

"Yes," Carla whispered, her eyes darting nervously around the room lest anyone overhear us.

"And you've been giving them little half smiles," I continued.

"Yes," she murmured, now confused at my question.

"Remember when little Willie came up and tugged on your skirt? Do you recall how you smiled that beautiful big smile of yours, turned toward him, and welcomed him into our grown-up conversation?"

"Yee-es," she answered haltingly.

"Well, I have a request, Carla. The next man who smiles at you, I want you to give him that same big smile you gave Willie. I want you to turn toward him just like you did then. Maybe even reach out and touch his arm like you did Willie's, and then welcome him into our conversation."

"Oh Leil, I couldn't do that."

"Carla, do it!" Sure enough, within a few minutes, another attractive man wandered our way and smiled. Carla played her role to perfection. She flashed her beautiful teeth, turned fully toward him, and said, "Hello, come join us." He wasted no time accepting Carla's invitation.

After a few moments, I excused myself. Neither noticed my departure because they were in animated conversation. The last glimpse I had of my friend at the party was her floating out the door on the arm of her new friend.

Just then the technique I call the *Big-Baby Pivot* was born. It is a skill that will help you win whatever your heart desires from whatever type of beasts you encounter in the social or corporate jungle.

TECHNIQUE #5:
THE BIG-BABY PIVOT

Give everyone you meet the *Big-Baby Pivot*. The instant the two of you are introduced, reward your new acquaintance. Give the warm smile, the total-body turn, and the undivided attention you would give a tiny tyke who crawled up to your feet, turned a precious face up to yours, and beamed a big toothless grin. Pivoting 100 percent toward New Person shouts "I think you are very, very special."

Remember, deep inside *everyone* is a big baby rattling the crib, wailing out for recognition of how very special he or she is.

The next technique reinforces their suspicion that they are, indeed, the center of the universe.

6 Hello Old Friend

The Secret to Making People Like You

A very wise man with the funny name of Zig[9] once told me, "People don't care how much you know until they know how much you care . . . about them." Zig Ziglar is right. The secret to making people like you is showing how much you like *them*!

Your body is a twenty-four-hour broadcasting station revealing to anyone within eyeshot precisely how you feel at any given moment. Even if your *Hang by Your Teeth* posture is gaining their respect, your *Flooding Smile* and *Big-Baby Pivot* are making them feel special, and your *Sticky Eyes* are capturing their hearts and minds, the rest of your body can reveal any incongruence. Every inch—from the crinkle of your forehead to the position of your feet—must give a command performance if you want to effectively present an "I care about you" attitude.

Unfortunately, when meeting someone, our brains are in overdrive. Remember Shakespeare's Julius Caesar? He said of Cassius, he "has a lean and hungry look . . . he thinks too much . . . such men are dangerous." So it is with our brains when conversing with a new acquaintance. Our brains become lean. (Some of us are fighting off shyness. Others are frantically sizing up the situation.) And hungry (we're deciding what, if anything, we want from this potential relationship). So we think too much instead of responding with candid, unself-conscious friendliness. Such actions are dangerous to impending friendship, love, or commerce.

When our bodies are shooting off 10,000 bullets of stimuli every second, a few shots are apt to misfire and reveal shyness or hidden hostility. We need a technique to assure every shot aims right at the heart of our subject. We need to trick our bodies into reacting perfectly.

To find it, let's explore the only time we *don't* need to worry about any shyness or negativity slipping out through our body language. It's when we feel none. That happens when we're chatting with close friends. When we see someone we love or feel completely comfortable with, we respond warmly from head to toe without a thought. Our lips part happily. We step closer. Our arms reach out. Our eyes become soft and wide. Even our palms turn up and our bodies turn fully toward our dear friend.

How to Trick Your Body into Doing Everything Right

Here's a visualization technique that accomplishes all that. It guarantees that everyone you encounter will feel your warmth. I call it *Hello Old Friend*.

When meeting someone, play a mental trick on yourself. In your mind's eye, see him or her as an old friend, someone you had a wonderful relationship with years ago. But somehow you lost track of your friend. You tried so hard to find your good buddy, but there was no listing in the phone book. No information on-line. None of your mutual friends had a clue.

Suddenly, WOW! What a surprise! After all those years, the two of you are reunited. You are so happy.

That's where the pretending stops. Obviously, you are not going to try to convince New Person that the two of you are really old friends. You are not going to hug and kiss and say, "Great to see you again!" or "How have you been all these years?" You merely say, "Hello," "How do you do," "I am pleased to meet you." But, inside, it's a very different story.

You will amaze yourself. The delight of rediscovery fills your face and buoys up your body language. I sometimes jokingly say if you were a light, you'd beam on the other person. If you were a dog, you'd be wagging your tail. You make New Person feel very special indeed.

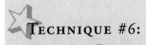

TECHNIQUE #6:
HELLO OLD FRIEND

When meeting someone, imagine he or she is an old friend (an old customer, an old beloved, or someone else you had great affection for). How sad, the vicissitudes of life tore you two asunder. But, holy mackerel, now the party (the meeting, the convention) has reunited you with your long-lost old friend!

The joyful experience starts a remarkable chain reaction in your body from the subconscious softening of your eyebrows to the positioning of your toes—and everything between.

In my seminars, I first have people introduce themselves to another participant before they've learned the *Hello Old Friend* technique. The group chats as though at a pleasant semiformal gathering. Later I ask them to introduce themselves to another stranger, imagining they are old friends. The difference is extraordinary. When they're using *Hello Old Friend*, the room comes alive. The atmosphere is charged with good feeling. The air sparkles with happier, high-energy people. They are standing closer, laughing more sincerely, and reaching out to one another. I feel like I'm attending a terrific bash that's been going on for hours.

Not a Word Need Be Spoken

The *Hello Old Friend* technique even supersedes language. Whenever you're traveling in countries where you don't speak the native tongue, be sure to use it. If you find yourself with a group of people who are all speaking a language unknown to you, just imagine them to be a group of your old friends. Everything is fine except they momentarily forgot how to speak English. In spite of the fact you won't understand a word, your whole body still responds with congeniality and acceptance.

I've used the *Hello Old Friend* technique while traveling in Europe. Sometimes my English-speaking friends who live there tell me their European colleagues say I am the friendliest American they've ever met. Yet, we'd never spoken a word between us!

A Self-Fulfilling Prophesy

An added benefit to the *Hello Old Friend* technique is it becomes a self-fulfilling prophesy. When you act as though you like someone, you start to *really* like them. An Adelphi University study called, appropriately, "Believing Another Likes or Dislikes You: Behaviors Making the Beliefs Come True" proved it.[10] Researchers told volunteers to treat unsuspecting subjects as though they liked them. When surveyed later, the results showed the volunteers wound up genuinely liking the subjects. The unsuspecting subjects were also surveyed. These respondents expressed much higher respect and affection for the volunteers who pretended they liked them. What it boils down to is: Love begets love, like begets like, respect begets respect. Use the *Hello Old Friend* technique and you will soon have many new "old friends" who wind up genuinely liking you.

You now have all the basics to come across to everyone you meet as a Somebody, a friendly Somebody. But your job isn't over yet. In addition to being liked, you want to appear credible, intelligent, and sure of yourself. Each of the next three techniques accomplishes one of those goals.

7 Limit the Fidget

How to Come Across
as 100 Percent Credible

I have a friend, a highly respected headhunter named Helen. Helen makes terrific hires for her clients. I once asked her the secret of her success. She said, "Probably because I can almost always tell when an applicant is lying."

"How can you tell?"

She said, "Well, just last week, I was interviewing a young woman for a position as marketing director for a small firm. Throughout the interview, the applicant had been sitting with her left leg crossed over her right. Her hands were comfortably resting in her lap and she was looking directly at me.

"I asked her salary. Without swerving her eyes from mine, she told me. I asked if she enjoyed her work. Still looking directly at me, she said, 'yes.' Then I asked her why she left her previous job."

Helen said, "At that point, her eyes fleetingly darted away before regaining eye contact with me. Then, while answering my question, she shifted in her seat and crossed her right leg over her left. At one point, she put her hands up to her mouth."

Helen said, "That's all I needed. With her words she was telling me she felt her 'growth opportunities were limited at her previous firm.' But her body told me she was not being entirely forthright."

Helen went on to explain the young woman's fidgeting alone wouldn't prove she was lying. Nevertheless, it was enough, she said, that she wanted to pursue the subject further.

Helen continued, "So I tested it. I changed the subject and went back to more neutral territory. I asked her about her goals for the future. Again, the girl stopped fidgeting. She folded her hands in her lap as she told me how she'd always wanted to work in a small company in order to have hands-on experience with more than one project.

"Then I repeated my earlier question. I asked again if it was *only* the lack of growth opportunity that made her leave her previous position. Sure enough, once again, the woman shifted in her seat and momentarily broke eye contact. As she continued talking about her last job, she started rubbing her forearm."

Helen continued to probe until she finally uncovered the truth. The applicant had been fired due to a nasty disagreement with the marketing director she worked for.

Human resources professionals who interview applicants and police officers who interrogate suspected criminals are trained to detect lies. They know specifically what signals to look for. The rest of us, although not knowledgeable about specific clues to deceit, have a sixth sense when someone is not telling us the truth.

Just recently a colleague of mine was considering hiring an in-house booking agent. After interviewing one fellow she said to me, "I don't know. I don't really think he has the success he claims."

"You think he's lying to you?" I asked.

"Absolutely. And the funny thing is I can't tell why. He looked right at me. He answered all my questions directly. There was just something that didn't seem right."

Employers often feel this way. They have a gut feeling about someone but they can't put their finger on it. Because of that, many large companies turn to the polygraph. The polygraph, or

lie detector, is a mechanical apparatus designed to detect if someone is lying. Banks, drugstores, and grocery stores rely heavily on
it for preemployment screening. The FBI, Justice Department, and
most police departments have used the polygraph on suspects.
And the interesting part is the polygraph is not a lie detector at
all! All the machine can do is detect fluctuations in our autonomic
nervous system—changes in breathing patterns, sweating, flush-
ing, heart rate, blood pressure, and other signs of emotional
arousal.

So is it accurate? Well, yes, often it is. Why? Because when
the average person tells a lie, he or she is emotionally aroused and
bodily changes do take place. When that happens, they fidget.
Experienced or trained liars, however, can fool the polygraph.

Beware the *Appearance* of Lying, Even When You're Telling the Truth

Problems arise for us when we are not lying, but are feeling emotional or intimidated by the person we are talking with. A young
man telling an attractive woman about his business success might
shift his weight. A woman talking about her company's track
record to an important client could rub her neck.

More problems arise out of the atmosphere. A businessman
who doesn't feel nervous at all could loosen his collar because the
room is hot. A politician giving a speech outdoors could blink
excessively because the air is dusty. Even though erroneous, these
fidgety movements give their listeners the sense something just isn't
right or a gut feeling they're lying.

Professional communicators are alert to this hazard. They
consciously squelch any signs anyone could mistake for shiftiness.
They fix a constant gaze on their listener. They never put their
hands on their faces. They don't massage their arm when it tin-
gles, or rub their nose when it itches. They don't loosen their collar when it's hot or blink because it's sandy. They don't wipe away
tiny perspiration beads in public or shield their eyes from the sun.
They suffer because they know fidgeting undermines credibility.
Consider the infamous September 25, 1960, televised presidential

debate between Richard Milhous Nixon and John Fitzgerald Kennedy. Political pundits speculate Nixon's lack of makeup, his fidgeting, and mopping his brow on camera lost him the election.

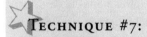

TECHNIQUE #7:
LIMIT THE FIDGET

Whenever your conversation really counts, let your nose itch, your ear tingle, or your foot prickle. Do not fidget, twitch, wiggle, squirm, or scratch. And above all, keep your paws away from your puss. Hand motions near your face and all fidgeting can give your listener the gut feeling you're fibbing.

If you want to come across as an entirely credible Somebody, try to squelch all extraneous movement when your communication counts. I call the technique *Limit the Fidget*.

Now let's tackle intelligence. "What?" you ask. "Can people come across as more intelligent than they really are?" Well, did you ever hear of Hans, the counting horse? Hans was considered the most intelligent horse in history, and he used the technique I'm about to suggest.

8 ✦ Hans's Horse Sense

How to Make Them Say "You've Got Horse Sense"

A horse, a very clever horse named Hans, inspires this next technique. Hans was owned by Herr von Osten, a Berliner, who had trained Hans to do simple arithmetic by tapping his right front hoof. So prodigious was Hans's ability that the horse's fame quickly spread throughout Europe in the early 1900s. He became known as Clever Hans, the counting horse.

Herr von Osten taught Hans to do more than just add. Soon the horse could subtract and divide. In time, Clever Hans even mastered the multiplication tables. The horse became quite a phenomenon. Without his owner uttering a single word, Hans could count out the size of his audience, tap the number wearing glasses, or respond to any counting question they asked him.

Finally, Hans achieved the ultimate ability that separates man from animal—language. Hans "learned" the alphabet. By tapping out hoof beats for each letter, he answered any question about anything humans had read in a newspaper or heard on the radio. He could even answer common questions about history, geography, and human biology.

Hans made headlines and was the main topic of discussion at dinner parties throughout Europe. The "human horse" quickly attracted the attention of scientists, psychology professors, veterinarians, even cavalry officers. Naturally they were skeptical, so they established an official commission to decide whether the horse was a case of clever trickery or equine genius. Whatever their suspicions, it was obvious to all, Hans was a very smart horse. Compared to other horses, Hans was a Somebody.

Cut to today. Why is it when you talk with certain individuals you just know they are smarter than other people—that they are a Somebody? Often they're not discussing highfalutin subjects or using two-dollar words. Nevertheless, everybody knows. People say, "She's smart as a whip," "He doesn't miss a trick," "She picks up on everything," "He's got the right stuff," "She's got horse sense." Which brings us back to Hans.

The day of the big test arrived. Everyone was convinced it must be a trick orchestrated by Herr von Osten, Hans's owner. There was standing room only in the auditorium filled with scientists, reporters, clairvoyants, psychics, and horse lovers who eagerly awaited the answer. The canny commission members were confident this was the day they would expose Hans as chicanery because they, too, had a trick up their sleeves. They were going to bar von Osten from the hall and put his horse to the test all alone.

When the crowd was assembled, they told von Osten he must leave the auditorium. The surprised owner departed, and Hans was stranded in an auditorium with a suspicious and anxious audience.

The confident commission leader asked Hans the first mathematical question. He tapped out the right answer! A second. He got it right! Then a third. Then the language questions followed. *He got them all right!*

The commission was befuddled. The critics were silenced.

However, the public wasn't. With a great outcry, they insisted on a new commission. The world waited while, once again, the authorities gathered scientists, professors, veterinarians, cavalry officers, and reporters from around the world.

Only after this second commission put Hans to the test did the truth about the clever horse come out. Commission number two started the enquiry perfunctorily with a simple addition problem. This time, however, instead of asking the question out loud for all to hear, one researcher whispered a number in Hans's ear, and a second researcher whispered another. Everyone expected Hans to quickly tap out the sum. But Hans remained dumb! Aha! The researchers revealed the truth to the waiting world. Can you guess what that was?

Here's a hint: when the audience or researcher *knew* the answer, Hans did, too. Now can you guess?

People gave off very subtle body-language signals the moment Hans's hoof gave the right number of taps. When Hans started tapping the answer to a question, the audience would show subtle signs of tension. Then, when Hans reached the right number, they responded by an expulsion of breath or slight relaxation of muscles. Von Osten had trained Hans to stop tapping at that point, and therefore appear to give the right answer.

Hans was using the technique I call *Hans's Horse Sense*. He watched his audiences' reactions very carefully and planned his responses accordingly.

If a Horse Can Do It, So Can You

Have you ever been watching TV when the phone rings? Someone asks you to hit the mute button on the television so they can talk. Because there's no sound now, you watch the TV action more carefully. You see performers smiling, scowling, smirking, squinting, and scores of other expressions. You don't miss a bit of the story because, just from their expressions, you can tell what they're thinking. *Hans's Horse Sense* is just that—watching people, seeing how they're reacting, and then making your moves accordingly. Even while you're talking, keep your eyes on your listeners and watch how they're responding to what you're saying. Don't miss a trick.

Are they smiling? Are they nodding? Are their palms up? They like what they're hearing.

Are they frowning? Are they looking away? Are their knuckles clenched? Maybe they don't.

Are they rubbing their necks? Are they stepping back? Are their feet pointing toward the door? Maybe they want to get away.

You don't need a complete course in body language here. Already your life's experience has given you a good grounding in that. Most people know if their Conversation Partners step back or look away, they're not interested in what you're saying. When they think you're a pain in the neck they rub theirs. When they feel superior to you, they steeple their hands.

We'll explore more body-language specifics in Technique #77: *Eyeball Selling*. For the moment, all you need to do is tune to the silent channel being broadcast by the speaker.

TECHNIQUE #8:
HANS'S HORSE SENSE

Make it a habit to get on a dual track while talking. Express yourself, but keep a keen eye on how your listener is reacting to what you're saying. Then plan your moves accordingly.

If a horse can do it, so can a human. People will say you pick up on everything. You never miss a trick. You've got horse sense.

You now have eight techniques to help you come across as a confident, credible, and charismatic person who makes everyone he or she comes in contact with feel like a million. Let's explore one last technique in this section to put it all together and make sure you don't miss a beat.

9 Watch the Scene Before You Make the Scene

How to Make Sure You Don't Miss a Beat

You've seen professional skiing on television? The athlete at the top of the piste, every muscle primed and poised, waiting for the gun to propel him to ultimate victory. Look deeply into his eyes and you'll see he is having an out-of-body experience. In his mind's eye, the skier is swooshing down the slope, zapping back and forth between the poles, and sliding across the finish line in faster time than the world thought possible. The athlete is *visualizing*.

All athletes do it: divers, runners, jumpers, javelin throwers, lugers, swimmers, skaters, acrobats. They *visualize* their magic before performing it. They *see* their own bodies bending, twisting, flipping, flying through the air. They *hear* the sound of the wind, the splash in the water, the whirr of the javelin, the thud of its landing. They *smell* the grass, the cement, the pool, the dust. Before they move a muscle, professional athletes watch the whole movie, which, of course, ends in their own victory.

Sports psychologists tell us visualization is not just for top-level competitive athletes. Studies show mental rehearsal helps weekend athletes sharpen their golf, their tennis, their running, whatever their favorite activity. Experts agree if you see the pictures, hear the sounds, and feel the movements of your body in your mind *before* you do the activity, the effect is powerful.

"Twenty-Six Miles on My Mattress"

Psychological mumbo jumbo? Absolutely not! I have a friend, Richard, who runs marathons. Once, several years ago, a scant three weeks before the big New York marathon, an out-of-control car crashed into Richard's and he was taken to the hospital. He was not badly injured. Nevertheless, his friends were sorry for him because being laid up two weeks in bed would, naturally, knock him out of the big event.

What a surprise when, on that crisp November marathon morning in Central Park, Richard showed up in his little shorts and big running shoes.

"Richard, are you crazy? You're in no shape to run. You've been in bed these past few weeks!" we all cried out.

"My body may have been in bed," he replied, "but *I've* been running."

"What?" we asked in unison.

"Yep. Every day. Twenty-six miles, 385 yards, right there on my mattress." Richard explained that in his imagination he saw himself traversing every step of the course. He saw the sights, heard the sounds, and felt the twitching movements in his muscles. He *visualized* himself racing in the marathon.

Richard didn't do as well as he had the year before, but the miracle is he finished the marathon, without injury, without excessive fatigue. It was all due to visualization. Visualization works in just about any endeavor you apply it to—including being a terrific communicator.

Visualization works best when you feel totally relaxed. Only when you have a calm state of mind can you get clear, vivid images. Do your visualization in the quiet of your home or car before leaving for the party, the convention, or the big-deal meeting. See it all in your mind's eye ahead of time.

TECHNIQUE #9:

WATCH THE SCENE BEFORE YOU MAKE THE SCENE

Rehearse being the Super Somebody you want to be ahead of time. SEE yourself walking around with *Hang by Your Teeth* posture, shaking hands, smiling the *Flooding Smile*, and making *Sticky Eyes*. HEAR yourself chatting comfortably with everyone. FEEL the pleasure of knowing you are in peak form and everyone is gravitating toward you. VISUALIZE yourself a Super Somebody. Then it all happens automatically.

You now have the skills necessary to get you started on the right foot with any new person in your life. Think of yourself in these first moments like a rocket taking off. When the folks at Cape Kennedy aim a spacecraft for the moon, a mistake in the millionth of a degree at the beginning, when the craft is still on the ground, means missing the moon by thousands of miles. Likewise, a tiny body-language blooper at the outset of a relationship may mean you will never make a hit with that person. But with *Flooding Smile*, *Sticky Eyes*, *Epoxy Eyes*, *Hang by Your Teeth*, *Big-Baby Pivot*, *Hello Old Friend*, *Limit the Fidget*, *Hans's Horse Sense*, and *Watch the Scene Before You Make the Scene*, you'll be right on course to get whatever you eventually want from anybody—be it business, friendship, or love.

We now move from the silent world to the spoken word.

PART TWO

WHAT DO I SAY AFTER I SAY "HI"?

Small Talk, Your Verbal Welcome Mat

Just as the first glimpse should please their eyes, your first words should delight their ears. Your tongue is a welcome mat embossed with either "Welcome" or "Go Away!" To make your Conversation Partner feel welcome, you must master small talk.

Small talk! Can you hear the shudder? Those two little words drive a stake into the hearts of some otherwise fearless and undaunted souls. Invite them to a party where they don't know anyone, and it mainlines queasiness into their veins.

If this sounds familiar, take consolation from the fact that the brighter the individual, the more he or she detests small talk. When consulting for Fortune 500 companies, I was astounded. Top executives, completely comfortable making big talk with their boards of directors or addressing their stockholders, confessed they felt like little lost children at parties where the pratter was less than prodigious.

Small-talk haters, take further consolation from the fact that you are in star-studded company. Fear of small talk and stage fright are the same thing. The butterflies you feel in your stomach when you're in a roomful of strangers flutter 'round the tummies of top performers. Pablo Casals complained of lifelong stage fright. Carly Simon curtailed live performances because of it. A friend of mine who worked with Neil Diamond said he insisted the words to "Song Sung Blue," a tune he'd been crooning for forty years, be displayed on his teleprompter, lest fear freeze him into forgetfulness.

Is Small-Talk-a-Phobia Curable?

Someday, scientists say, communications fears may be treatable with drugs. They're already experimenting with Prozac to change people's personalities. But some fear disastrous side effects. The good news is that when human beings think, and genuinely feel, certain emotions—like confidence they have specific techniques to fall back on—the brain manufactures its own antidotes. If fear and distaste of small talk is the disease, knowing solid techniques like the ones we explore in this section is the cure.

Incidentally, science is beginning to recognize it's not chance or even upbringing that one person has a belly of butterflies and another doesn't. In our brains, neurons communicate through chemicals called neurotransmitters. Some people have excessive levels of a neurotransmitter called *norepinephrine*, a chemical cousin of adrenaline. For some children, just walking into a kindergarten room makes them want to run and hide under a table.

As a tot, I spent a lot of time under the table. As a preteen in an all-girls boarding school, my legs turned to linguine every time I had to converse with a male. In eighth grade, I once had to invite a boy to our school prom. The entire selection of dancing males lived in the dormitory of our brother school. And I only knew one resident, Eugene. I had met Eugene at summer camp the year before. Mustering all my courage, I decided to call him.

Two weeks before the dance, I felt the onset of sweaty palms. I put the call off. One week before, rapid heartbeat set in. I put the call off. Finally, three days before the big bash, breathing became difficult. Time was running out.

The critical moment, I rationalized, would be easier if I read from a script. I wrote out the following: "Hi, this is Leil. We met at camp last summer. Remember?" (I programmed in a pause where I hoped he would say yes.) "Well, National Cathedral School's prom is this Saturday night and I'd like you to be my date." (I programmed in another pause where I *prayed* he'd say yes.)

On Thursday before the dance, I could no longer delay the inevitable. I picked up the receiver and dialed. Clutching the phone waiting for Eugene to answer, my eyes followed perspiration droplets rolling down my arm and dripping off my elbow. A small salty puddle was forming around my feet. "Hello?" a sexy, deep male voice answered the dorm phone.

In faster-than-a-speeding-bullet voice, like a nervous novice telemarketer, I shot out, "Hi, this is Leil. We-met-at-camp—last-summer-remember?" Forgetting to pause for his assent, I raced on, "Well-National-Cathedral-School's-prom-is-this-Saturday-night-and-I'd-like-you-to-be-my-date."

To my relief and delight, I heard a big, cheerful "Oh that's great, I'd love to!" I exhaled my first normal breath all day. He continued, "I'll pick you up at the girl's dorm at seven thirty. I'll have a pink carnation for you. Will that go with your dress? And my name is Donnie."

Donnie? *Donnie!* Who said anything about Donnie?

Well, Donnie turned out to be the best date I had that decade. Donnie had buckteeth, a head full of tousled red hair, and communications skills that immediately put me at ease.

On Saturday night, Donnie greeted me at the door, carnation in hand and grin on face. He joked self-deprecatingly about how he was dying to go to the prom so, knowing it was a case of mistaken identity, he accepted anyway. He told me he was thrilled when "the girl with the lovely voice" called, and he took full responsibility for "tricking" me into an invitation. Donnie made me comfortable and confident as we chatted. First we made small talk and then he gradually led me into subjects I was interested in. I flipped over Donnie, and he became my very first boyfriend.

Donnie instinctively had the small-talk skills that we are now going to fashion into techniques to help you glide through small talk like a hot knife through butter. When you master them, you will be able, like Donnie, to melt the heart of everyone you touch.

The goal of *Talking the Winner's Way* is not, of course, to make you a small-talk whiz and stop there. The aim is to make you a dynamic conversationalist and forceful communicator. However, small talk is the first crucial step toward that goal.

10 The Mood Match

How to Start a Conversation Without Strangling It

You've been there. You're introduced to someone at a party or business meeting. You shake hands, your eyes meet . . . and suddenly your entire body of knowledge dries up and thought processes come to a screeching halt. You fish for a topic to fill the awkward silence. Failing, your new contact slips away in the direction of the cheese tray.

We want the first words falling from our lips to be sparkling, witty, insightful. We want our listeners to immediately recognize how riveting we are. I was once at a gathering where *everybody* was sparkling, witty, insightful, and riveting. It drove me berserk because most of these same everybodies felt they had to prove it in their first ten words or less!

Several years ago, the Mensa organization, a social group of extremely bright individuals who score in the country's top 2 percent in intelligence, invited me to be a keynote speaker at their annual convention. Their cocktail party was in full swing in the lobby of the hotel as I arrived. After checking in, I hauled my bags through the hoard of happy-hour Mensans to the elevator.

The doors separated and I stepped into an elevator packed with party goers. As we began the journey up to our respective floors, the elevator gave several sleepy jerks.

"Hmm," I remarked, in response to the elevator's sluggishness, "the elevator seems a little flaky." Suddenly, each elevator occupant, feeling compelled to exhibit his or her 132-plus IQ, pounced forth with a thunderous explanation. "It's obviously got poor rail-guide alignment," announced one. "The relay contact is not made up," declared another. Suddenly I felt like a grasshopper trapped in a stereo speaker. I couldn't wait to escape the attack of the mental giants.

Afterward, in the solitude of my room, I thought back and reflected that the Mensan's answers were, indeed, interesting. Why then did I have an adverse reaction?

I realized it was too much, too soon. I was tired. Their high energy and intensity jarred my sluggish state.

You see, small talk is not about facts or words. It's about music, about melody. Small talk is about putting people at ease. It's about making comforting noises together like cats purring, children humming, or groups chanting. You must first match your listener's mood.

Like repeating the note on the music teacher's harmonica, Top Communicators pick up on their listener's tone of voice and duplicate it. Instead of jumping in with such intensity, the Mensans could have momentarily matched my lethargic mood by saying, "Yes, it is slow, isn't it?" Had they then prefaced their information with, "Have you ever been curious why an elevator is slow?" I would have responded with a sincere "Yes, I have." After a moment of equalized energy levels, I would have welcomed their explanations about the rail-guard alignment or whatever the heck it was. And friendships might have started.

I'm sure you've suffered the aggression of a mood mismatch. Have you ever been relaxing when some overexcited hot-breathed colleague starts pounding you with questions? Or the reverse: you're late, rushing to a meeting, when an associate stops you and starts lazily narrating a long, languorous story. No matter how interesting the tale, you don't want to hear it now.

The first step in starting a conversation without strangling it is to match your listener's mood, if only for a sentence or two. When it comes to small talk, think music, not words. Is your listener adagio or allegro? Match that pace. I call it making a *Mood Match*.

Matching the Mood Can Make or Break the Sale

Matching customers' moods is crucial for salespeople. Some years ago, I decided to throw a surprise party for my best friend Stella. It was going to be a triple-whammy party because she was celebrating three events. One, it was Stella's birthday. Two, she was newly engaged. And three, Stella had just landed her dream job. She had been my buddy since grade school and I was floating on air over her birthday-engagement-congratulations bash.

I had heard one of the best French restaurants in town had an attractive back room for parties. About 5 P.M. one afternoon, I wafted happily into the restaurant and found the seated maitre d' languidly looking over his reservation book. I began excitedly babbling about Stella's triple-whammy celebration and asked to see that fabulous back room I'd heard so much about. Without a smile or moving a muscle, he said, "Zee room ees een zee back. You can go zee eet eef you like."

CRASH. What a party pooper! His morose mood kicked all the party spirit out of me, and I no longer wanted to rent his stupid space. Before I even looked at the room, he lost the rental. I left his restaurant vowing to find a place where the management would at least *appear* to share the joy of the happy occasion.

Every mother knows this instinctively. To quiet a whimpering infant, mama doesn't just shake her finger and shout, "Quiet down." No, mama picks baby up. Mama cries, "Ooh, ooh, oh," sympathetically matching baby's misery for a few moments. Mama then gradually transitions the two of them into hush-hush happy sounds. Your listeners are all big babies! Match their mood if you want them to stop crying, start buying, or otherwise come 'round to your way of thinking.

TECHNIQUE #10:

MAKE A MOOD MATCH

Before opening your mouth, take a "voice sample" of your listener to detect his or her state of mind. Take a "psychic photograph" of the expression to see if your listener looks buoyant, bored, or blitzed. If you ever want to bring people around to your thoughts, you must match their mood and voice tone, if only for a moment.

11 ⭐ Prosaic with Passion

"What's a Good Opening Line When I Meet People?"

I was once at a party where I spotted a fellow surrounded by a fan club of avid listeners. The chap was smiling, gesticulating, obviously enthralling his audience. I went over to hearken to this fascinating speaker. I joined his throng of admirers and eavesdropped for a minute or two. Suddenly, it dawned on me: the fellow was saying the most banal things! His script was dull, dull, dull. Ah, but he was delivering his prosaic observations with such passion. Therefore, he held the group spellbound. It convinced me that it's not all *what* you say, it's *how* you say it.

Often people ask me, "What's a good opening line when I meet people?" I give them the same answer a woman who once worked in my office always gave me. Dottie often stayed at her desk to work through lunch. Sometimes, as I was leaving for the sandwich shop, I'd ask her, "Hey Dottie, what can I bring you back for lunch?"

Dottie, trying to be obliging, would say, "Oh anything is fine with me."

"No, Dottie!" I wanted to scream. "Tell me what you want. Ham 'n' cheese on rye? Bologna on whole wheat, hold the mayo?

Peanut butter 'n' jelly with sliced bananas? Be specific. *Anything* is a hassle."

Frustrating though it may be, my answer to the opening-line question is "Anything!" because almost anything you say really *is* OK—as long as it puts people at ease and sounds passionate.

How do you put people at ease? By convincing them they are OK and that the two of you are similar. When you do that, you break down walls of fear, suspicion, and mistrust.

Why Banal Makes a Bond

Samuel I. Hayakawa was a college president, U.S. senator, and brilliant linguistic analyst of Japanese origin. He tells us this story that shows the value of, as he says, "unoriginal remarks."[11]

In early 1942, a few weeks after the beginning of World War II—at a time when there were rumors of Japanese spies—Hayakawa had to wait several hours in a railroad station in Oshkosh, Wisconsin. He noticed others waiting in the station were staring at him suspiciously. Because of the war, they were apprehensive about his presence. He later wrote, "One couple with a small child was staring with special uneasiness and whispering to each other."

So what did Hayakawa do? He made *unoriginal* remarks to set them at ease. He said to the husband that it was too bad the train should be late on so cold a night.

The man agreed.

"I went on," Hayakawa wrote, "to remark that it must be especially difficult to travel with a small child in winter when train schedules were so uncertain. Again the husband agreed. I then asked the child's age and remarked that their child looked very big and strong for his age. Again agreement, this time with a slight smile. The tension was relaxing.

After two or three more exchanges, the man asked Hayakawa, "I hope you don't mind my bringing it up, but you're Japanese, aren't you? Do you think the Japs have any chance of winning this war?"

"Well," Hayakawa replied, "your guess is as good as mine. I don't know any more than I read in the papers. But the way I figure it, I don't see how the Japanese, with their lack of coal and steel and oil . . . can ever beat a powerfully industrialized nation like the United States."

Hayakawa went on, "My remark was admittedly neither original nor well informed. Hundreds of radio commentators . . . were saying much the same thing during those weeks. But just because they were, the remark sounded familiar and was on the right side so that it was easy to agree with."

The Wisconsin man agreed at once with what seemed like genuine relief. His next remark was, "Say, I hope your folks aren't over there while the war is going on."

"Yes, they are," Hayakawa replied. "My father and mother and two young sisters are over there."

"Do you ever hear from them?" the man asked.

"How can I?" Hayakawa answered.

Both the man and his wife looked troubled and sympathetic. "Do you mean you won't be able to see them or hear from them until after the war is over?"

There was more to the conversation but the result was, within ten minutes they had invited Hayakawa—whom they initially may have suspected was a Japanese spy—to visit them sometime in their city and have dinner in their home. And all because of this brilliant scholar's admittedly common and unoriginal small talk. Top Communicators know the most soothing and appropriate first words should be, like Senator Hayakawa's, unoriginal, even banal. But not indifferent. Hayakawa delivered his sentiments with sincerity and passion.

Ascent from Banality

There is no need, of course, to stay with mundane remarks. If you find your company displays cleverness or wit, you match that. The conversation then escalates naturally, compatibly. Don't rush it or, like the Mensans, you seem like you're showing off.

The bottom line on your first words is to have the courage of your own triteness. Because, remember, people tune in to your tone more than your text.

TECHNIQUE #11:
PROSAIC WITH PASSION

Worried about your first words? Fear not, since 80 percent of your listener's impression has nothing to do with your words anyway. Almost anything you say at first is fine. No matter how prosaic the text, an empathetic mood, a positive demeanor, and passionate delivery make you sound exciting.

"Anything, Except Liverwurst!"

Back to Dottie waiting for her sandwich at her desk. Sometimes as I walked out the door scratching my head wondering what to bring her, she'd call after me, "Anything, except liverwurst, that is." Thanks, Dottie, that's a little bit of help.

Here's my "anything, except liverwurst" on small talk. Anything you say is fine as long as it is not complaining, rude, or unpleasant. If the first words out of your mouth are a complaint, BLAM, people label you a complainer. Why? Because that complaint is your new acquaintance's 100-percent sampling of you so far. You could be the happiest Pollyanna ever, but how will they know? If your first comment is a complaint, you're a griper. If your first words are rude, you're a creep. If your first words are unpleasant, you're a stinker. Open and shut.

Other than these downers, anything goes. Ask them where they're from, how they know the host of the party, where they bought the lovely suit they're wearing—or hundreds of etceteras. The trick is to ask your prosaic question with passion to get the other person talking.

Still feel a bit shaky on making the approach to strangers? Let's take a quick detour on our road to meaningful communicating. I'll give you three quickie techniques to meet people at parties—then nine more to make small talk not so small.

12 Always Wear a Whatzit

What's a *Whatzit*?

Singles proficient at meeting potential sweethearts without the benefit of introduction (in the vernacular, making a "pickup"), have developed a deliciously devious technique that works equally well for social or corporate networking purposes. The technique requires no exceptional skill on your part, only the courage to sport a simple visual prop called a *Whatzit*.

What's a *Whatzit*? A *Whatzit* is anything you wear or carry that is unusual—a unique pin, an interesting purse, a strange tie, an amusing hat. A *Whatzit* is any object that draws people's attention and inspires them to approach you and ask, "Uh, what's that?" Your *Whatzit* can be as subtle or overt as your personality and the occasion permit.

I wear around my neck an outmoded pair of glasses that resembles a double monocle. Often the curious have approached me at a gathering and asked, "Whatzit?" I explain it's a lorgnette left to me by my grandmother, which, of course, paves the way to discuss hatred of glasses, aging eyes, love or loss of grandmothers, adoration of antique jewelry—any way the inquisitor wants to take it.

Perhaps, unknowingly, you have fallen prey to this soon-to-be-legendary technique. At a gathering, have you ever noticed someone you would like to talk to? Then you've racked your brain to conjure an excuse to make the approach. What a bounty it was to discover that he or she was wearing some weird, wild, or wonderful something you could comment on.

The *Whatzit* Way to Love

Your *Whatzit* is a social aid whether you seek business rewards or new romance. I have a friend, Alexander, who carries Greek worry beads with him wherever he goes. He's not worried. He knows any woman who wants to talk to him will come up and say, "What's that?"

Think about it, gentlemen. Suppose you're at a party. An attractive woman spots you across the room. She wants to talk to you but she's thinking, "Well, Mister, you're attractive. But, golly, what can I say to you? You just ain't got no *Whatzit*."

Be a *Whatzit* Seeker, Too

Likewise, become proficient in scrutinizing the apparel of those you wish to approach. Why not express interest in the handkerchief in the tycoon's vest pocket, the brooch on the bosom of the rich divorcé, or the school ring on the finger of the CEO whose company you want to work for?

The big spender who, you suspect, might buy a hundred of your widgets has a tiny golf-club lapel pin? Say, "Excuse me, I couldn't help but notice your attractive lapel pin. Are you a golfer? Me, too. What courses have you played?"

Your business cards and your *Whatzit* are crucial socializing artifacts. Whether you are riding in the elevator, climbing the

TECHNIQUE #12:

ALWAYS WEAR A WHATZIT

Whenever you go to a gathering, wear or carry
something unusual to give people who find you the
delightful stranger across the crowded room an excuse
to approach. "Excuse me, I couldn't help but notice
your . . . what IS that?"

doorstep, or traversing the path to the party, make sure your
Whatzit is hanging out for all to see.

The next quickie technique was originated by doggedly determined politicians who don't let one partygoer escape if they think
he or she could be helpful to their campaigns. I call it the *Whoozat*
technique.

13 Whoozat?

What to Do When He's Got No *Whatzit*

Say you have scrutinized the body of the important business contact you want to meet. You've searched in vain from the tip of his cowlick to the toes of his boots. He's not sporting a single *Whatzit*.

If you strike out on finding something to comment on, resort to the *Whoozat* technique. Like a persistent politician, go to the party giver and say, "That man/woman over there looks interesting. Who is he/she?" Then ask for an introduction. Don't be hesitant. The party giver will be pleased you find one of the guests interesting.

If, however, you are loathe to pull the party giver away from his or her other guests, you still can perform *Whoozat*. This time, don't ask for a formal introduction. Simply pump the party giver for just enough information to launch you. Find out about the stranger's jobs, interests, hobbies.

Suppose the party giver says, "Oh, that's Joe Smith. I'm not sure what his job is, but I know he loves to ski." Aha, you've just been given the icebreaker you need. Now you make a beeline for Joe Smith. "Hi, you're Joe Smith, aren't you? Susan was just telling me what a great skier you are. Where do you ski?" You get the idea.

⭐ TECHNIQUE #13:
WHOOZAT?

Whoozat is the most effective, least used (by nonpoliticians) meeting-people device ever contrived. Simply ask the party giver to make the introduction, or pump for a few facts that you can immediately turn into icebreakers.

Now the third in our little trio of meeting-who-you-want tricks.

14 Eavesdrop In

"I Just Thought I'd Eavesdrop In and Say 'Hello'"

The woman you've decided you MUST meet is wearing no *Whatzit?* Can't find the host for the *Whoozat* technique? To make matters worse, she's deep in conversation with a group of her friends. Seems quite hopeless that you will maneuver a meeting, doesn't it?

No obstacle blocks the resolute politician, who always has a trick or ten up his or her sleeve. A politico would resort to the *Eavesdrop In* technique. Eavesdropping, of course, conjures images of clandestine activities—wire tapping, Watergate break-ins, spies skulking around in the murky shadows. Eavesdropping has historical precedent with politicians so, in a pinch, it comes naturally to mind.

At parties, stand near the group of people you wish to infiltrate. Then wait for a word or two you can use as a wedge to break into the group. "Excuse me, I couldn't help overhearing that you . . ." and then whatever is relevant here. For example "I couldn't help overhearing your discussion of Bermuda. I'm going there next month for the first time. Any suggestions?"

Now you are in the circle and can direct your comments to your intended.

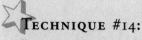

TECHNIQUE #14:

EAVESDROP IN

No *Whatzit*? No host for *Whoozat*? No problem!
Just sidle up behind the swarm of folks you want to infiltrate and open your ears. Wait for any flimsy excuse and jump in with "Excuse me, I couldn't help but overhear . . ."

Will they be taken aback? Momentarily.
Will they get over it? Momentarily.
Will you be in the conversation? Absolutely!

Let us now hop back on the train that first explored Small Talk City and travel to the land of Meaningful Communicating.

⭐ _15_ Never the Naked City

Don't Drop a Frozen Steak on Their Platter

You wouldn't dream of going to a party naked. And I hope you wouldn't dream of letting your conversation be exposed naked and defenseless against the two inevitable assaults "Where are you from?" and "What do you do?"

When asked these questions, most people, like clunking a frozen steak on a china platter, drop a brick of frozen geography or baffling job title on the asker's conversational platter. Then they slap on the muzzle.

You're at a convention. Everyone you meet will, of course, ask "And where are you from?" When you give them the short-form naked-city answer "Oh, I'm from Muscatine, Iowa" (or Millinocket, Maine; Winnemucca, Nevada; or _anywhere_ they haven't heard of), what can you expect except a blank stare? Even if you're a relatively big-city slicker from Denver, Colorado; Detroit, Michigan; or San Diego, California, you'll receive a panicked look from all but American history professors. They're rapidly racking their brains thinking "What do I say next?" Even the names of world-class burgs like New York, Chicago, Washington, and Los Angeles inspire less-than-riveting responses. When I tell people I'm from New York City, what are they expected to say? "Duh, seen any good muggings lately?"

Do humanity and yourself a favor. Never, *ever*, give just a one-sentence response to the question, "Where are you from?" Give the asker some fuel for his tank, some fodder for his trough. Give the hungry communicator something to conversationally nibble on. All it takes is an extra sentence or two about your city—some interesting fact, some witty observation—to hook the asker into the conversation.

Several months ago, a trade association invited me to be its keynote speaker on networking and teaching people to be better conversationalists. Just before my speech, I was introduced to Mrs. Devlin, who was the head of the association.

"How do you do?" she asked.

"How do you do?" I replied.

Then Mrs. Devlin smiled, anxiously awaiting a sample of my stimulating conversational expertise. I asked her where she was from. She plunked a frozen "Columbus, Ohio" and a big expectant grin on my platter. I had to quickly thaw her answer into digestible conversation. My mind thrashed into action. Leil's thought pattern: "Gulp, Columbus, Ohio. I've never been there, hmm. Criminy, what do I know about Columbus? I know a fellow named Jeff, a successful speaker who lives there. But Columbus is too big to ask if she knows him . . . and besides only kids play the 'Do-you-know-so-and-so' game." My panicked silent search continued. "I think it's named after Christopher Columbus . . . but I'm not sure, so I better keep my mouth shut on that one." Four or five other possibilities raced through my mind but I rejected them all as too obvious, too adolescent, or too off-the-wall.

I realized by now that seconds had passed, and Mrs. Devlin was still standing there with a slowly dissipating smile on her face. She was waiting for me (the "expert" who, within the hour, was expected to teach her trade association lessons on scintillating conversation) to spew forth words of wit or wisdom.

"Oh, Columbus, gee," I mumbled in desperation, watching

her face fall into the worried expression of a patient being asked by the surgeon, knife poised in hand, "Where's your appendix?"

I never came up with stimulating conversation on Columbus. But, just then, under the knife, I created the following technique for posterity. I call it *Never the Naked City*.

> ## TECHNIQUE #15:
> ## NEVER THE NAKED CITY
>
> Whenever someone asks you the inevitable, "And where are you from?" never, ever, unfairly challenge their powers of imagination with a one-word answer.
>
> Learn some engaging facts about your hometown that Conversational Partners can comment on. Then, when *they* say something clever in response to your bait, they think *you're* a great conversationalist.

Different Bait for Shrimp or Sharks

A fisherman uses different bait to bag bass or bluefish. And you will obviously throw out different conversational bait to snag simple shrimp or sophisticated sharks. Your hook should relate to the type of person you're speaking with. I'm originally from Washington, D.C. If someone at, say, an art gallery asked me where I was from, I might answer "Washington, D.C.—designed, you know, by the same city planner who designed Paris." This opens the conversational possibilities to the artistry of city planning, Paris, other cities' plans, European travel, and so forth.

At a social party of singles I'd opt for another answer. "I'm from Washington, D.C. The reason I left is there were seven women to every man when I was growing up." Now the conversation can turn to the ecstasy or agony of being single, the perceived lack of desirable men everywhere, even flirtatious possibilities.

In a political group, I'd cast a current fact from the constantly evolving political face of Washington. No need to speculate on the multitude of conversational possibilities *that* unlocks.

Where do you get your conversational bait? Start by phoning the chamber of commerce or historical society of your town. Search the World Wide Web and click on your town, or open an old-fashioned encyclopedia—all rich sources for future stimulating conversations. Learn some history, geography, business statistics, or perhaps a few fun facts to tickle future friends' funny bones.

The Devlin debacle inspired further research. The minute I got home, I called the Columbus Chamber of Commerce and the historical society. Say you, too, are from Columbus, Ohio, and your new acquaintance lays it on you: "Where are you from?" When you are talking with a businessperson, your answer could be, "I'm from Columbus, Ohio. You know many major corporations do their product testing in Columbus because it's so commercially typical. In fact, it's been called 'the most American city in America.' They say if it booms or bombs in Columbus, it booms or bombs nationally."

Talking with someone with a German last name? Tell her about Columbus's historic German Village with the brick streets and the wonderful 1850s-style little houses. It's bound to inspire stories of the old country. Your Conversation Partner's surname is Italian? Tell him Genoa, Italy, is Columbus's sister city.

Talking with an American history buff? Tell him that Columbus was, indeed, named after Christopher Columbus and that a replica of the Santa Maria is anchored in the Scioto River. Talking with a student? Tell her about the five universities in Columbus.

The possibilities continue. You suspect your Conversation Partner has an artistic bent? "Ah," you throw out casually, "Columbus is the home of artist George Bellows."

Columbusites, prepare some tasty snacks for askers even if you know nothing about them. Here's a goodie. Tell them you always have to say "Columbus, *Ohio*" because there is also a Columbus, *Arkansas*; Columbus, *Georgia*; Columbus, *Indiana*; Columbus, *Kansas*; Columbus, *Kentucky*; Columbus, *Mississippi*; Columbus,

Montana; Columbus, *Nebraska*; Columbus, *New Jersey*; Columbus, *New Mexico*; Columbus, *North Carolina*; Columbus, *North Dakota*; Columbus, *Pennsylvania*; Columbus, *Texas*; and Columbus, *Wisconsin.* That spreads the conversational possibilities to fifteen other states. Remember, as a quotable notable once said, "No man would listen to you talk if he didn't know it was his turn next."

A postscript to the hellish experience I had with Columbus. Months later, I mentioned the trauma to my speaker friend from Columbus, Jeff. Jeff explained his house was really in a smaller town just minutes outside Columbus.

"What town, Jeff?"

"Gahanna, Ohio. Gahanna means 'hell' in Hebrew," he said, and then went on to explain why he thought ancient Hebrew historians were clairvoyant.

Thanks, Jeff, I knew you'd never lay a naked city on any of your listeners.

16 Never the Naked Job

Answering the Inevitable

Third only to death and taxes is the assurance a new acquaintance will soon chirp, "And what do you do?" (Is it fitting and proper they should make that query? We'll pick up that sticky wicket later.) For the moment, these few defensive moves help you keep your crackerjack communicator credentials when asked the inevitable.

First, like *Never the Naked City*, don't toss a short-shrift answer in response to the asker's breathless inquiry. You leave the poor fish flopping on the deck when you just say your title: I'm an actuary, an auditor, an author, an astrophysicist. Have mercy so he or she doesn't don't feel like a nincompoop outsider asking, "What, er, kind of actuizing (auditing, authoring, or astrophysizing) do you do?"

You're an attorney. Don't leave it to laymen to try to figure out what you *really* do. Flesh it out. Tell a little story your Conversation Partner can get a handle on. For example, if you're talking with a young mother say, "I'm an attorney. Our firm specializes in employment law. In fact, now I'm involved in a case where a company actually discharged a woman for taking extra maternity leave that was a medical necessity." A mother can relate to that.

Talking with a business owner? Say "I'm an attorney. Our firm specializes in employment law. My current case concerns an employer who is being sued by one of her staff for asking personal questions during the initial job interview." A business owner can relate to that.

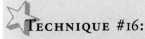

TECHNIQUE #16:
NEVER THE NAKED JOB

When asked the inevitable "And what do YOU do," you may think "I'm an economist," "an educator," "an engineer" is giving enough information to engender good conversation. However, to one who is not an economist, educator, or an engineer, you might as well be saying "I'm a paleontologist," "psychoanalyst," or "pornographer."

Flesh it out. Throw out some delicious facts about your job for new acquaintants to munch on. Otherwise, they'll soon excuse themselves, preferring the snacks back at the cheese tray.

Painful Memories of Naked Job Flashers

I still harbor painful recollections of being tongue-tied when confronted by naked job flashers. Like the time a fellow at a dinner party told me, "I'm a nuclear scientist." My weak "Oh, that must be fascinating" reduced me to a mental molecule in his eyes.

The chap on my other side announced, "I'm in industrial abrasives," and then paused, waiting for me to be impressed. My "Well, er, golly, you must have to be a shrewd judge of character to be in industrial abrasives" didn't fly either. We three sat in silence the rest of the meal.

Just last month a new acquaintance bragged, "I'm planning to teach Tibetan Buddhism at Truckee Meadows Community College," and then clammed up. I knew less about Truckee Meadows than I did about Tibetan Buddhism. Whenever people ask you what you do, give them some mouth-to-ear resuscitation so they can catch their breath and say *something*.

17 Never the Naked Introduction

Help Newlymets Through Their First Moments

"Susan, I'd like you to meet John Smith. John, this is Susan Jones." Duh, what do you expect John and Susan to say?

"Smith? Umm, that's S-M-I-T-H, isn't it?"

"Uh, er, golly, Susan, well, now, there's an interesting name."

Nice-try-forget-it. Don't blame John or Susan for being less than scintillating. The fault lies with the person who introduced the two the way most people introduce their friends to each other—with naked names. They cast out a line with no bait for people to sink their teeth into.

Big Winners may not talk a lot, but conversation never dies unwillingly in their midst. They make sure of it with techniques like *Never the Naked Introduction*. When they introduce people, they buy an insurance policy on the conversation with a few simple add-ons: "Susan, I'd like you to meet John. John has a wonderful boat we took a trip on last summer. John, this is Susan Smith. Susan is editor-in-chief of *Shoestring Gourmet* magazine."

Padding the introduction gives Susan the opportunity to ask what kind of boat John has or where the group went. It gives John an opening to discuss his love of writing. Or of cooking. Or of food. The conversation can then naturally expand to travel in general, life on boats, past vacations, favorite recipes, restaurants, budgets, diets, magazines, editorial policy—to infinity.

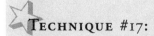

TECHNIQUE #17:
NEVER THE NAKED INTRODUCTION

When introducing people, don't throw out an unbaited hook and stand there grinning like Big Clam, leaving the newlymets to flutter their fins and fish for a topic. Bait the conversational hook to get them in the swim of things. Then you're free to stay or float on to the next networking opportunity.

If you're not comfortable mentioning someone's job during the introduction, mention their hobby or even a talent. The other day at a gathering, the hostess introduced a man named Gilbert. She said, "Leil, I'd like you to meet Gilbert. Gilbert's *gift* is sculpting. He makes beautiful wax carvings." I remember thinking, *gift*, now that's a lovely way to introduce someone and induce conversation.

Armed with these two personality enhancers, three conversation igniters, and three small extenders, it is time to take a step up the communications ladder. Let us now rise from small talk and seek the path to more meaningful dialogue. The next technique is *guaranteed* to make the exchange engrossing for your Conversation Partner.

⭐18 Be a Word Detective

Be a Sleuth on Their Slips of the Tongue

Even a well-intentioned husband who might ask his wife while making love, "Is it good for you, too, honey?" knows not to ask a colleague, "Is the conversation good for you, too?" Yet he wonders . . . we all do. With the following technique, set your mind at rest. You can definitely make the conversation hot for anyone you speak with. Like my prom date, Donnie, you will miraculously find subjects to engross your listeners. No matter how elusive the clue, Sherlock Holmes is confident he'll soon be staring right at it through his magnifying glass. Like the unerring detective, Big Winners know, no matter how elusive the clue, they'll find the right topic. How? They become *word detectives*.

I have a young friend, Nancy, who works in a nursing home. Nancy cares deeply about the elderly but often grumbles about how crotchety and laconic some of her patients are. She laments she has difficulty relating to them.

Nancy told me about one especially cantankerous old woman named Mrs. Otis, whom she could never get to open up to her. "One day," Nancy confided, "right after all those rainstorms we had last week, just to make conversation, I remarked to Mrs. Otis, 'Terrible storms we had last week, don't you think?' Well," Nancy continued, "Mrs. Otis practically jumped down my throat. She said in a snippy voice, 'It's been good for the plants.'" I asked Nancy how she responded to that.

"What could I say?" Nancy answered. "The woman was obviously cutting me off."

"Did you ever think to ask Mrs. Otis if she liked plants?"

"Plants?" Nancy asked.

"Well, yes," I suggested. "Mrs. Otis brought the subject up." I asked Nancy to do me a favor. "Ask her," I begged. Nancy resisted, but I persisted. Just to quiet me down, Nancy promised to ask "cantankerous old Mrs. Otis" if she liked plants.

The next day, a flabbergasted Nancy called me from work. "Leil, how did you know? Not only did Mrs. Otis *love* plants, she told me she'd been married to a gardener. Today I had a different problem with Mrs. Otis. I couldn't shut her up! She went on and on about her garden, her husband . . ."

Top Communicators know ideas don't come out of nowhere. If Mrs. Otis thought to bring up plants, then she must have some relationship with them. Furthermore, by mentioning the word, it meant subconsciously she wanted to talk about plants.

Suppose, for example, instead of responding to Nancy's comment about the rain with "It's good for the plants," Mrs. Otis had said, "Because of the rain, my dog couldn't go out." Nancy could then ask about her dog. Or suppose she grumbled, "It's bad for my arthritis." Can you guess what old Mrs. Otis wants to talk about now?

When talking with anyone, keep your ears open and, like a good detective, listen for clues. Be on the lookout for any unusual references: any anomaly, deviation, digression, or invocation of another place, time, person. Ask about it because it's the clue to what your Conversation Partner would *really* enjoy discussing.

If two people have something in common, when the shared interest comes up, they jump on it naturally. For example, if someone mentions playing squash (bird watching or stamp collecting) and the listener shares that passion, he or she pipes up, "Oh, you're a squasher (or birder or philatelist), too!"

Here's the trick: there's no need to be a squasher, birder, or philatelist to pipe up with enthusiasm. You can simply *Be a Word Detective*. When you pick up on the reference as though it excites you, too, it parlays you into conversation the stranger thrills to. (The subject may put your feet to sleep, but that's another story.)

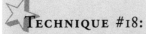

TECHNIQUE #18:
BE A WORD DETECTIVE

Like a good gumshoe, listen to your Conversation Partner's every word for clues to his or her preferred topic. The evidence is bound to slip out. Then spring on that subject like a sleuth on to a slip of the tongue. Like Sherlock Holmes, you have the clue to the subject that's hot for the other person.

Now that you've ignited stimulating conversation, let's explore a technique to *keep* it hot.

19 The Swiveling Spotlight

Sell Yourself with a Top Sales Technique

Several years ago, a girlfriend and I attended a party saturated with a hodgepodge of swellegant folks. Everyone we talked to seemed to lead a nifty life. Discussing the party afterward, I asked my friend, "Diane, of all the exciting people at the party, who did you enjoy talking to most?"

Without hesitation she said, "Oh by far, Dan Smith."

"What does Dan do?" I asked her.

"Uh, well, I'm not sure," she answered.

"Where does he live?"

"Uh, I don't know," Diane responded.

"Well, what is he interested in?"

"Well, we really didn't talk about his interests."

"Diane," I asked, "what *did* you talk about?"

"Well, I guess we talked mostly about me."

"Aha," I said to myself. Diane has just rubbed noses with a Big Winner.

As it turns out, I had the pleasure of meeting Big Winner Dan several months later. Diane's ignorance about his life piqued my curiosity so I grilled him for details. As it turns out, Dan lives in Paris, has a beach home in the south of France, and a mountain home in the Alps. He travels around the world producing sound and light shows for pyramids and ancient ruins—*and* he is an avid hang glider and scuba diver. Does this man have an interesting life or what? Yet Dan, when meeting Diane, said not one word about himself.

I told Dan about how pleased Diane was to meet him yet how little she learned about his life. Dan simply replied, "Well, when I meet someone, I learn so much more if I ask about *their* life. I always try to turn the spotlight on the other person." Truly confident people often do this. They know they grow more by listening than talking. Obviously, they also captivate the talker.

Several months ago at a speaker's convention, I was talking with a colleague, Brian Tracy. Brian does a brilliant job of training top salespeople. He tells his students of a giant spotlight that, when shining on their product, is not as interesting to the prospect. When salespeople shine the giant spotlight on the *prospect*, that's what makes the sale.

Salespeople, this technique is especially crucial for you. Keep your *Swiveling Spotlight* aimed away from you, only lightly on your product, and most brightly on your buyer. You'll do a much better job of selling yourself *and* your product.

TECHNIQUE #19
THE SWIVELING SPOTLIGHT

When you meet someone, imagine a giant revolving spotlight between you. When you're talking, the spotlight is on you. When New Person is speaking, it's shining on him or her. If you shine it brightly enough, the stranger will be blinded to the fact that you have hardly said a word about yourself. The longer you keep it shining away from you, the more interesting he or she finds you.

20 Parroting

Never Be Stuck for Something to Say Again

Moments arise, of course, when even conversationalists extraordinaire hit the wall. Some folks' monosyllabic grunts leave slim pickings even for masters of the *Be a Word Detective* technique.

If you find yourself futilely fanning the embers of a dying conversation (and if you feel for political reasons or human compassion that the conversation should continue), here's a foolproof trick to get the fire blazing again. I call it *Parroting* after that beautiful tropical bird that captures everyone's heart simply by repeating other people's words.

Have you ever, puttering around the house, had the TV in the background tuned to a tennis game? You hear the ball going back and forth over the net—klink-klunk, klink-klunk, klink . . . this time you don't hear the klunk. The ball didn't hit the court. What happened? You immediately look up at the set.

Likewise in conversation, the conversational ball goes back and forth. First you speak, then your partner speaks, you speak . . . and so it goes, back and forth. Each time, through a series of nods and comforting grunts like "um hum," or "umm," you let your

Conversation Partner know the ball has landed in your court. It's your "I got it" signal. Such is the rhythm of conversation.

"What Do I Say Next?"

Back to that frightfully familiar moment when it is your turn to speak but your mind goes blank. Don't panic. Instead of signaling verbally or nonverbally that you "got it," simply repeat, or *parrot*, the last two or three words your companion said, in a sympathetic, questioning tone. That throws the conversational ball right back in your partner's court.

I have a friend, Phil, who sometimes picks me up at the airport. Usually I am so exhausted that I rudely fall asleep in the passenger seat, relegating Phil to nothing more than a chauffeur.

After one especially exhausting trip some years ago, I flung my bags in his trunk and flopped onto the front seat. As I was dozing off, he mentioned he'd gone to the theater the night before. Usually I would have just grunted and wafted into unconsciousness. However, on this particular trip, I had learned the *Parroting* technique and was anxious to try it. "Theater?" I parroted quizzically.

"Yes, it was a great show," he replied, fully expecting it to be the last word on the subject before I fell into my usual sleepy stupor.

"Great show?" I parroted. Pleasantly surprised by my interest, he said, "Yes, it's a new show by Stephen Sondheim called *Sweeney Todd.*"

"*Sweeney Todd?*" I again parroted. Now Phil was getting fired up. "Yeah, great music and an unbelievably bizarre story . . ."

"Bizarre story?" I parroted. Well, that's all Phil needed. For the next half an hour, Phil told me the show's story about a London butcher who went around murdering people. I half dozed, but soon decided his tale of Sweeney Todd's cutting off peoples' heads was disturbing my sleepy reverie. So I simply backed up and parroted one of his previous phrases to get him on another track.

"You said it had great music?"

That did the trick. For the rest of the forty-five minute trip to my home, Phil sang me "Pretty Women," "The Best Pies in London," and other songs from *Sweeney Todd*—much better accompaniment for my demi-nap. I'm sure, to this day, Phil thinks of that trip as one of the best conversations we ever had. And all I did was parrot a few of his phrases.

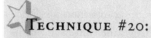

TECHNIQUE #20:
PARROTING

Never be left speechless again. Like a parrot, simply repeat the last few words your Conversation Partner says. That puts the ball right back in his or her court, and then all you need to do is listen.

Salespeople, why go on a wild goose chase for a customer's real objections when it's so easy to shake them out of the trees with *Parroting*?

Parroting Your Way to Profits

Parroting is also a can opener to pry open people's real feelings. Star salespeople use it to get to their prospect's emotional objections, which they often don't even articulate to themselves. A friend of mine, Paul, a used-car salesman, told me he credits a recent sale of a Lamborghini to *Parroting*.

Paul was walking around the lot with a prospect and his wife, who had expressed interest in a "sensible car." He was showing them every sensible Chevy and Ford on the lot. As they were looking at one very sensible family car, Paul asked the husband what he thought of it. "Well," he mused, "I'm not sure this car is right for me." Instead of moving on to the next sensible car, Paul parroted "Right for you?" Paul's questioning inflection signaled the prospect that he needed to say more.

"Well, er, yeah," the prospect mumbled. "I'm not sure it fits my personality."

"Fits your personality?" Paul again parroted.

"You know, maybe I need something a little more sporty."

"A little more sporty?" Paul parroted.

"Well, those cars over there look a little more sporty."

Aha! Paul's parrot had ferreted out which cars to show the customer. As they walked over toward a Lamborghini on the lot, Paul saw the prospect's eyes light up. An hour later, Paul had pocketed a fat commission.

Want to take a rest from talking to save your throat? This next technique gets your Conversation Partner off and running so all you have to do is listen (or even sneak off unnoticed as he or she chats congenially away).

21 Encore!

"Tell 'Em About the Time You . . ."

Every father smiles when his little tyke beseeches him at bedtime, "Daddy, Daddy, tell me the story again of the three little pigs" (or the dancing princesses, or how you and Mommy met). Daddy knows Junior enjoyed the story so much the first time, he wants to hear it again and again.

Junior inspires the following technique called *Encore!* which serves two purposes. *Encore!* makes a colleague feel like a happy dad, and it's a great way to give dying conversation a heart transplant.

I once worked on a ship that had Italian officers and mostly American passengers. Each week, the deck officers were required to attend the captain's cocktail party. After the captain's address in charmingly broken English, the officers invariably clumped together yakking it up in Italian. Needless to say, most of the passengers' grasp of Italian ended at macaroni, spaghetti, salami, and pizza.

As cruise director, it fell on my shoulders to get the officers to mingle with the passengers. My not-so-subtle tactic was to grab one of the officers' arms and literally drag him over to a smiling throng of expectant passengers. I would then introduce the officer and pray that either the cat would release his tongue, or a passenger would come up with a more original question than "Gee, if all you officers are here, who is driving the boat?" Never happened. I dreaded the weekly captain's cocktail party.

One night, sleeping in my cabin, I was awakened by the ship rocking violently from side to side. I listened and the engines were off. A bad sign. I grabbed my robe and raced up to the deck. Through the dense fog, I could barely discern another ship not half a mile from us. Five or six officers were grasping the starboard guardrail and leaning overboard. I rushed over just in time to see a man in the moonlight with a bandage over one eye struggling up our violently rocking ladder. The officers immediately whisked him off to our ship's hospital. The engines started again and we were on our way.

The next morning I got the full story. A laborer on the other ship, a freighter, had been drilling a hole in an engine cylinder. While he was working, a sharp needle-thin piece of metal shot like a missile into his right eye. The freighter had no doctor on board so the ship broadcast an emergency signal.

International sea laws dictate that any ship hearing a distress signal must respond. Our ship came to the rescue and the seaman, clutching his bleeding eye, was lowered into a lifeboat that brought him to our ship. Dr. Rossi, our ship's doctor, was successfully able to remove the needle from the workman's eye thus saving his eyesight.

Cut to the next captain's cocktail party. Once again I was faced with the familiar challenge of getting officers to mingle and make small talk with the passengers. I made my weekly trek to the laconic officers' throng to drag one or two away and, this time, my hand fell on the arm of the ship's doctor. I hauled him over to the nearest group of grinning passengers and introduced him. I then said, "Just last week Dr. Rossi saved the eyesight of a seaman on another ship after a dramatic midnight rescue. Dr. Rossi, I'm sure these folks would love to hear about it."

It was like a magic wand. To my amazement, it was as though Dr. Rossi was blessed instantly with the tongues of angels. His previously monosyllabic broken English became thickly accented eloquence. He recounted the entire story for the growing group of passengers gathering around him. I left the throng that Dr. Rossi enraptured to pull another officer over to an awaiting audience.

I grabbed the captain's stripe-covered arm, dragged him over to another pack of smiling passengers and said, "Captain Cafiero, why don't you tell these folks about the dramatic midnight rescue you made last week?" The cat released Cafiero's tongue and he was off and running.

Back to the throng to get the first officer for the next group. By now I knew I had a winner. "Signor Salvago, why don't you tell these folks how you awakened the captain at midnight last week for the dramatic midnight rescue?"

By then it was time to go back to extract the ship's doctor from the first bevy and take him to his next pack of passengers. It worked even better the second time. He happily commenced his *Encore!* for the second audience. As he chatted away, I raced back to the captain to pull him away for a second telling with another throng. I felt like the circus juggler who keeps all the plates spinning on sticks. Just as I got one conversation spinning, I had to race back to the first speaker to give him a whirl at another audience.

The captain's cocktail parties were a breeze for me for the rest of the season. The three officers loved telling the same story of their heroism to new people every cruise. The only problem was I noticed the stories getting longer and more elaborate each time. I had to adjust my timing in getting them to do a repeat performance for the next audience.

Play It Again, Sam

Encore! is the word appreciative audiences chant when they want another song from the singer, another dance from the dancer, another poem from the poet, and in my case, another storytelling from the officers. *Encore!* is the name of the technique you can use to request a repeat story from a prospect, potential employer, or valued acquaintance. While the two of you are chatting with a group of people, simply turn to him and say, "John, I bet everyone would love to hear about the time you caught that thirty-pound striped bass." Or, "Susan, tell everyone that story you just told me of how you rescued the kitten from the tree." He or she will, of course, demure. Insist! Your Conversation Partner is secretly loving it. The subtext of your request is "That story of yours was so terrific, I want my other friends to hear it." After all, only crowd pleasers are asked to do an *Encore!*

Technique #21:
Encore!

The sweetest sound a performer can hear welling up out of the applause is "Encore! Encore! Let's hear it again!" The sweetest sound your Conversation Partner can hear from your lips when you're talking with a group of people is "Tell them about the time you . . ."

Whenever you're at a meeting or party with someone important to you, think of some stories he or she told you. Choose an appropriate one from their repertoire that the crowd will enjoy. Then shine the spotlight by requesting a repeat performance.

One word of warning: make sure the story you request is one in which the teller shines. No one wants to retell the time they lost the sale, cracked up the car, or broke up the bar and spent the night in jail. Make sure your requested *Encore!* is a positive story where they come out the Big Winner, not the buffoon.

The next technique deals with sharing some positive stories of *your* life.

22 Ac-cen-tu-ate the Pos-i-tive

Endearing Little Flubs?

Often people think when they meet someone they like, they should share a secret, reveal an intimacy, or make a confession of sorts to show they are human too. Airing your youthful battle with bed wetting, teeth grinding, or thumb sucking—or your present struggle with gout or a goiter—supposedly endears you to the masses.

Well, sometimes it does. One study showed that if someone is above you in stature, their revealing a foible brings them closer to you.[12] The holes in the bottom of presidential candidate Adlai Stevenson's shoes charmed a nation, as did George Bush's shocking admission that he couldn't stomach broccoli.

If you're on sure footing, say a superstar who wants to become friends with a fan, go ahead and tell your devotees about the time you were out of work and penniless. But if you're *not* a superstar, better play it safe and keep the skeletons in the closet until later. People don't know you well enough to put your foible in context.

Later in a relationship, telling your new friend you've been thrice married, you got caught shoplifting as a teenager, and you got turned down for a big job may be no big deal. And that may be the extent of what could be construed as black marks on an otherwise flawless life of solid relationships, no misdemeanors, and an impressive professional record. But very early in a relationship, the instinctive reaction is "What else is coming? If he shares that with me so quickly, what else is he hiding? A closetful of ex-spouses, a criminal record, walls papered with rejection letters?" Your new acquaintance has no way of knowing your confession was a generous act, a well-intentioned revelation, on your part.

TECHNIQUE #22:
AC-CEN-TU-ATE THE POS-I-TIVE

When first meeting someone, lock your closet door and save your skeletons for later. You and your new good friend can invite the skeletons out, have a good laugh, and dance over their bones later in the relationship. But now's the time, as the old song says, to "ac-cen-tu-ate the pos-i-tive and elim-i-nate the neg-a-tive."

So far, in this section, you have found assertive methods for meeting people and mastering small talk. The next is both an assertive and defensive move to help spare you that pasty smile we tend to sport when we have no idea what people are talking about.

23 The Latest News . . . Don't Leave Home Without It

Your Most Important Prop

You've heard folks whine, "I can't go to the party, I haven't got a thing to wear." When was the last time you heard, "I can't go to the party, I haven't got a thing to say?"

When going to a gathering with great networking possibilities, you naturally plan your outfit and make sure your shoes will match. And, of course, you must have just the right tie or correct color lipstick. You puff your hair, pack your business cards, and you're off.

Whoa! Wait a minute. Didn't you forget the most important thing? What about the right conversation to enhance your image? Are you actually going to say *anything* that comes to mind, or *doesn't*, at the moment? You wouldn't don the first outfit your groping hand hits in the darkened closet, so you shouldn't leave your conversing to the first thought that comes to mind when facing a group of expectant, smiling faces. You will, of course, follow your instincts in conversation. But at least be prepared in case inspiration doesn't hit.

The best way to assure you're conversationally in the swing of things is to listen to a newscast just before you leave. What's happening right now in the world—all the fires, floods, air disasters, toppled governments, and stock market crashes—pulverizes into great conversational fodder, no matter what crowd you're circulating in.

It is with some embarrassment that I must attribute the following technique to a businesswoman in the world's oldest profession. For a magazine article I was writing, I interviewed one of the savviest operators in her field, Sidney Biddle Barrows, the famed Mayflower Madam.

Sydney told me she had a house rule when she was in business. All of her female "independent contractors" were directed to keep up with the daily news so they could be good conversationalists with their clients. This was not just Sidney's whim. Feedback from her employees had revealed that 60 percent of her girls' work hour was spend in chatting, and only 40 percent in satisfying the customers' needs. Thus she instructed them to read the daily newspaper or listen to a radio broadcast before leaving for an appointment. Sidney told me when she initiated this rule, her business increased significantly. Reports came back from her clients complimenting her on the fascinating women she had working for her. The consummate businesswoman, Ms. Barrows always strove to exceed her customers' expectations.

TECHNIQUE #23:

THE LATEST NEWS . . . DON'T LEAVE HOME WITHOUT IT

The last move to make before leaving for the party—even after you've given yourself final approval in the mirror—is to turn on the radio news or scan your newspaper. Anything that happened *today* is good material. Knowing the big-deal news of the moment is also a defensive move that rescues you from putting your foot in your mouth by asking what everybody's talking about. Foot-in-mouth is not very tasty in public, especially when it's surrounded by egg-on-face.

Ready for the big leagues of conversation? Let's go . . .

PART THREE

How to Talk Like the Big Boys 'n' Girls

Welcome to the Human Jungle

When two tigers prowling through the jungle chance upon each other in a clearing, they look at each other. They freeze. Instinctively they calculate, "If our staring came to hissing—came to scratching—came to clawing—who would win? Which of us has the stronger survival skills?"

Tigers in the wilderness differ little from the urban upright animals inhabiting the corporate jungle (or singles jungle or social jungle). Humans start the process by looking at each other and talking. In the business world, while smiling and uttering "How do you do?" "Hello," "Howdy," or "Hi," they are, like tigers, instinctively, instantaneously, sizing each other up.

They're not calculating the length of each other's claws or the sharpness of their teeth. They're judging each other on a weapon far more powerful to survival as they have defined it. Humans are judging each other's *communications skills*. Although they may not know the names of the specific studies first proving it, they sense the truth: *85 percent of one's success in life is directly due to communications skills.*[13]

They may not be familiar with the U.S. Census Bureau's recent survey showing employers choose candidates with good communications skills and attitude way over education, experience, and training.[14] But they know communications skills get people to the top. Thus, by observing each other carefully during casual conversing, it becomes almost immediately evident to both which is the Bigger Cat in the human jungle.

It doesn't take long for people to recognize who is an "important" person. One cliché, one insensitive remark, one overanxious reaction, and you can be professionally or personally demoted. You can lose a potentially important friendship or business contact. One stupid move and you can tumble off the corporate or social ladder.

The techniques in this section will help assure you make all the right moves so this doesn't happen. The following communications skills give you a leg up to start your ascent to the top of any ladder you choose.

24 ⟩ What Do You Do—NOT!

"And What Do *You* Do? Hmm?"

To size each other up, the first question little cats flat-pawedly ask each other is, "And what do *you* do?" Then they crouch there, quivering their whiskers and twitching their noses, with an obvious "I'm going to pronounce silent judgment on you after you answer" look on their pusses.

Big Cats *never* ask outright, "What do you do?" (Oh they find out, all right, in a much more subtle manner.) By not asking the question, the Big Boys and Girls come across as more principled, even spiritual. "After all," their silence says, "a man or woman is far more than his or her job."

Resisting the tempting question also shows their sensitivity. With so much downsizing, rightsizing, and capsizing of corporations these days, the blunt interrogation evokes uneasiness. The job question is not just unpleasant for those who are "between engagements." I have several gainfully employed friends who hate being asked, "And what do you do?" (One of these folks cuts cadavers for autopsies, the other is an IRS collection agent.)

Additionally, there are millions of talented and accomplished women who have chosen to devote themselves to motherhood. When the cruel corporate question is thrust at them, they feel guilty. The rude interrogation belittles their commitment to their families. No matter how the women answer, they fear the asker is only going to hear a humble "I'm just a housewife."

There is yet another reason Big Boys and Girls avoid asking, "What do you do?" Their abstinence from the question leads listeners to believe that they are in the habit of soaring with a high-flying crowd. Recently I attended a posh party on Easy Street. (I suspect they invited me as their token working-class person.) I noticed no one was asking anyone what they did—because these swells didn't *do* anything. Oh, some might have a ticker tape on the bed table of their mansion to track investments. But they definitely did not *work* for a living.

The final benefit to not asking, "What do you do?" is it throws people off guard. It convinces them you are enjoying their company for who they are, not for any crass networking reason.

TECHNIQUE #24:
WHAT DO YOU DO–NOT!

A sure sign you're a Somebody is the conspicuous absence of the question, "What do you do?" (You determine this, of course, but not with those four dirty words that label you as either (1) a ruthless networker, (2) a social climber, (3) a gold-digging husband or wife hunter, or (4) someone who's never strolled along Easy Street.)

The Right Way to Find Out

So how do you find out what someone does for a living? (I thought you'd never ask.) You simply practice the following eight words. All together now: "How . . . do . . . you . . . spend . . . most . . . of . . . your . . . time?"

"How do you spend most of your time?" is the gracious way to let a cadaver cutter, a tax collector, or a capsized employee off the hook. It's the way to reinforce an accomplished mother's choice. It's the way to assure a spiritual soul you see his or her inner beauty. It's a way to suggest to a swell that you reside on Easy Street, too.

Now, suppose you've just made the acquaintance of someone who *does* like to talk about his or her work? Asking, "How do you spend most of your time?" also opens the door for workaholics to spout off, "Oh golly," they mock moan, "I just spend all my time working." That, of course, is your invitation to grill them for details. (Then they'll talk your ear off.) Yet the new wording of your question gives those who are somewhere between "at leisure" and "work addicted" the choice of telling you about their job or not. Finally, asking "How do you spend most of your time?" instead of "And what do you do?" gives *you* your Big Cat stripes right off.

25 The Nutshell Resume

Socially Submitting Your Oral Resume

Now, having said that, 99 percent of the people you meet will, of course, ask "And what do you do?" Big Winners, realizing someone will *always* ask, are fully prepared for the interrogation.

Many folks have one written resume for job seeking. They type it up and then trudge off to the printer to get a nice neat stack to send to all prospective employers. The resume lists their previous positions, dates of employment, and education. Then, at the bottom, they might as well have scribbled, "Well, that's me. Take it or leave it." And usually they get left. Why? Because prospective employers do not find enough specific points in the resume that relate *directly* to what their firm is seeking.

Boys and Girls in the Big Leagues, however, have bits and bytes of their entire work experience tucked away in their computers. When applying for a job, they punch up only the appropriate data and print it out so it looks like it just came from the printer.

My friend Roberto was out of work last year. He applied for two positions. One was for sales manager of an ice cream company. The other was head of strategic planning for a fast-food chain. He did extensive research and found the ice cream company had deep sales difficulties and the food chain had long-range international aspirations. Did he send the same resume to each? Absolutely not. His resume never deviated one iota from the truth of his background. However, for the ice cream company, he highlighted his experience turning a small company around by doubling its sales in three years. For the food chain, he underscored his experience working in Europe and his knowledge of foreign markets.

Both firms offered Roberto the job. Now he could play them off against each other. He went to each, explaining he'd like to work for them but another firm was offering a higher salary or more perks. The two firms started bidding against each other for Roberto. He finally chose the food chain at almost double the salary they originally offered him.

To make the most of every encounter, personalize your verbal resume with just as much care as you would your written curriculum vitae. Instead of having one answer to the omnipresent "What do you do?" prepare a dozen or so variations, depending on who's asking. For optimum networking, every time someone asks about your job, give a calculated oral resume in a nutshell. Before you submit your answer, consider what possible interest the asker could have in you and your work.

"Here's How My Life Can Benefit Yours"

Top salespeople talk extensively of the "benefit statement." They know, when talking with a potential client, they should open their conversation with a benefit statement. When my colleague Brian makes cold calls, instead of saying "Hello, my name is Brian Tracy. I'm a sales trainer," he says, "Hello, my name is Brian Tracy from the Institute for Executive Development. Would you be interested in a proven method that can increase your sales from 20 to 30 percent over the next twelve months?" That is his benefit statement. He highlights the specific benefits of what he has to offer to his prospect.

My hairdresser Gloria, I discovered, gives a terrific benefit statement to everyone she meets. That's probably why she has so many clients. In fact, that's how she got *me* as a client. When I met Gloria at a convention, she told me she was a hairdresser who specialized in flexible hairstyles for the businesswoman. She casually mentioned she has many clients who choose a conservative hairstyle for work that they can instantly convert to a feminine style for social situations. "Hey, that's me," I said to myself, fingering my stringy little ponytail. I asked for her card and Gloria became my hairdresser.

Then, several months later, I happened to see Gloria at another event. I overheard her chatting with a stylish grey-haired woman at the buffet table. Gloria was saying ". . . and we specialize in a wonderful array of blue rinses." Now that was news to me! I didn't remember seeing one grey head in her salon.

As I was leaving the party, Gloria was out on the lawn talking animatedly with the host's teenage daughters. "Oh yeah," she was saying, "like we specialize in these really cool up-to-the-minute styles." Good for you, Gloria!

Like Gloria the hairdresser, give your response a once-over before answering the inevitable "What do you do?" When someone asks, never give just a one-word answer. That's for forms. If business networking is on your mind, ask yourself, "How could my professional experience *benefit* this person's life?" For example, here are some descriptions various people might put on their tax return:

> real estate agent
> financial planner
> martial arts instructor
> cosmetic surgeon
> hairdresser

Any practitioner of the above professions should reflect on the benefit his or her job has to humankind. (Every job has some benefit or you wouldn't get paid to do it.) The advice to the folks above is

> Don't say "real estate agent." Say "I help people moving into our area find the right home."

Don't say "financial planner." Say "I help people plan their financial future."

Don't say "martial arts instructor." Say "I help people defend themselves by teaching martial arts."

Don't say "cosmetic surgeon." Say "I reconstruct people's faces after disfiguring accidents." (Or, if you're talking with a woman "of a certain age," as the French so gracefully say, tell her, "I help people to look as young as they feel through cosmetic surgery.")

Don't say "hairdresser." Say "I help a woman find the right hairstyle for her particular face." (Go, Gloria!)

Putting the benefit statement in your verbal *Nutshell Resume* brings your job to life and makes it memorable. Even if your new acquaintance can't use your services, the next time he or she meets someone moving into the area, wanting to plan their financial future, thinking of self defense, considering cosmetic surgery, or needing a new hairstyle, who comes to mind? Not the unimaginative people who gave the tax-return description of their jobs, but the Big Winners who painted a picture of helping people with needs.

A Nutshell Resume for Your Private Life

The *Nutshell Resume* works in nonbusiness situations, too. Since new acquaintances will always ask you about yourself, prepare a few exciting stock answers. When meeting a potential friend or loved one, make your life sound like you will be a fun person to know.

As a young girl, I wrote novels in my mind about my life. "Leil, squinting her eyes against the torrential downpour, bravely reached out the window into the icy storm to pull the shutters tight and keep the family safe from the approaching hurricane." Big deal—Mama asked me to close the windows when it started to rain. Still, marching toward the open window, I fancied myself the family's brave savior.

You don't need to be quite so melodramatic in your self-image, but at least punch up your life to sound interesting and dedicated.

TECHNIQUE #25:
THE NUTSHELL RESUME

Just as job-seeking top managers roll a different written resume off their printers for each position they're applying for, let a different true story about your professional life roll off your tongue for each listener. Before responding to "What do you do," ask yourself, "What possible interest could this person have in my answer? Could he refer business to me? Buy from me? Hire me? Marry my sister? Become my buddy?

Wherever you go, pack a nutshell about your own life to work into your communications bag of tricks.

26 Your Personal Thesaurus

Easy Path to the Verbally Elite

Did you ever hear someone try to say a word that was just too darn big for their tongue? By the smile on the speaker's face and the gleam in his eye as the word limped off his lips, you knew he was really proud of it. (To make matters worse, he probably used the word incorrectly, inappropriately, and maybe even mispronounced it. Ouch.)

The world perceives people with rich vocabularies to be more creative, more intelligent. People with larger vocabularies get hired quicker, promoted faster, and listened to a whole lot more. So Big Winners use rich, full words, but they never sound inappropriate. The phrases slide gracefully off their tongues to enrich their conversation. The words *fit*. With the care that they choose their tie or their blouse, Big Players in life choose words to match their personalities and their points.

The startling good news is that the difference between a respected vocabulary and a mundane one is only about fifty words! You don't need much to sound like a Big Winner. A mere few dozen wonderful words will give everyone the impression that you have an original and creative mind.

Acquiring this super vocabulary is easy. You needn't pore over vocabulary books or listen to tapes of pompous pontificators with impossible British accents. You don't need to learn two-dollar words that your grandmother, if she heard, would wash out of your mouth with soap.

All you need to do is think of a few tired, overworked words you use every day—words like *smart, nice, pretty,* or *good.* Then grab a thesaurus or book of synonyms off the shelf. Look up that common word even *you* are bored hearing yourself utter every day. Examine your long list of alternatives.

For example, if you turn to the word *smart,* you'll find dozens of synonyms. There are colorful, rich words like *ingenious, resourceful, adroit, shrewd,* and many more. Run down the list and say each out loud. Which ones fit your personality? Which ones seem right for *you?* Try each on like a suit of clothes to see which feel comfortable. Choose a few favorites and practice saying them aloud until they become a natural staple of your vocabulary. The next time you want to compliment someone on being smart, say, you'll be purring

"Oh, that was so *clever* of you."
"My how *resourceful.*"
"That was *ingenious.*"
Or maybe, "How *astute* of you."

And Now, for Men Only

Gentlemen, we women spend a lot of time in front of the mirror (as if you didn't know). When I was in college, it used to take me a full fifteen minutes to fix myself up for a date. Every year since, I've had to add a few minutes. I'm now up to an hour and a half gussying myself up for an evening out.

Gentlemen, when your wife comes down the staircase all dolled up for a night out, or you pick a lady up for dinner, what do you say? If you make no comment except, "Well, are you ready to go?" how do you think that makes the lady feel?

I have one friend, Gary, a nice gentleman who occasionally takes me to dinner. I met him about twelve years ago, and I'll never forget the first time he arrived on my doorstep for our date. He said, "Leil, you look great." I adored his reaction!

I saw Gary a month or so later. On my doorstep again, "Leil, you look great." The precise same words as the first time, but I still appreciated it.

It's been *twelve long years* now that this gentleman and I have been friends. I see him about once every two months, and every darn time it's the same old comment, "Leil, you look great." (I think I'll show up one evening in a flannel nightshirt and a mud pack on my face. I swear Gary will say, "Leil, you look great.")

During my seminars, to help men avoid Gary's mistake, I ask every male to think of a synonym for *pretty*, or *great*. Then I bring up one woman and several men. I ask each to pretend he is her husband. She has just come down the stairs ready to go out to dinner. I ask each to take her hand and deliver his compliment.

"Darla," one says, "you look *elegant*."

"Ooh!" Every woman in the room sighs.

"Darla," says another, taking her hand, "you look *stunning*."

"Ooh!" Every woman in the room swoons.

"Darla," says the third, putting her hand between his, "You look *ravishing*."

"Ooooh!" By now every woman in the room has gone limp.

Pay attention men! Words work on us women.

More Unisex Suggestions

Suppose you've been at a party and it was wonderful. Don't tell the hosts it was *wonderful*. Everybody says that. Tell them it was a *splendid* party, a *superb* party, an *extraordinary* party. Hug the hosts and tell them you had a *magnificent* time, a *remarkable* time, a *glorious* time.

The first few times you say a word like *glorious*, it may not roll comfortably off your tongue. Yet you have no trouble with the word *wonderful*. Hmm, *glor-i-ous* doesn't have any more syllables than *won-der-ful*. Neither does it have any more difficult sounds to pronounce. Vocabulary is all a matter of familiarity. Use your new favorite words a few times and, just like breaking in a new pair of shoes, you'll be very comfortable wearing your glorious new words.

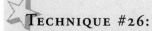

TECHNIQUE #26:
YOUR PERSONAL THESAURUS

Look up some common words you use every day in the thesaurus. Then, like slipping your feet into a new pair of shoes, slip your tongue into a few new words to see how they fit. If you like them, start making permanent replacements.

Remember, only fifty words makes the difference between a rich, creative vocabulary and an average, middle-of-the-road one. Substitute a word a day for two months and you'll be in the verbally elite.

27 ★ Kill the Quick "Me, Too!"

Let Them *Discover* Your Similarity

Tigers prowl with tigers, lions lurk with lions, and little alley cats scramble around with other little alley cats. Similarity breeds attraction. But in the human jungle, Big Cats know a secret. When you *delay* revealing your similarity, or let them discover it, it has much more punch.

Whenever someone mentions a common interest or experience, instead of jumping in with a breathless, "Hey, me, too! I do that, too" or "I know all about that," let your Conversation Partner enjoy talking about it. Let her go on about the country club before you tell her you're a member, too. Let him go on analyzing the golf swing of Arnold Palmer before you start casually comparing the swings of golf greats Greg, Jack, Tiger, and Arnie. Let her tell you how many tennis games she's won before you just happen to mention your USTA ranking.

Several years ago, I was telling a new acquaintance how much I love to ski. He listened with interest as I indulged in a detailed travelogue of places I'd skied. I raved about the various resorts. I analyzed the various conditions. I discussed artificial versus natural snow. It wasn't until near the end of my monologue that I finally had the sense to ask my new acquaintance if he skied. He replied, "Yes, I keep a little apartment in Aspen."

Cool! If he'd jumped in and told me about his ski pad right after I first told him how much I liked skiing, I'd have been impressed. Mildly. However, waiting until the *end* of our conversation—and then revealing he was such an avid skier that he kept an Aspen ski pad—made it unforgettable.

Here's the technique I call *Kill the Quick "Me, Too!"* Whenever people mention an activity or interest you share, let them enjoy discussing their passion. Then, when the time is right, *casually* mention you share their interest.

Oh, I Must Have Been Boring You!

I waited weeks for the opportunity to try it out. Finally the moment presented itself at a convention. A new contact began telling me about her recent trip to Washington, D.C. (She had no idea that Washington was where I grew up.) She told me all about the Capitol, the Washington monument, the Kennedy Center, and how she and her husband went bicycling in Rock Creek Park. (Momentarily I forgot I was keeping my mouth shut to practice my new technique. I was genuinely enjoying hearing about these familiar sights from a visitor's perspective.)

I asked her where she stayed, where she dined, and if she had a chance to get into any of the beautiful Maryland or Virginia suburbs. At one point, obviously pleased by my interest in her trip, she said, "You sound like you know a lot about Washington."

"Yes," I replied. "It's my hometown, but I haven't been back there in ages."

"Your hometown!" she squealed. "My goodness, why didn't you tell me? I must have been boring you."

"Oh, not at all," I replied honestly. "I was enjoying hearing about your trip so much, I was afraid you'd stop if I told you." Her big smile and barely audible "Oh gosh" let me know I had won a new friend.

When someone starts telling you about an activity he has done, a trip she has made, a club he belongs to, an interest she has—anything that you share—bite your tongue. Let the teller relish his or her own monologue. Relax and enjoy it, too, secretly knowing how much pleasure your Conversation Partner will have when you reveal you share the same experience. Then, when the moment is ripe, casually disclose your similarity. And be sure to mention how much you enjoyed hearing about his or her shared interest.

TECHNIQUE #27:
KILL THE QUICK "ME, TOO!"

Whenever you have something in common with someone, the longer you wait to reveal it, the more moved (and impressed) he or she will be. You emerge as a confident Big Cat, not a lonely little stray, hungry for quick connection with a stranger.

PS: Don't wait *too* long to reveal your shared interest or it will seem like you're being tricky.

28 ⭐ Comm-YOU-nication

Be a YOU-Firstie

"SEX! Now that I have your attention . . . " Two-bit comics have been using that gag from the days when two bits bought a foursquare meal. However, Big Winners know there's a three-letter word more potent then *SEX* to get people's attention. That word is *YOU*.

Why is *YOU* such a powerful word? Because when we were infants, we thought we were the center of the universe. Nothing mattered but ME, MYSELF, and I. The rest of the shadowy forms stirring about us (which we later learned were other people) existed solely for what they could do for us. Self-centered little tykes that we were, our tiny brains translated every action, every word, into, "How does that affect ME?"

Big Winners know we haven't changed a bit. Adults camouflage their self-centeredness under a mask of civilization and politeness. Yet the human brain still immediately, instinctively, and unfailingly translates everything into terms of "How does that affect ME?"

For example, suppose, gentlemen, you want to ask a colleague, Jill, if she would like to join you for dinner. So you say to her, "There's a really good new Indian restaurant in town. Will you join me there for dinner tonight?"

Before answering, Jill is thinking to herself, "By 'good' does he mean the food or the atmosphere or both?" Her reverie continues, "Indian cuisine, I'm not sure. *He* says it's good. However, will *I* like it?" While thinking, Jill hesitates. You probably take her hesitation personally, and the joy of the exchange diminishes.

Suppose, instead, you had said to her, "Jill, YOU will really love this new Indian restaurant. Will you join me there this evening for dinner?" Phrasing it that way, you've already subliminally answered Jill's questions and she's more apt to give you a quick yes.

The pleasure-pain principle is a guiding force in life. Psychologists tell us everyone automatically gravitates toward that which is pleasurable and pulls away from that which is painful. For many people, *thinking* is painful.

So Big Winners (when they wish to control, inspire, be loved by, sell to people, or get them to go to dinner) do the thinking for them. They translate everything into the other person's terms by starting as many sentences as they can with that powerful little three-letter word, *YOU*. Thus, I call the technique *Comm-YOU-nication*.

Comm-YOU-nicate When You Want a Favor

Putting YOU first gets a much better response, especially when you're asking a favor, because it pushes the asker's pride button. Suppose you want to take a long weekend. You decide to ask your boss if you can take Friday off. Which request do you think he or she is going to react to more positively? "Can I take Friday off, Boss?" Or this one: "Boss, can YOU do without me Friday?"

In the first case, Boss had to translate your "Can I take Friday off" into "Can *I* do without this employee Friday?" That's an extra thought process. (And you know how some bosses hate to think!)

However, in the second case, "Boss, can YOU do without me Friday," you did Boss's thinking for her. Your new wording made managing without you a matter of pride for Boss. "Of course," she said to herself. "I can manage without your help Friday."

Comm-YOU-nicate Your Compliments

Comm-YOU-nication also enriches your social conversation. Gentlemen, say a lady likes your suit. Which woman gives you warmer feelings? The woman who says, "I like your suit." Or the one who says, "YOU look great in that suit."

Big Players who make business presentations use *Comm-YOU-nication* to excellent advantage. Suppose you're giving a talk and a participant asks a question. He likes to hear you say, "That's a good question." However, consider how much better he feels when you tell him, "YOU'VE asked a good question."

Salespeople, don't just tell your prospects, "It's important that . . . " Convince them by informing them, "YOU'LL see the importance of . . . "

When negotiating, instead of, "The result will be . . . " let them know, "YOU'LL see the result when you . . ."

Starting sentences with *YOU* even works when talking to strangers on the street. Once, driving around San Francisco hopelessly lost, I asked people walking along the sidewalk how to get to the Golden Gate Bridge. I stopped a couple trudging up a hill. "Excuse me," I called out the window, "I can't find the Golden Gate Bridge." The pair looked at each other and shrugged with that "How stupid can these tourists get" look on their faces. "That direction," the husband mumbled, pointing straight ahead.

Still lost, I called out to the next couple I encountered. "Excuse me, where's the Golden Gate Bridge?" Without smiling, they pointed in the opposite direction.

Then I decided to try *Comm-YOU-nication*. When I came upon the next strolling couple, I called out the window, "Excuse me, could YOU tell me where the Golden Gate Bridge is?"

"Of course," they said, answering my question literally. You see, by phrasing the question that way, it was a subtle challenge. I was asking, in essence, "Are you *able* to give me directions?" This hits them in the pride button. They walked over to my car and gave me explicit instructions.

Hey, I thought. This *YOU* stuff really works. To test my hypothesis, I tried it a few more times. I kept asking passersby my three forms of the question. Sure enough, whenever I asked, "Could YOU tell me where . . ." people were more pleasant and helpful than when I started the question with *I* or *Where*.

⭐ **TECHNIQUE #28:**

COMM-YOU-NICATION

Start every appropriate sentence with *YOU*. It immediately grabs your listener's attention. It gets a more positive response because it pushes the pride button and saves them having to translate it into "me" terms.

When you sprinkle *YOU* as liberally as salt and pepper throughout your conversation, your listeners find it an irresistible spice.

I'm sure when they recover the flight box from the Fall of Man under a fig leaf in the Garden of Eden, it will convince the world of the power of the word *YOU*. Eve did not *ask* Adam to eat the apple. She did not *command* him to eat the apple. She didn't even say, "Adam, *I* want you to eat this apple." She phrased it (as all Big Winners would), "*YOU* will love this apple." That's why he bit.

Comm-YOU-nication Is a Sign of Sanity

Therapists calculate inmates of mental institutions say *I* and *me* twelve times more often than residents of the outside world. As patients' conditions improve, the number of times they use the personal pronouns also diminishes.

Continuing up the sanity scale, the fewer times you use *I*, the more sane you seem to your listeners. If you eavesdrop on Big Winners talking with each other, you'll notice a lot more *you* than *I* in their conversation.

The next technique concerns a way Big Winners are *silently* YOU-oriented.

29 The Exclusive Smile

"I Don't Smile at Just Anybody"

Have you ever seen those low-budget mail-order fashion catalogues that use the same model throughout? Whether she is engulfed in a wedding gown or partially clad in a bikini, her face sports the same plastic smile. Looking at her, you get the feeling if you rapped on her forehead, a tiny voice would come back saying "Nobody's in here."

Whereas models in more sophisticated magazines have mastered a myriad of different expressions: a flirtatious "I've got a secret" smile on one page; a quizzical "I think I'd like to get to know you but I'm not sure" smile on the next; and a mysterious Mona Lisa smile on the third. You feel there's a brain running the operation somewhere inside that beautiful head.

I once stood in the receiving line of the ship I worked on, along with the captain, his wife, and several other officers. One passenger with a radiant smile started shaking hands down our line. When he got to me, he flashed a shimmering smile, revealing teeth as even and white as keys on a new piano. I was transfixed. It was as though a brilliant light had illuminated the dim ballroom. I wished him a happy cruise and resolved to find this charming gentleman later.

Then he was introduced to the next person. Out of the corner of my eye, I saw his identical glistening grin. A third person, the same grin. My interest began to dwindle.

When he gave his fourth indistinguishable smile to the next person, he started to resemble a Cheshire cat. By the time he was introduced to the fifth person, his consistent smile felt like a strobe light disturbing the ambiance of the ballroom. Strobe Man went on flashing everybody the same smile down the line. I had no further interest in talking with him.

Why did this man's stock shoot high in my ticker one minute and plummet the next? Because his smile, although charming, reflected no special reaction to *me*. Obviously, he gave the same smile to everybody and, by that, it lost all its specialness. If Strobe Man had given each of us a slightly *different* smile, he would have appeared sensitive and insightful. (Of course, if his smile had been just a tad bigger for me than for the others, I couldn't have waited for the formalities to be over to seek him out in the crowded ballroom.)

Review Your Repertoire of Smiles

If your job required you to carry a gun, you would, of course, learn all about the moving parts before firing it. And before taking aim, you would carefully consider whether it would murder, maim, or merely wound your target. Since your smile is one of your biggest communications weapons, learn all about the moving parts and the effect on your target. Set aside five minutes. Lock your bedroom or bathroom door so your family doesn't think you've gone off the deep end. Now stand in front of the mirror and flash a few smiles. Discover the subtle differences in your repertoire.

Just as you would alternate saying "Hello," "How do you do," and "I am pleased to meet you" when being introduced to a group of people, vary your smile. Don't use the same on each. Let each of your smiles reflect the nuances of your sentiment about the recipient.

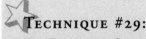

TECHNIQUE #29:
THE EXCLUSIVE SMILE

If you flash everybody the same smile, like a Confederate dollar, it loses value. When meeting groups of people, grace each with a *distinct* smile. Let your smiles grow out of the beauty Big Players find in each new face.

If one person in a group is more important to you than the others, reserve an especially big, flooding smile just for him or her.

In Defense of the Quickie

There are times, I discovered, when the quick put-on smile works. For example, when you want to engineer the acquaintance of someone to whom you have not had the opportunity to be introduced. (In the vernacular, that's "pick them up.")

The smile's pickup power was proven for posterity by solemn researchers at the University of Missouri. They conducted a highly controlled study entitled "Giving Men the Come-on: Effect of Eye Contact and Smiling in a Bar Environment."[15] (I kid you not.) To prove their hypothesis, female researchers made eye contact with unsuspecting male subjects enjoying a little libation in a local drinking establishment. Sometimes, the female researchers followed their glance with a smile. In other cases, no smile.

The results? I quote the study: "The highest approach behavior, 60 percent, was observed in the condition in which there was smiling." That translates into layman's English: "The guy came over 60 percent of the time when the lady smiled." Without the smile, he "made the approach only 20 percent of the time." So, yes, a smile works for those who wish to pick somebody up.

However, in situations where the stakes are higher, try the *Flooding Smile* from the first section, and now the *Exclusive Smile*.

30 ⭐ Don't Touch a Cliché with a Ten-Foot Pole

The Quickest Way to Tell a Jerk

Do you remember that scene from the movie classic *Annie Hall* where Diane Keaton is first meeting Woody Allen? As she's chatting with him, we hear her private thoughts. She's musing to herself, "Oh I hope he's not a jerk like all the others."

One of the quickest ways to make a Big Winner think you are, well, a jerk, is to use a cliché. If you're chatting with a Top Communicator and even innocently remark "Yes, I was *tired as a dog*," or "She was *cute as a button*," you've unknowingly laid a linguistic bomb.

Big Winners silently moan when they hear someone mouth a trite overworn phrase. Oh sure, just like rest of us, Big Winners find themselves feeling *fit as a fiddle*, *happy as a lark*, or *high as a kite*. Like the rest of humanity, they consider some of their acquaintances *crazy as a loon*, *nutty as a fruitcake*, or *blind as a bat*. Because many of them work hard, many of them are as *busy as a bee* and get *rich as Croesus*.

Yet would any of them describe themselves in those words? *Not in a coon's age!* Why? Because when a Big Winner hears your cliché, you might as well be saying, "My powers of imagination are impoverished. I can't think of anything original to say, so I must fall back on these trite overworn phrases." Mouthing a common cliché around uncommonly successful people brands you as uncommonly common.

Technique #30:
Don't Touch a Cliché with a Ten-Foot Pole

Be on guard. Don't use any clichés when chatting with Big Winners. Don't even *touch one with a ten-foot pole*. Never? Not even *when hell freezes over?* Not unless you want to sound *dumb as a doorknob*.

Instead of coughing up a cliché, roll your own clever phrases by using the next technique.

31 Use Jawsmith's Jive

You've Got Pro's Equipment

They say the pen is mightier than the sword. It is, but the tongue is even mightier than the pen. Our tongues can bring crowds to laughter, to tears, and often to their feet in shouting appreciation. Orators have moved nations to war or brought lost souls to God. And what is their equipment? The same eyes, ears, hands, legs, arms, and vocal chords you and I have.

Perhaps a professional athlete has a stronger body or a professional singer is blessed with a more beautiful singing voice than the one we were doled out. But the professional speaker starts out with the same equipment we all have. The difference is, these jawsmiths use it *all*. They use their hands, they use their bodies, and they use specific gestures with heavy impact. They think about the space they're talking in. They employ many different tones of voice, they invoke various expressions, they vary the speed with which they speak . . . and they make effective use of silence.

You may not have to make a formal speech anytime soon, but chances are sometime (probably very soon) you're going to want people to see things your way, whether it's persuading your family to spend their next vacation at Grandma's, or convincing the stockholders in your multimillion-dollar corporation that it's time to do a takeover, do it like a pro. Get a book or two on public speaking and learn some of the tricks of the trade. Then put some of that drama into your everyday conversation.

A Gem for Every Occasion

If stirring words help make your point, ponder the impact of powerful phrases. They've helped politicians get elected ("Read My Lips, No New Taxes") and defendants get acquitted ("If it doesn't fit, you must acquit.")

If George Bush had said, "I promise not to raise taxes," or Johnny Cochran, during O. J. Simpson's criminal trial, had said, "If the glove doesn't fit, he must be innocent," their bulky sentences would have slipped in and out of the voter's or juror's consciousness. As every politician and trial lawyer knows, neat phrases make powerful weapons. (If you're not careful, your enemies will later use them against you—read my lips!)

One of my favorite speakers is a radio broadcaster named Barry Farber who brightens up late-night radio with sparkling similes. Barry would never use a cliché like *nervous as a cat on a hot tin roof.* He'd describe being nervous about losing his job as "I felt like an elephant dangling over a cliff with his tail tied to a daisy." Instead of saying he looked at a pretty woman, he'd say, "My eyeballs popped out and dangled by the optic nerve."

When I first met him, I asked, "Mr. Farber, how do you come up with these phrases?"

"My daddy's Mr. Farber. I'm Barry," he chided (his way of saying, "Call me Barry"). He then candidly admitted, although some of his phrases are original, many are borrowed. (Elvis Presley used to say, "My daddy's Mr. Presley. Call me Elvis.") Like all professional speakers, Barry spends several hours a week gleaning through books of quotations and humor. All professional speakers do. They collect bon mots they can use in a variety of situations—most especially to scrape egg off their faces when something unexpected happens.

Many speakers use author's and speaker's agent Lilly Walters's face-saver lines from her book, *What to Say When You're Dying on the Platform.*[16] If you tell a joke and no one laughs, try "That joke was designed to get a silent laugh—and it worked." If the microphone lets out an agonizing howl, look at it and say, "I don't understand. I brushed my teeth this morning." If someone asks you a question you don't want to answer, "Could you save that question until I'm finished—and well on my way home?" All pros think of holes they might fall into and then memorize great escape lines. You can do the same.

Look through books of similes to enrich your day-to-day conversations. Instead of *happy as a lark* try "happy as a lottery winner" or "happy as a baby with its first ice cream cone." Instead of *bald as an eagle*, try "bald as a new marine" or "bald as a bullfrog's belly." Instead of *quiet as a mouse*, try "quiet as an eel swimming in oil" or "quiet as a fly lighting on a feather duster."

Find phrases that have visual impact. Instead of a cliché like *sure as death and taxes*, try "as certain as beach traffic in July" or "as sure as your shadow will follow you." Your listeners can't *see* death or taxes. But they sure can see beach traffic in July or their shadow following them down the street.

Try to make your similes relate to the situation. If you're riding in a taxi with someone, "as sure as that taxi meter will rise" has immediate impact. If you're talking with a man walking his dog, "as sure as your dog is thinking about that tree" adds a touch of humor.

Make 'Em Laugh, Make 'Em Laugh, Make 'Em Laugh

Humor enriches any conversation. But not jokes starting with, "Hey didja hear the one about . . . ?" Plan your humor and make it relevant. For example, if you're going to a meeting on the budget, look up *money* in a quotation book. In an uptight business situation, a little levity shows you're at ease.

Once, during an oppressive financial meeting, I heard a top executive say, "Don't worry, this company has enough money to stay in business for years—unless we pay our creditors." He broke the tension and won the appreciation of all. Later I saw a similar quote in a humor book attributed to Jackie Mason, the comedian. So what? The exec still came across as Cool Communicator with his clever comment.

Big Players who want to be quoted in the media lie awake at night gnawing the pillow trying to come up with phrases the press will pick up. A Michigan veterinarian named Timothy, a heavy hitter in his own field but completely unknown outside it, made national headlines when he planned to attach a pair of feet to a rooster who lost his to frostbite. Why? Because he called it a "drumstick transplant."

I don't know if a French woman, Jeanne Calment, then officially the world's oldest person, was looking for publicity on her 122nd birthday. But she made international headlines when she told the media, "I've only ever had one wrinkle, and I'm sitting on it."

Mark Victor Hansen, a Big Player in his own field but once relatively unknown outside of it, was propelled into national prominence when he came up with a catchy name for his book coauthored with Jack Canfield, *Chicken Soup for the Soul.* He told me his original title was *101 Pretty Stories.* How far would that have gone? Soon the world was lapping up, among others, his *Chicken Soup for the Woman's Soul, Chicken Soup for the Teenage Soul, Chicken Soup for the Mother's Soul, Chicken Soup for the Christian Soul,* plus second, third, and fourth servings of chicken soup in hardcover, paperback, audiocassette, videocassette, and calendars.

A Word of Warning

No matter how good your material is, it bombs if it doesn't fit the situation. I learned this the hard way during my cruise ship days. On a cruise to England I decided to give my passengers a reading of the English love poems of Elizabeth Barrett and Robert Browning. You know, "How do I love thee? Let me count the ways." It was a BIG hit. The passengers loved it and raved for days. I couldn't walk out on deck without some passenger turning to me and affectionately echoing, "How do I love thee?"

Naturally I got a pretty swollen head over this performance and fancied myself an eminent poetry reader. I decided to reward the passengers on the next cruise (which was a cruise to the Caribbean and didn't go anywhere in the neighborhood of England) with my spectacular reading of the English love poems. WHAT A BOMB! Passengers avoided me on the deck for the rest of the cruise. "How did you *bore* me? Let me count the ways."

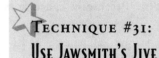

TECHNIQUE #31:
USE JAWSMITH'S JIVE

Whether you're standing behind a podium facing thousands, or behind the barbecue grill facing your family, you'll move, amuse, and motivate with the same skills.

Read speakers' books to cull quotations, pull pearls of wisdom, and get gems to tickle their funny bones. Find a few bon mots to let casually slide off your tongue on chosen occasions. If you want to be notable, dream up a crazy quotable.

Make 'em rhyme, make 'em clever, or make 'em funny. Above all, make 'em relevant.

32 ✦ Call a Spade a Spade

Big Winners Call It Like It Is

If you stepped into an elevator full of people speaking Hungarian, you might not recognize they were Hungarian unless you spoke their language. However, the minute you opened your mouth, *they'd* recognize you're *not* Hungarian.

It's the same with the Big Cats. If you overhear several of them speaking, you might not recognize they're Big Cats. However, the minute you opened your mouth *they'd* recognize *you're* not a Big Cat, unless you spoke their lingo.

What are some differences between a Big Cat's growl and a little cat's insignificant hiss? One of the most blatant is euphemisms. Big Cats aren't afraid of real words. They call a spade a spade. Words like *toilet paper* don't scare them. Little cats hide behind *bathroom tissue*. If somebody is rich, Big Cats call it *rich*. Little cats, oh so embarrassed at the concept of talking about money in polite company, substitute the word *wealthy*. When little cats use a substitute word or euphemism, they might as well be saying, "Whoops, you are better than I am. I'm in polite company now and so I'll use the nicey-nice word."

Big Cats are anatomically correct—no cutesy words for body parts. They'll say *breasts* when they mean breasts. When they say *knockers,* they mean decorative structures that hang on the front door. And *family jewels* are in the safe on the wall.

If a Big Cat is ever in doubt about a word, he or she simply resorts to French. If they feel the word *buttocks* is debatable, *derriere* will do quite nicely, thank you.

TECHNIQUE #32:
CALL A SPADE A SPADE

Don't hide behind euphemisms. Call a spade a spade. That doesn't mean Big Cats use tasteless four-letter words when perfectly decent five- and six-letter ones exist. They've simply learned the King's English, and they speak it.

Here's another way to tell the Big Players from the little ones just by listening to a few minutes of their conversation.

33 Trash the Teasing

Another Dead Giveaway

Once I was at a small dinner party given by the president of an advertising agency, Louis, and his wife, Lillian. The evening started with cocktails, followed by a gourmet meal accompanied by a selection of excellent wines. The conversation had been convivial, the cuisine delicious, and the wine very fine. And very plentiful. At the end of the evening, Louis raised his glass to make a toast. A few wine droplets sloshed out of his glass onto the tablecloth.

A pretty young woman who was the date of a new art director named Bob giggled and said, "I can tell you're feeling no pain."

Shock waves went around the table. Everyone froze. The host was indeed a bit inebriated. However, alluding to Louis being a little looped, even in jest, was as though the woman had suddenly smashed the crystal chandelier above the table with her dinner plate.

One guest quickly covered the girl's horrifying gaffe by lifting her glass and saying "None of us are. No one in the company of Louis and Lillian could ever feel any pain. Here's to a truly wonderful evening."

Louis then continued with his toast to the wonderful company, and no one was feeling pain any longer. *Except* Bob. He knew his date's innocent teasing was a black mark, if not in his personnel file, on his personal file.

The next sure sign of little cathood is teasing. Little cats go around patting their friends' paunches and saying, "Enjoying that cheesecake, huh?" Or looking at their balding heads and saying, "Hey, hair today, gone tomorrow, huh?" They think it's hilarious to make a quip at someone else's expense and say "You don't have an inferiority complex. You are inferior! Hardy har har."

TECHNIQUE #33:
TRASH THE TEASING

A dead giveaway of a little cat is his or her proclivity to tease. An innocent joke at someone else's expense may get you a cheap laugh. Nevertheless, the Big Cats will have the last one. Because you'll bang your head against the glass ceiling they construct to keep little cats from stepping on their paws.

Never, ever, make a joke at anyone else's expense. You'll wind up paying for it, dearly.

34 ⭐ It's the Receiver's Ball

Keep Your Eye on Who's Catching the Ball

In ancient Egypt, the pharaoh treated the humblest message runner like a prince when he arrived at the palace, *if* he brought good news. However, if the exhausted runner had the misfortune to bring the pharaoh unhappy news, his head was chopped off.

Shades of that spirit pervade today's conversations. Once a friend and I packed up some peanut butter and jelly sandwiches for an outing. As we waltzed happily out the door, picnic basket in hand, a smiling neighbor, rocking away on his porch, looked up at the sky and said, "Oh boy, bad day for a picnic. The newscast says it's going to rain." I wanted to rub his face in my peanut-butter and jelly sandwich. Not for his gloomy weather report, for his *smile*.

Several months ago I was racing to catch a bus. As I breathlessly shoved my handful of cash across the Greyhound counter, the grinning sales agent gushed, "Oh that bus left five minutes ago." Dreams of decapitation!

It's not the *news* that makes someone angry. It's the unsympathetic attitude with which it's delivered. Everyone must give bad news from time to time, and winning professionals do it with the proper attitude. A doctor advising a patient she needs an operation does it with compassion. A boss informing an employee he didn't get the job takes on a sympathetic demeanor. Grief counselors at airports after fatal crashes share the grief-stricken sentiment of relatives. Big Winners know, when delivering any bad news, they should share the sentiment of the receiver.

Unfortunately, many people are not aware of this sensitivity. When you're weary from a long flight, has a hotel clerk cheerfully chirped that your room isn't ready yet? When you had your heart set on the roast beef, has your waiter merrily warbled that he just served the last piece? When you needed cash for the weekend, has your bank teller gleefully told you your account is overdrawn? It makes you as traveler, diner, or depositor want to put your fist right through their insensitive grins.

Had my neighbor told me of the impending rainstorm with sympathy, I would have appreciated his warning. Had the Greyhound salesclerk sympathetically informed me that my bus had already left, I probably would have said, "Oh, that's all right. I'll catch the next one." Big Winners, when they bear bad news, deliver bombs with the emotion the bombarded person is sure to have.

TECHNIQUE #34:
IT'S THE RECEIVER'S BALL

A football player wouldn't last two beats of the time clock if he made blind passes. A pro throws the ball with the receiver always in mind.

Before throwing out any news, keep your receiver in mind. Then deliver it with a smile, a sigh, or a sob. Not according to how *you* feel about the news, but how the *receiver* will take it.

Big Winners know how to give bad news to people. They also know how *not* to give any news to anyone, even when people are pressuring them. Let's explore that next.

35 The Broken Record

When You Don't Want to Answer (and Wish They'd Shut the Heck Up)

One of my clients, a ministar in the furniture business, recently separated from her husband and business partner, a megastar in the furniture business. They suffered a long and messy divorce that resulted in them keeping the business jointly, but not having to deal with each other.

Soon after the divorce, I was at an industry convention with my client, Barbara. Since she and her husband Frank were both beloved in the industry, people were curious what had happened and how it affected their company. But, of course, no one dared ask outright. And Barbara was offering no explanations.

I was seated next to Barbara at the gala farewell dinner. Apparently one of her colleagues at the table couldn't contain her curiosity any longer. During dessert, she leaned over to Barbara and in a hushed voice asked, "Barbara, what happened with you and Frank?"

Barbara, unruffled by the rude question, simply took a spoonful of her cherries jubilee and said, "We've separated, but the company is unaffected."

Not satisfied with that answer, the woman pumped harder. "Are you still working together?"

Barbara took another bite of her dessert and repeated in precisely the same tone of voice, "We've separated, but the company is unaffected."

The frustrated interrogator was not going to give up easily. "Are you both still working in the company?"

Barbara, appearing not the least disturbed by the woman's incontinent insistence, scooped the last cherry out of her dish, smiled, looked directly at her, and said in the identical tone of voice, "We've separated, but the company is unaffected."

That shut her up. Barbara had shown her Big Winner's badge by using the *Broken Record* technique, the most effective way to curtail an unwelcome cross-examination.

Technique #35:
The Broken Record

Whenever someone persists in questioning you on an unwelcome subject, simply repeat your original response. Use *precisely* the same words in *precisely* the same tone of voice. Hearing it again usually quiets them down. If your rude interrogator hangs on like a leech, your next repetition never fails to flick them off.

36 Big Shots Don't Slobber

How Big Players Handle a Celebrity

Suppose you've just settled in for dinner at a nice restaurant. You look over at the next table, and who do you see? Is it really he? Could it possibly be? It's gotta be a look-alike. No, it isn't! It really is . . . Woody Allen. (Substitute any celebrity here: your favorite movie star, politician, broadcaster, boss who owns the company that owns the company you work for.) And there the celestial body is in the flesh, sitting not ten feet from you. What should you do?

Nothing! Let the star enjoy a brief moment of anonymity. If he or she should cast a glance in your direction, give a smile and a nod. Then waft your gaze back to your dining companion. You will be a lot cooler in the eyes of your dinner partner if you take it all in your stride.

Now, if you just can't resist this once-in-a-lifetime opportunity to press the flesh of the Megastar and tell him or her of your admiration, here's how to do it with grace. Wait until you or the luminary are leaving the restaurant. After the check has been paid and you will obviously not be taking much of his or her time, you may make your approach. Say something like, "Mr. Allen, I just want to tell you how much pleasure your wonderful films have given me over the years. Thank you so much."

Did you pick up the subtlety here? You are not *complimenting* his work. "After all," he might well ask himself, "who are you to judge whether I am a great filmmaker or not?" You can only speak from your own perspective. You do this by telling him how much pleasure his work has given you.

If it's your boss's boss's boss's boss whom the fates have sent to bask in your adulation, do the same. Do not say "Bill" or "Mr. Gates, you really run a great company."

"Lowly geek," he thinks, "who are you to judge?" Instead, tell him what an honor it is to work for him. Obviously this is not the moment to detail the intricacies of your improvements on image-editing software for digitizing photographs.

Then let your body language express that if Woody or Bill or other Megastar wants to leave it at that, you are happy with the exchange. If, however, Megastar is captivated by you (or has had so much liquid merriment that he or she has decided to mingle with the masses tonight), then all bets are off. You're on your own. Enjoy! *Until* you pick up the first body-language sign that they would like to end it. Think of yourself as a ballroom dance student waltzing with your teacher. He leads, you follow. And he tells you when the waltz is over.

Incidentally, if Megastar is with a companion and your conversation goes on for more than a few moments, direct some comments at the companion. If the satellite is in such stellar company, he or she is probably also an accomplished person.

Felicia, a friend of mine, is a talented trial lawyer who is married to a local TV-show host. Because Tom is on television, people recognize him wherever they go, and Felicia gets ignored. Felicia tells me how frustrating it is, even for Tom. Whenever they go to a party, people gush all over Tom, and Felicia's fascinating work hardly ever gets mentioned. She and Tom used to love going out to dinner, but now they hide out at home in the evenings. Why? Because they can't stand the interruptions of overly effervescent fans.

"I Love What You *Used* to Be (You Has-Been)"

Another sensitivity: the film star is probably obsessed with his last film, the politician with her last election, a corporate mogul with his last takeover, an author with her last novel—and so forth. So when discussing the star's, the politician's, the mogul's, the author's, or any VIP's work, try to keep your comments to current or recent work. Telling Woody Allen how much you loved his 1980 film *Stardust Memories* would not endear you to him. "What about all my wonderful films since?" thinks he. Stick to the present or very recent past if possible.

⭐ TECHNIQUE #36:
BIG SHOTS DON'T SLOBBER

People who are VIPs in their own right don't slobber over celebrities. When you are chatting with one, don't compliment her work, simply say how much pleasure or insight it's given you. If you do single out any one of the star's accomplishments, make sure it's a recent one, not a memory that's getting yellow in her scrapbook.

If the Queen Bee has a drone sitting with her, find a way to involve him in the conversation.

A final celebrity codicil: Suppose you are fortunate enough to have one at your party. To shine some star light on your party, don't ask the TV host to "say a few words." Don't ask the singer to sing a song. What looks effortless to the rest of us because they seem so comfortable performing, is *work* for them. You wouldn't ask an accountant guest to look over your books. Or a dentist to check out your third left molar. Let the dignitary drink. Let the luminary laugh. Celebrities are people, too, and they like their time off.

37 Never the Naked Thank You

The Final Touch

To wrap up our section on sounding like the Big Boys and Girls, here is a simple and gracious little maneuver. It not only signals people you're a Top Communicator, it encourages them to keep doing nice things for you. Or complimenting you. Or doing business with you. Or loving you. It is very short. It is very sweet. It is very simple. You can use it with everyone in your life. When it becomes instinctive, you'll find yourself using it every day.

Very simply, never let the word *thank you* stand naked and alone. Always make it thank you *for* something. People use the bare exposed *thank you* so often that people don't even hear it anymore. When we buy the morning newspaper, we flash a naked *thank you* at the vendor when he gives us our nickel's change. Is that the same *thank you* you want to give a valued customer who makes a big purchase in your store? Or a loved one who cooks you a delicious dinner?

Whenever the occasion warrants more than an unconscious acknowledgment, dress up your *thank you* with the reason:

Thank you *for* coming.
Thank you *for* being so understanding.

Thank you *for* waiting.
Thank you *for* being such a good customer.
Thank you *for* being so loving.

Often, when I disembark an airplane, the captain and first officer are standing by the cockpit door to bid the passengers farewell. I say, "Thanks for getting us here." Admittedly, that's carrying *Never the Naked Thank You* to extremes, but it has a surprising effect. They fall all over themselves with "Oh, thanks for flying with us!"

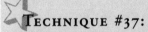

TECHNIQUE #37:

NEVER THE NAKED THANK YOU

Never let the words *thank you* stand alone. From A to Z, always follow it with *for*: from "Thank you for asking" to "Thank you for zipping me up."

Thank you for reading this section of *Talking the Winner's Way*! Now let us move on to another conversation challenge, how to talk knowledgeably with everyone—from groups of accountants to Zen Buddhists—no matter how little you might have in common.

PART FOUR

How to Be an Insider in Any Crowd

What Are They All Talking About?

Has it ever happened to you? Everyone at the party is speaking gobbledygook. They're all discussing faulty audits, code constraints, or the library market—and you have no idea what they're talking about. It's because everybody at the party is an accountant, an architect, or a publisher—and you're not.

So you stand there with a pasty smile on your face not opening your mouth. If you do, you fear the wrong thing will come out. Paranoia sets in. Everybody will snicker at you. You're an *outsider*. So you suffer in silence.

In high school I suffered a massive Silent Outsider Syndrome, especially around males. All they wanted to talk about was cars. I knew nothing about cars. The only time I'd ever set foot in a "body shop" was to get a suntan.

Well, one fateful day, Mama came home with a gift for me that transformed my teenage existence from shy to sociable. It was a book on all the current model cars and their differences over and under the hood. One reading, and I became fluent in Fords, Chevys, and Buicks. I no longer hyperventilated when boys said words like *carburetor, alternator, camshaft,* or *exhaust manifold.*

I didn't need to learn a lot, just enough to ask the right questions to get the guys talking. When I'd learned to speak "car" with the boys, it worked wonders for my social life.

Cut to today. We grown-up boys and girls also have our favorite topics which usually involve our work or our hobbies. When we're with people in our own field or who share interests, we open up like small-town gossips. (Even engineers who have a constant case of cat-got-their-tongue start gabbing about greasy turbines and various projects when they're together.) To outsiders, our conversation sounds like gobbledygook. But we know precisely what it's about. It's our own *job*beldygook or *hobby*dygook.

You fear you'll find yourself in a party of squash players when you're the type of person who'd rather be *in* court than *on* court? Don't panic hearing words like *lobbing* and *hitting rails* roll off the squash players' tongues. So what if the only experience you've ever had with squash was the mashed acorn variety on your plate next to the turkey last Thanksgiving. All you need is the few techniques that follow.

Just as anglers throw out a dragonfly to get the fish to bite, all you have to do is throw out the *right* questions to get people to open up. Dale Carnegie's adage, "show sincere interest and people will talk," only goes so far. As they say in poker, "it takes jacks or better to open." And in conversation, it takes cursory *knowledge* or better about their field to get them to really open up. You must have knowledgeable curiosity, the kind that makes you sound like you're worth talking to.

In this section, we explore techniques that are "Open Sesames" to get people gabbing with you like an insider.

38 Scramble Therapy

To Be a Modern-Day Renaissance Man or Woman

Whenever friends visit my hometown, New York City, I warn them "Never ask anyone riding in the subway for directions."

"Because I'll get mugged?" they fearfully ask.

"No, just because you'll never get where you're going!" Most Big Apple subway riders know only two things about the subway: where they get on and where they get off. They know nothing about the rest of the system. Most people are like NYC strap-hangers when it comes to their hobbies and interests. They know their own pastimes, but all the others are like unvisited stations.

My unmarried (and wishing she weren't) friend Rita has a bad case of bowler's thumb. Every Wednesday night she's bowling up a storm with her friends. She is forever discussing her scores, her averages, and her high game. Another single and searching friend, Walter, is into white-water rafting. He talks endlessly with his paddling friends about which rivers he's run, which outfitters he's gone with, and which class rapids he prefers. Thinking my two single friends might hit it off, I introduced Walter the paddler to Rita the bowler and mentioned their respective passions.

"Oh you're a bowler!" said Walter.

"Yes," Rita smiled demurely, awaiting more questions about her big bowling turn-on. Walter was silent.

Masking her disappointment, Rita said, "Uh, Leil tells me you're into water rafting." Walter smiled proudly, awaiting further friendly interrogation on paddling. "Uh, that must be exciting. Isn't it dangerous?" was the best Rita could do.

"No, it's not dangerous," Walter patronizingly responded to her typical outsider's question. Then the conversation died.

During the deafening silence, I remember thinking, if Rita had run just *one* river, if Walter had bowled just *one* game, their lives might be different now. Conversation could have flowed, and who knows what else might have flowered.

Go Fly a Kite!

The *Scramble Therapy* technique is salvation from such disappointing encounters. It will transform you into a modern-day Renaissance man or woman who comfortably can discuss a variety of interests.

Scramble Therapy is, quite simply, scrambling up your life and participating in an activity you'd never think of indulging in. Just one out of every four weekends, do something totally out of your pattern. Do you usually play tennis on weekends? This weekend, go hiking. Do you usually go hiking? This weekend, take a tennis lesson. Do you bowl? Leave that to your buddies this time. Instead, go white-water rafting. Oh, you were planning on running some rapids like you do every warm weekend? Forget it, go bowling.

Go to a stamp exhibition. Go to a chess lecture. Go ballooning. Go bird watching. Go to a pool hall. Go kayaking. Go fly a kite! Why? Because it will give you conversational fodder *for the rest of your life.* From that weekend on, you'll sound like an insider with all the hikers, stamp collectors, ballooners, birders, billiards players, kayakers, and kitists you ever meet. Just by doing their activity once.

If you take a piece of blue litmus paper and dip it in a huge vat of acid, the tip turns pink. If you take another blue litmus paper and dip it into just one minuscule drop of acid on a glass slide, the tip turns just as pink. Compare this to participating in an activity just one time. A sampling gives you 80 percent of the conversational value. You learn the insider's questions to ask. You start using the right terms. You'll never be at a loss again when the subject of extracurricular interests comes up—which it always does.

Do You Speak Scuba?

I'm not a certified scuba diver. However, six years ago in Bermuda I saw a sign: "Resort Dives, $25, no Scuba experience necessary." In just three hours, I received the best crash course in talking with scuba divers the world offers.

First I was given a quick lesson in the pool. Then, struggling to stay erect under the weight of my oxygen tank, regulator, buoyancy compensator, and weight belt, I went clumping out to the dive boat. Sitting there on the rocking dinghy, fondling my mask and fins like worry beads, I overheard the certified divers asking each other insider questions:

> "Where were you *certified*?"
> "Where have you *dived*?"
> "Do you prefer *wrecks* or *reefs*?"
> "Ever done any *night diving*?"
> "Are you into *underwater photography*?"
> "Do you *dive on a computer*?"
> "What's your longest *bottom time*?"
> "Did you ever get *the bends*?"

Why the italicized words? Those are scuba lingo. I now speak scuba. To this day, whenever I meet divers, I have the right questions to ask, and subjects to discuss. And the right ones to avoid. (Like how much I like seafood. That's like telling a cat lover how much you love tender barbecued kitten.) I can now ask my new friends which of the scuba hot spots they've been to—Cozumel, Cayman, Cancun. Then, if I want to really show off, I ask if they've been to Truk Lagoon in the Far Pacific, the Great Barrier Reef in Australia, or the Red Sea.

All the insider terms now roll comfortably off my tongue. Before my *Scramble Therapy* experience I'd be calling their beloved wrecks and reefs "sunken ships" and "coral." Understandable words, but not scuba words. Not *insider* words. Upon meeting a scuba diver, I probably would have asked, "Oh scuba diving. That must be interesting. Uh, aren't you afraid of sharks?" Not a good way to get off on the right fin with a diver.

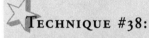

TECHNIQUE #38:
SCRAMBLE THERAPY

Once a month, scramble your life. Do something you'd *never* dream of doing. Participate in a sport, go to an exhibition, hear a lecture on something totally out of your experience. You get 80 percent of the right lingo and insider questions from just one exposure.

Think about it! Suppose at a dinner party, the table conversation turns to scuba diving. If you, too, had done your one-time-only dive, you'd ask your diving dinner companion if he likes night diving, or whether he prefers diving on wrecks or reefs. (He'll never believe it when you tell him the deepest water you've ever submerged yourself in is your own bathtub.)

Then you turn to the bungee jumper seated on your left and ask him, "Do you prefer chest-waist jumps or ankle jumps?" If the conversation then changes to tennis, or martial arts, or chess, or coin collecting, or even bird watching, you can keep up and keep the conversation going. What a guy! What a gal!

39 Learn a Little Jobbledygook

Surviving Bafflegab

Even more insidious than hobby-talk is job-speak, or Jobble-dygook. I still harbor social nightmares of the evening I attended a party thrown by a couple who worked in computer database management. As I walked in the door, I overheard one chap saying to another, "When the domain relational calculus is restricted to safe expressions, it's equivalent to the turple relational . . ."

That's all I stayed around for. I knew I wasn't going to understand one *bit* or *byte* of conversation the rest of the evening. It made me long for the days when a *mouse* meant the furry little fellow who loves cheese, *windows* were the kind you bought drapes for, and *the web* was something spiders trapped flies in. I knew I was going to need some *technical support* if I was going to be compatible with this crowd.

I decided then and there to learn some of the opening questions database management types ask each other. Which I did. Now I can't wait for a second chance at that crowd because I'm armed with questions like "What raid level are you using?" and "What data warehousing product do you use?"

All you need are a few insider opening questions to get you started with any group. You ask questions, listen to the responses, and indulge in elementary on-target conversation with them for a moment or two about their field. (Then change the subject ASAP! You don't want to fake you are more knowledgeable about their field than you really are.)

It's All in the Opening Question

A tennis player can tell immediately from just appraising your opening serve how good a player you are. Is it going to be great playing with you, or a real bore? It's the same in communicating. Just from your verbal opening serve, someone knows if it's going to be interesting talking with you about their life or interests— or dull, dull, dull.

For example, suppose I'm introduced to someone and the first words out of her mouth are, "Oh, you're a writer. When are you going to write the great American novel?" Yikes, I know I'm talking with someone who is unfamiliar with my world. We'll chat, but I prefer to change the subject. And soon, my Conversation Partner.

If, however, my new acquaintance says, "Oh you're a writer. Do you write fiction or nonfiction?" Bingo! Now I know I'm with a person who knows about my world. Why? Because that is the first question *all* writers ask each other. I enjoy talking to this inquisitor because I presume she has more insights into the writing world. Even if we quickly get off the subject of writing, she has come across as a well-informed individual.

Every job, *every* sport, *every* interest has insider opening questions that everybody in the same field asks—and its dumb outsider questions that they never ask each other. When an astronaut meets another astronaut, he asks, "What missions have you been on?" (*Never* "How do you go to the bathroom up there?") A dentist asks another dentist, "Are you in general practice or do you have a specialty?" (*Never* "Heard any good pain jokes lately?")

The good news is, beginning Jobbledygook is an easy language. There's no need to master buzzwords, only a few opening questions to make you sound like an insider. Then, here's the fun part, when you tell them you're *not* connected to their field, they're all the more impressed. "What a knowledgeable person!" they say to themselves.

"Help! Everybody There Will Be an Artist."

It's not hard to harvest good Jobbledygook. Let's say you've been invited to a gallery opening where you'll be meeting many artists. If you don't speak artist, go through your Rolodex to see if you have an artist friend or two.

Aha, you found one. Well, sort of. Your friend Sally attended art school. You call her up and ask, "Sally, I know this sounds silly but I've been invited to an event where I'm bound to be talking with a lot of artists. Could you give me a few good questions to ask?" Sally might find your query a tad unusual, but your diligence should impress her.

Maybe she'll say, "Well, ask artists what *medium* they work in."

"Medium?" you ask.

"Sure," she'll tell you. "That's the insider's way to ask if they work with acrylics, oil, charcoal, pen, etc."

"Oh."

"Don't ask artists to describe their work," she warns. "They feel theirs is a visual medium that can't be described."

"Oh."

"And don't ask them if their work is in a gallery."

"Oh?"

"That could be a sore point. Instead ask 'Is there anyplace I might see your work?' They'll love that because, even if they're not represented by a gallery, they can invite you to their studio to possibly buy their work."

Technique #39:
Learn a Little Jobbledygook

Big Winners speak Jobbledygook as a second language. What is Jobbledygook? It's the language of other professions.

Why speak it? It makes you sound like an insider.

How do you learn it? You'll find no Jobbledygook cassettes in the language section of your bookstore, but the lingo is easy to pick up. Simply ask a friend who speaks the lingo of the crowd you'll be with to teach you a few opening questions. The words are few and the rewards are manifold.

That's all you need to get started—two good opening art questions and a warning against the most-asked dumb outsider question.

Let's say you've given a great opening serve with the right question on their job. You've slammed a swift ball dead center into their conversational court. Happily, thinking they're with an ace player, they answer your question. Then they put a little spin on the ball and send it lobbing right back into your court and it's time for a follow-up question. Whoops, what to do now?

If you don't want to come out of the bluffer's closet just yet, you must master the next technique, *Baring Their Hot Button*.

40 Baring Their Hot Button

Elementary Doc-Talk

I have a friend, John, a physician, who recently married a charming Japanese woman, Yamika. John told me the first time they were invited to a party to meet many of John's colleagues, Yamika was panic-stricken. She wanted to make a good impression, yet she was tense about talking to American doctors. John was the only one she'd ever met, and during their romance they didn't spend a whole lot of time discussing medicine.

John told her, "Don't worry about it, Yami. They all ask each other the same old questions. When you meet them, just ask, 'What's your specialty' and 'Are you affiliated with a hospital?'

"Then, to get into deeper conversation," he continued, "throw out questions like 'How's your relationship with your hospital?' or 'How's the current medical environment affecting you?' These are hot issues with doctors because everything's changing in health care."

John said Yamika delivered the lines verbatim. She circulated the party asking the various doctors' specialties and inquiring about their affiliations and relationships with their hospitals. As a result, she was the hit of the party. Many of John's colleagues later congratulated him on having found such a charming and insightful woman.

Getting the Real Grabber

It's not just doctors. *Every* profession has concerns that are all the buzz within the industry. The rest of the world, however, knows little about these fixations. For example, independent booksellers constantly complain that big superstore chains are taking over the industry. Accountants lie awake nights worrying about liability insurance for faulty audits. And dentists grind their teeth over OSHA and EPA regulations. Oh, us writers, too. We're always belly-aching about magazines not paying us for electronic rights to our precious words.

Suppose some hapless soul were unlucky enough to find himself in a party of writers. Making conversation with these folks (who seldom know what they think until they see what they say) is no easy task for one who is accustomed to communicating in the spoken word. However, if before the party the nonwriter had called just one writer acquaintance and asked about the burning issues, he'd have had hot conversation with the wordsmiths all evening. I call the technique *Baring Their Hot Button*.

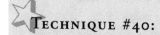

TECHNIQUE #40:
BARING THEIR HOT BUTTON

Before jumping blindly into a bevy of bookbinders or a drove of dentists, find out what the hot issues are in their fields. Every industry has burning concerns the outside world knows little about. Ask your informant to bare the industry buzz. Then, to heat the conversation up, push those buttons.

Back to the art show you're about to attend. You can't let Sally hang up yet. She's given you the two best opening questions for artists. But don't let her go until you get the real conversational grabber. Ask her the hottest issues going on in the art world. She might think a minute and then say, "Well, there's always art prices."

"Art prices?" you ask.

"Yes," she explains. "For example, in the 1980s the art world was very market-driven. Prices went sky high because some investors and status seekers paid exorbitant amounts. We feel that kind of took art away from the masses."

Wow, now you're really armed with some good insider art talk!

See You at the Big One!

While you're at it, don't forget to grill your informant for special insider greetings to use when you're with their gang. For example, actresses cringe if they hear "good luck" before a show, but they smile at well-wishers who say "Break a leg!"

"Break a leg," however, is not appropriate for runners before a marathon. That's the last thought they want to have! The only thing they want to break is their personal record. Try "Have a personal best!"

Firefighters who work on shift seldom see each other except, of course, at the biggest blazes. Thus the firefighters' greeting "See ya at the big one!"

Once, driving in a sleepy town you have to work at getting lost in, I succeeded. I was hopelessly turned around. Happily, I spotted the firehouse and a couple of bored firefighters lounging out front.

"Excuse me, can you tell me the way back to Route 50?" I called out the window. I could tell from their attitude they thought I was an idiot. Nevertheless, they lethargically pointed me in the right direction. As I drove off, I called out, "Thanks guys, see ya at the big one!" In the rearview mirror I saw huge smiles break out on their faces as they stood up in unison and waved good-bye. The disoriented dizzy blond driving off had won their respect with their insider salute.

41 Read Their Rags

Extra! Extra! Learn Even More About Their Lives

Let's say your paper carrier has just hurled the newspaper from his bike to your front door. You pour a cup of coffee and get comfortable to catch up on what's happening in the world. Your world, that is. Do you flip first to the international news? The fashion section? The sports page? The entertainment section? Maybe the comics?

Whichever section you usually flip to first, tomorrow DON'T. Turn to *any* other section, preferably one you hardly ever read. Why? Because it will familiarize you with other worlds so that you can soon discuss anything with anybody, no matter how little you have in common.

How about the real estate section? Yawn. Maybe you don't find real estate especially engrossing. However, sooner or later you're going to find yourself with a group of people who are discussing properties, deals, and today's market. Scanning the real estate section just once every few weeks will keep you *au courant* with their conversation.

The advertising column? Maybe you think the world would be a far far better place without Madison Avenue. But your bottom line won't be better off if you can't hold your own discussing matters with the marketing maven you've just contracted to advertise your company's widgets. Just a few peeks at the advertising news section and you'll soon be chatting about *campaigns* and *creative* people, and doing *print* or *TV*. Instead of saying *words*, you'll be saying *copy*. Instead of *the agency*, you'll be bandying about real insider terms like *the shop*.

Using outsider words is one of the biggest giveaways that you are not in the know. On the ship, if a passenger asked any of my staff, "How long have you been working on the boat?" they'd squelch a groan. Cruise staffers proudly worked on a *ship*, and the word *boat* revealed the passenger as a real landlubber.

The right word can perform conversational miracles. In the receiving line, whenever passengers asked our laconic captain, "When did you first become a master?" or "What was your first command?" he would hold up the entire line of people snaking around the ballroom waiting to shake his hand. Captain Cafiero would enthusiastically recount his naval history to the savvy inquirer who might have just learned the words *master* or *command* last week in the newspaper shipping notices. (If the passenger had simply said, "How long have you been a captain?" or "What was your first boat?" he or she would have gotten the captain's usual Italian gentleman's version of the bum's rush.)

Soon you'll become addicted to the high that establishing rapport with so many people gives you. All it takes is reading different sections of the newspaper.

Pump Their Pulp for Even More Fuel

Then, when you crave a bigger hit of insider lingo, start reading trade journals. Those are the closed-circulation magazines that go to members of various industries. Ask your friends in different jobs to lend you one so you'll have even more fuel for the conversational fire.

All industries have one or two. You'll see big glossy rags with names like *Automotive News*, *Restaurant Business*, *Pool and Spa News*, *Trucking Industry*, and even *Hogs Today* for people in the pig business. (Excuse me, they call themselves *swine practitioners.* Hey, you never know when, to make your next big sale, it will help to speak pig.) Any one issue will give you a sample of their lingo and inform you of the hottest issues in that field.

When it comes to peoples' hobbies and interests, browse through magazines on running, working out, bicycling, skiing, swimming, surfing. Large magazine stores carry biker rags, boxer rags, bowler rags, even bull-riding rags. You'll find thousands of special-interest magazines published every month.

Several years ago, I got hooked on buying a different one each week. It paid off quickly when a potential consulting client invited me to dinner at her home. She had a beautiful garden and, thanks to *Flower and Garden Magazine,* I could throw out insider terms like *ornamentals, annuals,* and *perennials.* I could even keep up when the discussion turned to the advantages of growing from seeds or bulbs.

Because I was so fluent in flower, she invited me to take a longer walk with her to see her private back gardens. As we strolled, I gradually changed the subject from chrysanthemums to the consulting work I could do for her company. Who was leading whom down the garden path?

TECHNIQUE #41:
READ THEIR RAGS

Is your next big client a golfer, runner, swimmer, surfer, or skier? Are you attending a social function filled with accountants or Zen Buddhists—or anything between? There are untold thousands of monthly magazines serving every imaginable interest. You can dish up more information than you'll ever need to sound like an insider with anyone just by reading the rags that serve their racket. (Have you read your latest copy of *Zoonooz* yet?)

Is the world getting smaller, or are we getting bigger? Today's Renaissance man or woman is comfortable and confident anywhere. The next technique helps you be an insider wherever you find yourself on the planet, and it saves you from fulfilling the world's fantasy of "the ugly American."

42 Clear "Customs"

How to Be a Global Insider

Say you're traveling abroad on business. What's the first thing on your to-do list? Get a passport and a phrase book, right? After all, who wants to wander around Rome not knowing how to ask for a restroom? Or be thirsty in Kuala Lumpur not knowing how to ask for a Coke? However, there's something most of us forget to pack, often to dire consequences—a book on international customs.

A friend of mine, a fellow speaker named Geraldine, was excited about her first speech in Japan. To be comfy on her long flight to Tokyo, she donned her favorite designer jeans and a casual jacket. Fourteen hours and 6,737 miles later, four impeccably dressed Japanese gentlemen greeted her at Narita Airport. Smiling and bowing low, they handed her their business cards. With her carry-on bag in one hand, Geri took their cards with the other. She thanked them, glanced briefly at the cards, and packed them safely into her back pocket. She then pulled one of her business cards out of her purse and, sensitive to the fact that they might have difficulty pronouncing Geraldine, wrote her nickname "Geri" above her printed name. The gentlemen hovered over her card, turning it over to examine it a few times, before one of them put it in his briefcase.

When the five of them arrived at the hotel, they invited Geri for tea in the lobby. While sipping tea, the gentlemen presented her with a small gift which she eagerly opened. One of Geri's most charming qualities is her instinctive warmth and effusiveness. She was thrilled with the gift and, in typical Geri style, she squealed, "Oh, it's beautiful!" as she gave each of the gentlemen a little hug.

At this point, the four Japanese gentlemen stood up in unison like four frowning Siamese twins and, bowing only very slightly, mumbled "Sayonara" and promptly left. Poor Geri was flabbergasted. What did she do wrong?

Everything! First, the jeans. Even if you're coming off a bicycle in Asia, you do not meet clients casually dressed. The second mistake was Geri's vulgar handling of their business cards. In Asia, the business card is one of the most important protocol tools. It is always presented and accepted reverently with both hands. (Except in Moslem Asia where the left hand is considered unclean.)

Geri then put their cards away much too quickly. In Asia, people use business cards as a conversation starter. You chat about each other's cards and work and do not put theirs away until they gently and respectfully place yours in safekeeping. Shoving it into her back jeans pocket was the ultimate disrespect.

Geri didn't discover her fourth gaffe until she returned home. One of her colleagues, Bill, a seasoned business traveler, analyzed the fiasco for her. Bill told her the reason the gentlemen had turned Geraldine's card over and over when she gave it to them at the airport was to find her name, title, and company printed in Japanese on the other side. The flip side of Geri's card was, of course, blank.

Then, fifth horror of horrors, Geri should not have written on the card. Cards in Asia are not exactly sacred, but one should never deface them with messy handwriting.

The sad tale of Geri and the Japanese gets worse. Bill broke the bad news to her: she should not have opened the gift in front of her clients. Why? Because in a land where saving face is critical, it would be embarrassing to discover the gift they gave was not as nice as the one they received. (Yikes, Geri hadn't even given them a gift!) Gaffe number seven.

Geri's little squeal when receiving the gift was also a boo-boo. In Asia, the lower the tone of voice, the higher the rank. The final flub was, of course, giving the gentlemen a thank-you hug. Hugging, highly revered in certain parts of the world is, in Japan, absolutely unacceptable with a new client.

Needless to say, Geri has not been invited back to Japan. However, she does have a gig coming up in El Salvador. This time she's smart. She's studying up on the customs there. Happily, she's finding she can hug to her heart's content. However she shouldn't use her (or anybody else's) first name. Oh, and she must not introduce herself as an "American." After all, Salvadorans are Americans, too!

The differences 'round the world go on and on. Whenever I travel, I have to hit myself over the head and realize I'm not in the anything-goes ol' USA. I love to travel in jeans, I'm an incurable hugger, and I can't wait to see what's in a gift box anybody gives me. However, whenever I plan to leave Uncle Sam's shores, I check on foreign customs to see how much of myself I can be.

There are some excellent books on international customs. You'll find the names of a few in the notes.[17-19]

TECHNIQUE #42:
CLEAR "CUSTOMS"

Before putting one toe on foreign soil, get a book on dos and taboos around the world. Before you shake hands, give a gift, make gestures, or even compliment anyone's possessions, check it out. Your gaffe could gum up your entire gig.

Don't be like another hapless colleague of mine who almost blew a big business deal with a Brazilian. Just before signing the contract, he gave the OK sign with his thumb and forefinger. Little did he know he was telling his new business partner to go have intercourse with himself. You never know until it's too late.

Now we come to where being an insider shows immediate, tangible, and calculable rewards. And where being an outsider really hurts—right in your pocket or purse.

$\overset{\star}{43}$ Bluffing for Bargains

Getting What You Want
at the Insider Price

Never underestimate human ingenuity when it comes to getting what you want. Many people expand the adage, *All's fair in love and war* to *All is fair in love, war, and buying what I want.* To get a table at a posh restaurant on a busy night, using a celebrity name is an old ploy. My favorite maitre d' told me he gets a lot of Robert De Niros phoning in a reservation. When their party of six or eight arrives, he hears, "I'm so sorry, Rob wasn't feeling well this evening."

One woman, frustrated when her fake celebrity name didn't work, shouted at him, "Look, who the hell do I have to be to get a table? I'll be anyone you want me to be, Goldie Hawn, Steffi Graf, Fergie—just *tell* me." Some people try a last-minute approach. They simply walk up to the maitre d' at an overbooked restaurant, point to any name on the reservation book and say, "That's us."

You'll witness the same cunning at overbooked hotels. Several months ago I was checking into a popular hotel for which, fortunately, I had a confirmed reservation. A loudmouthed man in front of me in line shouted at the desk clerk, "Whaddaya mean, no room? I'm staying in this hotel tonight. If you don't have a room, I'm sleeping right here on the floor." His temper tantrum was not working.

"And I warn you," he continued, "I sleep in the nude!"

He got a room.

These crafty childish tactics are not recommended. Rather, I suggest a more principled technique called *Bluffing for Bargains.* It was born one afternoon sitting with an insurance broker, Mr. Carson. He was trying to sell me a homeowner's policy. Of course I wanted the most coverage for the least cash. Carson was a smooth operator and he was patiently explaining to me in layman's terms the benefits of certain riders he was pushing.

Just as he started discussing disasters like wars and hurricanes, his phone rang. With apologies, he picked up the receiver. It was one of his colleagues. Suddenly a metamorphosis took place before my eyes. The sophisticated salesman became a palsy-walsy regular down-home kinda guy chatting it up with his old buddy about *umbrellas.* I thought they were discussing the weather.

Then the conversation turned to *floaters.* I now assumed they were talking about an eye problem. It took a while for me to realize that umbrella policies and floaters were part of the insurancese they were speaking.

A few minutes later, Carson said, "Yeah, OK, so long, buddy," and put the phone down. He cleared his throat and again transmogrified back into the formal sales agent patiently defining damages and deductibles to a naive client.

Sitting there listening to bafflegab like *subrogation* and *pro rata liability,* I began to ponder: If Carson's colleague who just called wanted to buy insurance, he would have gotten a much better policy, much cheaper. In practically every industry, vendors give two prices on goods or services—one to insiders, and one to you and me.

Before I let myself get angry about this, I thought it through. Is it unfair? Not really. If the vendor doesn't have to spend time being salesman or psychologist answering the endless stream of novice questions, he can afford to give his best price. Carson wouldn't have had to take twenty minutes explaining to his colleague (as he did to me) why, if a tornado takes your house, it's considered "an act of God." Therefore, you lose. When knowledgeable associates buy products, the vendor is happily reduced to nothing more than a purchasing agent. For very little work, he makes a small profit and is satisfied.

A little bit of knowledge goes a long way when you're buying something. If you have insight into your real estate broker's bottom line, he's more apt to give you the better price. If you are facile with the insider words caterers and car salesmen use to pad their profits, if you're savvy to techniques moving companies and mechanics use to bilk the unsuspecting, if you are on the lookout for lawyers' methods of fattening fees—in short, *if you know the ropes,* you will not get ripped off. You don't need to know a lot, just a few insider terms. The pro assumes, since you are conversant in some esoteric industry terms, you also know the best deal and rock-bottom price.

No one put it better than my housepainter, Iggy. "Sure," he told me, "you gotta know how to talk to a painter. Not me, but a lotta them other guys, they're gonna get whatever they can. It's only human nature. Especially if you're a woman and you deal with 'em smart, like I'm gonna tell you how, their hair will stand on end. They'll say to themselves, 'Hey, dis is no babe in the woods. I better deal straight.'"

"OK, Iggy, how?"

He said, "Tell them guys, 'Look the walls need very little *prepping.* You're not going to have to spend much time *scraping* and *spackling.* It's a clean job.'" Iggy told me these few sentences alone can save you hundreds of dollars. Why? Right away the painter knows you know the score and that the most time-consuming part for him is preparing the surface (*prepping* in painterese). Therefore, it's his biggest markup item.

"Then," Iggy continued, "when you tell 'em there will be no *cutting in* (painting two colors next to each other), your price goes down again. Be sure and tell 'em not to leave any *holidays* (unpainted or sparsely painted spots) and you get a more careful job." I'm only sorry I don't have an Iggy in every field to give me a crash course in how to deal.

How to Deal When There's No Iggy in Your Life

Here's how to get the best price and the best deal from anyone. Find your Iggy Informer. If you have a friend in the business, get the lingo from him. If not, instead of going straight to the vendor you want to buy from, visit several others first. Talk with them. Learn a little lingo from each.

For instance, suppose you want to buy a diamond. Instead of going right to your favorite jewelry shop and asking dumbbell diamond questions, go to the competition. Make friends with the salesclerk and pick up a few gems of diamondese. You'll learn jewelers say *stones,* not *diamonds.* When you're talking about the top of the stone, they say *table;* the widest part is the *girdle;* the bottom is the *cutlet.* If the stone looks yellow, don't say *yellow,* say *cape.* If you see flaws, don't say *flaws,* say *inclusions* or *gletz.* If you still don't like the stone, don't say "I'd like to see something better," say *finer.* (Don't ask me why. That's just the way the diamond crowd talks.)

Then, when you've got your lingo down, go to where you want to buy. Because you now speak diamond, you get a much better price.

⭐ **TECHNIQUE #43:**
BLUFFING FOR BARGAINS

The haggling skills used in ancient Arab markets are alive and well in contemporary America for big-ticket items. Your price is much lower when you know how to deal.

Before every big purchase, find several vendors—a few to learn from and one to buy from. Armed with a few words of industryese, you're ready to head for the store where you're going to buy.

Soon you'll be asking furriers where the *skins* were *dressed,* moving companies for their ICC performance record, and lawyers the hourly rate of paralegals and associates. Then these folks, like Iggy the painter, will say to themselves, "Hey, dis is no babe in the woods—I better deal straight."

Let us now delve deeper into the world of being an insider. This time we explore how to give your Conversation Partner the sense that you share not only experiences, but the heavy stuff. You share beliefs and values in life.

PART FIVE

WHY, WE'RE JUST ALIKE!

We're Like Peas in a Pod

If you squint your eyes and look up carefully at a flight of birds, you'll see finches flying with finches, swallows soaring with swallows, and yellow birds winging it with yellow birds. The avian apartheid escalates. You'll never see a barn swallow with a bank swallow, or even a yellow bird hanging out with a yellow finch. Somebody said it shorter: *Birds of a feather flock together.*

Happily, humans are smarter than birds. In one respect, at least: we have brains capable of overcoming bias. Really smart human beings work together, play together, and break bread together. Does that mean their comfort level is high? Well, that depends on the human being. Our purpose here is not to examine the absurdity of apartheid. It is to leave no stone unturned in making sure people are *completely* comfortable doing business or pleasure with you.

It has been proven beyond a doubt, people are most receptive to those they feel have the same values in life. In one study, individuals were first given a personality and beliefs test.[20] They were then paired off with a partner and told to go spend time together. Before meeting, half the couples were told they were very similar in beliefs to their partner. The other half were told they were dissimilar. Neither statement was true.

However, when quizzed afterward on how much they liked each other, partners who believed they were similar liked each other a lot more than the couples who thought themselves to be dissimilar, demonstrating we have a predisposition toward people we believe are just like us. We are most comfortable giving our business and friendship to those we feel share our values and beliefs in life. To that end I offer six techniques to create sensations of similarity with everyone you wish.

Along with making more profound rapport with customers, friends, and associates, using the following techniques develops a deeper understanding and empathy with people of all races and backgrounds. They also open doors that might otherwise be closed to you.

⭐ 44 ⯈ Be a Copyclass

Watch Their Every Move

Just like the finch flaps its wings faster than the gliding eagle, people of different backgrounds *move* differently. For example, westerners used to the wide-open plains stand farther from each other. Easterners, systematically sardined into subways and crowded busses, stand closer. Asian Americans make modest movements. Italian Americans make massive ones.

At teatime, the finishing-school set genuflects and gracefully lowers derrieres onto the sofa. When the ladies reach for a cup, they hold the saucer in one hand and the cup in the other, pinkie ever so slightly extended. Folks who never finished *any* manners school make a fanny dive in the middle of the sofa and clutch the cup with both hands.

Is one right? Is the other wrong? No. However, Top Communicators know when doing business with a derriere-dipping pinkie extender or a fanny-plopping two-fisted mug grabber, they darn well should do the same. People feel comfortable around people who move just like they do.

I have a friend who travels the country giving an outrageous seminar called "How to Marry the Rich." Genie was once in a

Las Vegas casino when a television reporter asked if she could tell the real rich from the great pretenders.

"Of course," Genie answered.

"All right," challenged the reporter. "Who is the wealthiest man in this room?" Convened at the next table were three men in tailored suits (Hayward of Mayfair, London, no doubt), hand-made shirts (Charvet of Place Vendôme in Paris, no doubt), and sipping scotch (single-malt Laphroaig from the Scottish island of Islay, no doubt). The reporter, naturally, assumed Genie would choose one of these likely candidates.

Instead, with the scrutiny of a hunting dog, Genie's eyes scanned the room. Like a trained basset hound, she instinctively pointed a long red fingernail at a fellow in torn jeans at a corner table. She murmured, "He's *very* rich."

Flabbergasted, the reporter asked Genie, "How can you tell?"

"He moves like old money," she said. "You see," Genie went on to explain, "there's moving like *old* money. There's moving like *new* money. And there's moving like *no* money." Genie could tell the unlikely chap in the corner was obviously sitting on big assets, and all because of the way he moved.

TECHNIQUE #44:
BE A COPYCLASS

Watch people. Look at the way they move. Small movements? Big movements? Fast? Slow? Jerky? Fluid? Old? Young? Classy? Trashy?

Pretend the person you are talking to is your dance instructor. Is he a jazzy mover? Is she a balletic mover? Watch his or her body, then *imitate* the style of movement. That makes your Conversation Partner subliminally real comfy with you.

They're Buying *You*, Too

If you're in sales, copy not only your customer's class but the class of your product as well. I live in a section of New York City called Soho, which is a few blocks above the famous-for-being-trashy Canal Street. Often, clutching my purse tightly and dodging the crowds on Canal Street, I'll pass a pickpocket-turned-salesman-for-the-day. He furtively looks around and flashes a greasy handkerchief at me with a piece of jewelry on it. "Psst, wanna buy a gold chain?" His nervous thief's demeanor alone could get him arrested.

Now, about sixty blocks uptown, you'll find the fashionable and very expensive Tiffany's jewelry store. Occasionally, clutching my fantasies of being able to afford something therein, I stroll through the huge gilt doors. Imagine one of the impeccably dressed sales professionals behind the beveled glass counters furtively looking around and saying to me, "Psst, wanna buy a diamond?"

No sale!

Match your personality to your product. Selling handmade suits? A little decorum please. Selling jeans? A little cool, please. Selling sweat suits? A little sporty, please. And so on for whatever you're selling. Remember, *you* are your customers' buying experience. Therefore you are part of the product they're buying.

 ## 45 Echoing

"We're Like Peas in a Pod"

Have you ever been gabbing with a new acquaintance and, after a few moments, you've said to yourself, "This person and I think alike! We're on the same wavelength." It's a fabulous feeling, almost like falling in love.

Lovers call it *chemistry.* New friends talk of *instant rapport,* and business people say *a meeting of minds.* Yet it's the same magic, that sudden sense of warmth and closeness, that strange sensation of "Wow, we were old friends at once!"

When we were children, making friends was easier. Most of the kids we met grew up in the same town and so they were on our wavelength. Then the years went by. We grew older. We moved away. Our backgrounds, our experiences, our goals, our lifestyles became diverse. Thus, we fell off each other's wavelengths.

Wouldn't it be great to have a magic surfboard to help you hop right back on *everybody's* wavelength whenever you wanted? Here it is, a linguistic device that gets you riding on high rapport with everyone you meet. If you stand on a mountain cliff and shout "hello-oh" across the valley, your identical "hello-oh" thunders back at you. I call the technique *Echoing* because, like the mountain, you echo your Conversation Partner's precise words.

It All Started Across the Ocean

In many European countries, you'll hear five, ten, or more languages within the language. For example, in Italy, the Sicilians from the south speak a dialect that seems like gobbledygook to northern Italians. In an Italian restaurant, I once overheard a diner discover his waiter was also from Udine, a town in northeastern Italy where they speak the Friulano dialect. The diner stood up and hugged the waiter like he was a long-lost brother. They started babbling in a tongue that left the other Italian waiters shrugging.

In America we have dialects, too. We just aren't conscious of them. In fact we have thousands of different words, depending on our region, our job, our interests, and our upbringing. Once, when traveling across the country, I tried to order a *soda* like a Coke or 7-Up in a highway diner. It took some explaining before the waitress understood I wanted what she called a *pop*. Perhaps because the English-speaking world is so large, Americans have a vaster choice of words for the same old stuff than any language I've encountered.

Family members find themselves speaking alike. Friends use the same words, and associates in a company or members in a club talk alike. Everyone you meet will have his or her own language that subliminally distinguishes them from outsiders. The words are all English, but they vary from area to area, industry to industry, and even family to family.

The Linguistic Device That Says "We're on the Same Wavelength"

When you want to give someone the subliminal feeling you're just alike, use *their* words, not yours. Suppose you are selling a car to a young mother who tells you she is concerned about safety because she has a young *toddler*. When explaining the safety features of the car, use her word. Don't use whatever word you call your kids. Don't even say "*child*-protection lock," which was in your sales manual. Tell your prospect, "No *toddler* can open the window because of the driver's control device." Even call it a "*toddler*-protection lock." When Mom hears *toddler* coming from your lips, she feels you are "family" because that's how all her relatives refer to her little tyke. Suppose your prospect had said *kid* or *infant*. Fine, echo any word she used. (Well, almost any word. If she'd said my *brat,* you might want to pass on *Echoing* this time.)

Echoing at Parties

Let's say you are at a party. It's a huge bash with many different types of people. You are first chatting with a lawyer who tells you her *profession* is often maligned. When it comes your turn to speak, say *profession* too. If you say *job,* it puts a subconscious barrier between you.

Next you meet a construction worker who starts talking about his *job.* Now you're in trouble if you say, "Well, in my *profession* . . ." He'd think you were being hoity-toity.

After the lawyer and the construction worker, you talk to several freelancers—first a model, then a professional speaker, finally a pop musician. All three of these folks will use different words for their work. The model brags about her *bookings.* The professional speaker might say bookings, but he is more apt to boast of his speaking *engagements.* A pop musician might say, "Yeah, man, I get a lot of *gigs.*" It's tough to memorize what they all call their work. Just keep your ears open and echo their word after they say it.

Echoing goes beyond job names. For example if you are chatting with a boat owner and you call his boat an *it,* he labels you a real landlubber. (He reverently refers to his beloved boat, of course, as a *she.*) If you listen carefully, you hear language subtleties you never dreamed existed. Would you believe using the wrong synonym for a seemingly uncomplicated word like *have* labels you a know-nothing in somebody else's world? For example, cat lovers purr about *having* cats. But horse people would say *owning* horses. And fish folk don't *own* fish. They talk about *keeping* fish. Hey, no big deal. But if you use the wrong word, your Conversation Partner will assume, correctly, that you are a stranger in his or her hobbyland.

The Peril of *Not* Echoing

Sometimes you lose out by not *Echoing*. My friend Phil and I were talking with several guests at a party. One woman proudly told the group about the wonderful new ski *chalet* she had just purchased. She was looking forward to inviting her friends up to her little *chalet* in the mountains.

"That's wonderful," said Phil, secretly hoping for an invitation. "Where exactly is your *cabin*?" KERPLUNK! There went Phil's chances for an invitation to the lady's *chalet*.

I couldn't resist. After the conversation, I whispered to my friend, "Phil, why did you insult that woman by calling her *chalet* a *cabin*?" Phil scratched his head and said, "What do you mean insult her? *Cabin* is a beautiful word. My family has a cabin in Cape Cod and I grew up loving the word, the associations, the joy of a cabin." (In other words, the connotations of *cabin*.) Well, fine, Phil. The word *cabin* may be beautiful to you, but obviously the skier preferred the word *chalet*.

Professional Echoing

In today's sales environment, customers expect salespeople to be problem solvers, not just vendors. They feel you don't grasp their industry's problems if you don't speak their language.

I have a friend, Penny, who sells office furniture. Among her clients are people in publishing, advertising, broadcasting, and a few lawyers. Penny's sales manual says *office* furniture. However, she told me, if she used the word *office* with all of her clients, they'd assume she knew nothing about their respective industries.

She told me her client, the purchasing officer in advertising, talks about his advertising *agency*. Penny's publishing client says publishing *house*. The lawyers talk about furniture for their *firm*, and her radio clients use the word *station* instead of office. "Hey," Penny says, "it's their salt mine. They can call it whatever the heck they please. And," she added, "if I want to make the sale, I'd better call it the same thing."

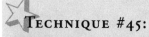

TECHNIQUE #45:
ECHOING

Echoing is a simple linguistic technique that packs a powerful wallop. Listen to the speaker's arbitrary choice of nouns, verbs, prepositions, adjectives—and echo them back. Hearing their words come out of your mouth creates subliminal rapport. It makes them feel you share their values, their attitudes, their interests, their experiences.

Echoing Is Politically Correct Insurance

Here's a quiz: You're talking with a pharmacist and you ask her, "How long have you worked at the drugstore?" What's wrong with that question?

Give up? It's the word *drugstore*. Pharmacists abhor the word because it conjures up many industry problems. They're used to hearing it from outsiders, but it's a tip-off that they are unaware of, or insensitive to, their professional problems. They prefer *pharmacy.*

Recently, at a reception, I introduced one of my friends, Susan, as a day-care worker. Afterward Susan begged, "Leil, puleeze do not call me a *day*-care worker. We're *child*-care workers." Whoops! Time and recent history quickly make certain terms archaic.

A group's intense preference for one word is not arbitrary. Certain jobs, minorities, and special-interest groups often have a history the public is not sensitive to. When that history has too much pain attached to it, people invent another word that doesn't have bitter connotations.

I have a dear friend, Leslie, who is in a wheelchair. She says whenever anyone says the word *handicapped,* she cringes. Leslie says it makes her feel less than whole. "We prefer you say *person with a disability.*" She then gave a moving explanation. "We people with disabilities are the same as every other able-bodied person." We say "AB," she added. "ABs go through life with all the same baggage we do. We just carry one extra piece, a disability."

It's simple. It's effective. To show respect and make people feel close to you, *Echo* their words. It makes you a more sensitive communicator—and keeps you out of trouble every time.

46 Potent Imaging

Old-Boy Analogies Are Unsportsmanlike Conduct with the Girls

I recently had to make a presentation to fifteen men in a corporate meeting. "OK," I said to myself as I stood up, "fifteen Martians and one Venusian." No problem! I'd read *Men Are from Mars, Women Are from Venus.* I'd explored neurological differences in men's and women's brains. I knew all about gender-specific body-language signals. Hey, I teach communications differences. I was well prepared to talk to these men, get my point across, and fend any questions.

Everything started out fine. I'd conceived my presentation clearly and concisely, developed each theme, and presented it flawlessly. Then, I sat down and confidently invited questions and open discussion.

That's when it fell apart. All I remember is a horrifying barrage of questions couched in football analogies.

"Do you think we *dropped the ball* on that one?" one man asked.

"Yeah," another responded. "But can we make a *fumble recovery?*"

Those two I understood. However, when it got to *pass coverage* and *intentional grounding,* I started to lose it. When one guy raved about a *Hail Mary pass* being needed to save the deal, I suffered the ultimate humiliation. I had to ask, "Uh, what does that mean?" The guys looked at each other knowingly, and then smiled condescendingly as they explained it to me.

That night I had sadistic fantasies of fifteen women running the company and one man left scratching his head as we bandied about childbirth analogies.

"We won't get his new proposal 'till the third *trimester,*" reports the account exec.

"Yeah, but that's six months away. Let's get it by *C-section,*" responds the comptroller.

"Why bother?" asks the marketing VP. "All his ideas are developed *in vitro* anyway."

"I'm about to go into *postpartum depression,*" murmurs the CEO. The lone male employee is left as confused and humiliated as I was in the face of football analogies.

Ahem, the aim of this book is not to feed fiendish fantasies, but to improve communications. To that end, I offer the following technique based on analogies, not just football analogies.

On-Target Analogies Hit Bull's-Eye

Analogies can be an effective communications tool—*if* you evoke images from the life of the person you are talking to. Men don't use football analogies to obfuscate matters or to confuse women, but to clarify situations for each other. Analogies from the sport bring situations to life for men because generally they watch more football than women.

Moving on to other sports analogies: everyone knows what the speaker means when he or she hears, "We'll never *strike out* with this solution." Nevertheless, a baseball fan would find it a more compelling image as he would analogies like *caught on the fly, hitting the dirt,* or *throwing a spit ball.*

You've heard people say, "This solution is right *on target.*" We all understand it. But the phrasing would be more dramatic for archery enthusiasts. If your listener were a bowler, speaking of *gutter balls* or *big splits* would bring whatever you were discussing to life. If your business buddies were basketball fans, analogies like *hook shot* or *air ball* would land right in their basket. If your client wrestles, saying *feints* and *scissor holds* would be the way to grab him.

These analogies might sound farfetched to you. But they are potent communications tools when they envoke your Conversation Partner's world. Why not use the most powerful terms possible to get your point across and make the sale? I call the technique *Potent Imaging.*

TECHNIQUE #46:
POTENT IMAGING

Does your customer have a garden? Talk about *sowing the seeds* for success. Does your boss own a boat? Tell him or her about a concept that will *hold water* or *stay afloat.* Maybe he is a private pilot? Talk about a concept really *taking off.* She plays tennis? Tell her it really hits the *sweet spot.*

Evoke your listener's interests or lifestyle and weave images around it. To give your points more power and punch, use analogies from your listener's world, not your own. *Potent Imaging* also tells your listeners you think like them and hints you share their interests.

Pardon me while I return momentarily to my sadistic fantasies of the hopelessly confused lone male employee. The all-female management team is now arguing the corporate strategy using, not football of course, but ballet analogies.

"I say let's do the corporate takeover *allegro*," she suggests.

"Nah, you gotta go *adagio* in these matters," her colleague responds.

"But what if they do a *tour jeté* while we're poised in *fifth*?"

"C'mon did you ever see a good *pas seul* from their president?"

The top woman settles it. "I say let's just give him a little *révérence*, and then a *grand battement* in the balls."

47 Employ Empathizers

Beyond "Yep, Uh Huh, Yeah"

While listening to someone talk, we often vocalize "uh huh" or purr throaty little "umm" sounds to reassure the speaker we have heard their words. In fact, with some it's such a habit, the noises escape their throats unconsciously. My friend Phil is a consummate, constant, and incontinent "ummer" whenever I'm talking. Occasionally, if I'm feeling contentious after he's given one of his agreeable "umms" in response to something I've said, I challenge him with, "OK, Phil, what did I say?"

"Uh, well, gosh . . ." Phil has no idea. It's not his fault. He's male. Men are especially guilty of the not-really-listening umm habit. Once, when I was on a monologue about nothing in particular, Phil was on a real umm roll. To test his listening skills, I slipped in, "Yes, this afternoon I think I'll go out and get tattooed all over my body."

Phil nodded his habitual "uh huh."

Well, umming is better than a blank stare. However, it's not the choice of Top Communicators. Try replacing your umms with full-blown empathizers.

What Are Empathizers?

Empathizers are simple, short, supportive statements. Unlike "uh huh," they are complete sentences such as "I can appreciate you decided to do that," or "That really is exciting." Empathizers can be one-sentence positive critiques like "Yes, that was the honorable thing to do" or "It's charming you felt that way."

When you respond with complete sentences instead of the usual grunts, not only do you come across as more articulate, your listener feels that you *really* understand.

TECHNIQUE #47:
EMPLOY EMPATHIZERS

Don't be an unconscious ummer. Vocalize complete sentences to show your understanding. Dust your dialogue with phrases like "I see what you mean." Sprinkle it with sentimental sparklers like "That's a lovely thing to say." Your empathy impresses your listeners and encourages them to continue.

Of course, you pay a price. In order to use the right empathizers, you *do* need to listen.

Now let's fine-tune this technique and explore *advanced* empathizing.

48 Anatomically Correct Empathizers

A Sound Idea

About ten years ago, I had a roommate named Brenda. Brenda was a tap dance teacher who didn't just tap dance to make a living. She lived to tap. Posters of Bill "Bojangles" Robinson and Charles "Honi" Coles plastered her walls. She didn't walk around the house. She *tapped* her way from room to room. It was noisy but at least, when a phone call came for Brenda, I never had trouble finding her.

Once I asked Brenda when she got interested in tap. She said, "From the moment I first opened my ears." Her *ears*? I thought, that's strange. Most people say "from the moment I opened my eyes." At that moment, I realized Brenda "saw" the world more through her ears than her eyes.

We all perceive the world through five senses. We *see* the world. We *hear* the world. We *feel* the world. We *smell* the world. And we *taste* the world. Therefore, we talk in terms of those five senses. Proponents of neurolinguistic programming (NLP) tell us, for each person, one sense is stronger than others. For Brenda, it was her hearing.

Brenda told me she grew up in a dark apartment below street

level in New York City. She remembers, as an infant, hearing the pitter-patter of feet walking just above her crib on the sidewalk. As a toddler, her tiny ears were bombarded with honking horns, shrieking sirens, and tire chains slapping the icy streets. She especially remembers the clumpety-clomp of police horses' hoofs on the pavement outside her window. Her first perceptions of the outside world came to her through her ears. To this day, sound dominates her life. Brenda, the tap dancer, is an auditory person.

Since neurolinguists suggest invoking our listener's strongest sense, I tried a few auditory references on Brenda. Rather than saying, "That *looks* good to me," I'd say "That *sounds* good." Instead of saying, "I *see* what you mean," I'd say, "I *hear* you." When I used these auditory references, I felt she paid more attention.

So I started listening very carefully to all my friends to discover which was their primary perception. Sometimes I'd hear visual references like

I *see* what you mean.
That *looks* good to me.
I can't *picture* myself doing that.
I take a *dim view* of that idea.
From my *perspective* . . .

Wow, I thought I was really on to something!

A Wrinkle Develops

But then, whoops, at other times, I'd hear that same friend say

Yeah, I *hear* you.
Sure, that *sounds* good to me.
I kept *saying* to myself it would work.
That has a negative *ring* to it.
He really *tuned out* on the whole idea.
Something *tells* me . . .

This wasn't going to be quite as easy as I'd expected. However, I wasn't ready to give up.

Once Brenda and I went skiing with several friends. That night we were at a party. One of our friends was telling a group of people, "The ski slopes were beautiful. Everything was so crystal clear and white."

"A visual person?" I asked myself.

Another skier added, "The feel of the fresh snow on our faces was terrific."

"Aha, a kinesthetic person," I mused silently.

Sure enough, just then, Brenda said, "Today was so silent. The only sound you could hear was the wind in your ears as you came swooshing down the slopes." That little riff convinced me there was something to it.

However, I still found it difficult to discern one's primary sense.

A Simple Solution

Here's what I've found does work, and it doesn't take too much detective work on your part. I call the technique *Anatomically Correct Empathizers*, and it's easy to master. Unless it is *obvious* the person you are speaking with is primarily visual, auditory, or kinesthetic, simply respond in his or her mode of the moment. Match your empathizers to the current sense someone is talking through. For example, suppose a business colleague describing a financial plan says, "With this plan, we can see our way clear in six months." Since this time she's using primarily visual references, say "I *see* what you mean" or "You really have a *clear picture* of that situation."

If, instead, your colleague had said, "This plan has a good ring to it," you'd substitute auditory empathizers like "It does *sound* great" or "I *hear* you."

A third possibility. Suppose she had said, "I have a gut feeling this plan will work." Now you give her a *kinesthetic* empathizer like "I can understand how you *feel*," or "You have a good *grasp* of that problem."

TECHNIQUE #48:
ANATOMICALLY CORRECT EMPATHIZERS

What part of their anatomy are your associates talking though? Their eyes? Their ears? Their gut?

For visual people, use visual empathizers to make them think you *see* the world the way they do. For auditory folks, use auditory empathizers to make them think you *hear* them loud and clear. For kinesthetic types, use kinesthetic empathizers to make them think you *feel* the same way they do.

What about the other two senses, taste and smell? Well, I've never run up against any gustatory or olfactory types. But you could always compliment a chef by saying, "That's a *delicious* idea." And if you are talking to your dog (olfactory, of course), tell him "The whole idea *stinks*."

The next technique helps create affinity with a single word.

49 › The Premature *We*

"We Talked Like Old Friends at Once"

By just eavesdropping for a few moments on any two people chatting, you could tell a lot about their relationship. You could tell if they were new acquaintances or old friends. You could tell whether a man and a woman were strangers or a couple.

You wouldn't even need to hear friends call each other *pal, buddy,* or *mate.* You wouldn't need to hear a man and a woman whisper *dear, sweetheart,* or *turtle dove.* It wouldn't matter *what* they were discussing, or even their tone of voice. You could even be blindfolded and tell a lot about their relationship because the technique I'm about to share has nothing to do with body language.

How? A fascinating progression of conversation unfolds as people become closer. Here's how it develops:

LEVEL ONE: CLICHÉS

Two strangers talking together primarily toss clichés back and forth. For instance, when chatting about the universally agreed-upon world's dullest subject, the weather, one stranger might say to the other, "Beautiful sunny weather we've been having." Or, "Boy, some rain, huh?" That's level one, clichés.

LEVEL TWO: FACTS

People who know each other but are just acquaintances often discuss facts. "You know, Joe, we've had twice as many sunny days this year to date as last." Or, "Yeah, well, we finally decided to put in a swimming pool to beat the heat."

LEVEL THREE: FEELINGS AND PERSONAL QUESTIONS

When people become friends, they often express their feelings to each other, even on subjects as dull as the weather. "George, I just love these sunny days." They also ask each other personal questions: "How about you, Betty? Are you a sun person?"

LEVEL FOUR: *WE* STATEMENTS

Now we progress to the highest level of intimacy. This level is richer than facts and creates more rapport than feelings. It's *we* and *us* statements. Friends discussing the weather might say, "If we keep having this good weather, it'll be a great summer." Lovers might say, "I hope this good weather keeps up for *us* so *we* can go swimming on our trip."

A technique to achieve the ultimate verbal intimacy grows out of this phenomenon. Simply use the word *we* prematurely. You can use it to make a client, a prospect, a stranger feel you are already friends. Use it to make a potential romantic partner feel the two of you are already an item. I call it the *Premature We*. In casual conversation, simply cut through levels one and two. Jump straight to three and four.

Ask your prospect's feelings on something the way you would query a friend. ("George, how do you feel about the new governor?") Then use the pronoun *we* when discussing anything that might affect the two of you. ("Do you think *we're* going to prosper during his administration?") Make it a point to concoct *we* sentences, the kind people instinctively reserve for friends, lovers, and other intimates. ("I think *we'll* survive while the governor's in office.")

The word *we* fosters togetherness. It makes the listener feel connected. It gives a subliminal feeling of "you and me against the cold, cold world." When you prematurely say *we* or *us*, even to strangers, it subconsciously brings them closer. It subliminally hints you are already friends. At a party, you might say to someone standing behind you at the buffet line, "Hey, this looks great. They really laid out a nice spread for *us*." Or, "Uh-oh, *we're* going to get fat if we let ourselves enjoy all of this."

TECHNIQUE #49:
THE PREMATURE *WE*

Create the sensation of intimacy with someone even if you've met just moments before. Scramble the signals in their psyche by skipping conversational levels one and two, and cutting right to levels three and four. Elicit intimate feelings by using the magic words *we, us,* and *our.*

Well, we have just explored how to copy our Conversation Partners' movements with *Be a Copyclass, Echo* their words, evoke *Potent Images* from their world, create a bond through their primary sense with *Anatomically Correct Empathizers,* and establish subliminal friendship with words like *we.*

What else do friends, lovers, and close associates have in common? A *history.* The final technique in this section is a device to give a fairly new acquaintance the warm and fuzzy feeling the two of you have been together for a long, long time.

⭐ 50 Instant History

Our Own Private Joke

Lovers whisper phrases in each others' ears that mean nothing to anyone but themselves. Friends crack up over a few words that sound like gobbledygook to anyone overhearing them. Close business associates chuckle about shared experiences.

One company I've worked with has seen *reengineering, empowerment, TQM,* and *team building* come and go in one decade. At company parties, the employees never fail to crack up over the time when the whole company—managers to mail-room clerks—scrambled up a twenty-nine-foot pole together all in the name of team building. The CEO slipped down the pole and broke his big toe. At the next weekly meeting, the CEO shook his crutch and caustically announced, "No more team exercises!" Thus, the death of team building—and the birth of a private joke.

Out of shared experiences like this, a company culture grows. These employees have a history, and a language to go with it. To this day, whenever they want to put an abrupt end to any idea, they say, "Let's shake a crutch at it" or "Let's slide that one down the flagpole." They all smile. Nobody knows what they mean except fellow employees.

The playwright Neil Simon, sometimes with a single word, can make an entire Broadway audience understand two performers onstage are either married or longtime friends. The actor simply says something to the actress that makes no sense to the audience. Then both of them laugh uproariously. Everybody gets the message: these two people are an item.

Every time my friend Daryl and I meet, we don't say "Hello." We say "Quack." Why? We met at a party five years ago and, in our first conversation, Daryl told me he grew up on a duck farm. When I told him I'd never seen a duck farm, he performed the best human imitation of a duck I'd ever seen. He flipped his head side to side looking at me first out of one eye, then the other, all the while flapping his arms and quacking. I got such a laugh out of his performance that it inspired him to do a full flat-footed duck waddle for me. It was contagious. Together we waddled around the room flapping and quacking. We made absolute fools of ourselves that evening.

The next day, my phone rang. I picked up the receiver to hear, not "Hello, this is Daryl," but simply, "Quack." I'm sure that's what started our friendship. To this day, every time I hear his "Quack" on the phone, it floods me with happy, if a tad embarrassing, memories. It recalls our history and renews our friendship no matter how long it's been since we last quacked at each other.

TECHNIQUE #50:
INSTANT HISTORY

When you meet a stranger you'd like to make less a stranger, search for some special moment you shared during your first encounter. Then find a few words that reprieve the laugh, the warm smile, the good feelings the two of you felt. Now, just like old friends, you have a history together, an *Instant History*.

With anyone you'd like to make part of your personal or professional future, look for special moments together. Then make them a refrain.

Now What's Left?

Chemistry, charisma, and confidence are three characteristics shared by Big Winners in all walks of life. Part One helped us make a dynamic, confident, and charismatic first impression with body language. In Two, we put smooth small-talk lyrics to our body ballet. Then in Three, we seized hints from the Big Boys and Girls so we're contenders for life's Big League. Part Four rescued us from being tongue-tied with folks with whom we have very little in common. And in Five, we learned techniques to create instant chemistry, instant intimacy, instant rapport.

What's left? You guessed it—making people feel really good about themselves. But compliments are a dangerous weapon in today's world. One mishandling and you can butcher the relationship. Let us now explore the power of praise, the folly of flattery, and how you can use these potent tools effectively.

PART SIX

The Power of Praise, the Folly of Flattery

Praise Reappraised

Kids are experts at getting what they want. Perched on papa's knee, "Oh Daddy, you're so wunnerful. I know you'll buy me that new doll." The next morning with mama in the supermarket, "Oh Mommy, I love you. You're the most bestest mommy in the world. I know you'll buy me that chocolate munchie."

From the hungry infant's instinctive cooing as mommy approaches the crib to the car salesman's calculated praise as the prospect walks into the showroom, compliments come naturally to people when they want something from somebody. In fact, compliments are the most widely used and thoroughly endorsed of all getting-what-you-want techniques. When Dale Carnegie wrote "Begin with praise," fifteen million readers took it to heart. Most of us still think praise is the path to extracting what we want from someone.

And yes, if it's as simple as dolls from daddy and munchies from mommy, it may be. But the business world has changed dramatically since Dale Carnegie's day. In today's world, not every smiling flatterer has the power to procure through praise.

The Malaise of Unskilled Praise

You give someone a compliment. You smile, waiting to see the warm feelings engulf the recipient. You may have to wait a long time.

If he or she has a speck of suspicion your praise is self-serving, it has the opposite effect. If your compliment is insincere or unskilled, it can wreck your chances of ever being trusted by that person again. It can abort a potential relationship before it ever gets off the runway.

However, skilled praise is a different story. When done well, it gives the relationship immediate liftoff. It can make a sale, win a new friend, or rejuvenate a marriage on a golden anniversary.

What is the difference between praise that lifts and flattery that flattens? Many factors enter the equation. They include your sincerity, timing, motivation, and wording. They also involve the recipient's self-image, professional position, experience with compliments, and judgment of your powers of perception. Of course it entails the relationship between the two of you and how long you have known each other. If you're complimenting someone by phone, e-mail, or snail mail, it even involves subtleties such as whether you've ever seen their face, either in person or a photograph.

Mind boggling, isn't it? Sociologists' research shows: (1) a compliment from a new person is more potent than from someone you already know, (2) your compliment has more credibility when given to an unattractive person or an attractive person whose face you've never seen, (3) you are taken more seriously if you preface your comments by some self-effacing remark—but only if your listener perceives you as higher on the totem pole. If you're lower, your self-effacing remark reduces your credibility. Complicated, this complimenting stuff.

Rather than dizzying ourselves with the surfeit of specific studies, let's just put some terrific techniques in our little bag of tricks. Each of the following meets all the criteria of social scientists' findings. Here are nine effective ways to praise in the new millennium.

〽️51 Grapevine Glory

Depend on Their Keen Sense of Rumor

The risk in giving a compliment face-to-face is, of course, that the distrustful recipient will assume you are indulging in shameless obsequious pandering to achieve your own greedy goals.

It's a sad reality about compliments. If you lay a big one out of the blue on your boss, your prospect, or your sweetie, the recipient will probably think you're brownnosing. Your main squeeze will assume you're suffering guilt over something you've done. So what's the solution? Hold back your sincere esteem?

No, simply deliver it through the grapevine. The grapevine has long been a trusted means of communication. From the days when Catskills comics insisted the best ways to spread news were "telephone, telegraph, and tell-a-woman," we have known it works. Unfortunately the grapevine is most often associated with bad news, the kind that goes in one ear and over the back fence. But the grapevine need not be laden only with scuttlebutt and sour grapes. Good news can travel through the same filament. And when it arrives in the recipient's ear, it is all the more delectable. This is not a new discovery. Back in 1732, Thomas Fuller wrote, "He's my friend that speaks well of me behind my back." We're more apt to trust someone who says nice things about us when we aren't listening than someone who flatters us to our face.

No-Risk Praise (Do It Behind Their Back)

Instead of telling someone directly of your admiration, tell someone who is close to the person you wish to compliment. For instance, suppose you want to be in the good graces of Jane Smith. Don't directly compliment Jane. Go to her close associate Diane Doe and say, "You know, Jane is a very dynamic woman. She said something so brilliant in the meeting the other day. Someday she'll be running this company." I place ten-to-one odds your comment will get back to Jane via the grapevine in twenty-four hours. Diane will tell her friend, "You should hear what so 'n' so said about you the other day."

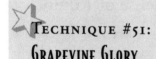

TECHNIQUE #51:
GRAPEVINE GLORY

A compliment one hears is never as exciting as the one he *overhears.* A priceless way to praise is not by telephone, not by telegraph, but by *tell-a-friend.* This way you escape possible suspicion that you are an apple-polishing, bootlicking, egg-sucking, back-scratching sycophant trying to win brownie points. You also leave recipients with the happy fantasy that you are telling the whole world about their greatness.

When you gave *Grapevine Glory* to Jane, Diane became the carrier pigeon of that compliment. Which leads us to the next technique where *you* become the carrier pigeon of other people's compliments.

52 ⭐ Carrier Pigeon Kudos

Bring Joy to the World Like the Brave Little Birdies

Carrier pigeons have a long and valiant history. The dauntless winged messengers, often maimed by shellfire and dying after delivering their messages, have saved the lives of thousands. One tenacious little bird named Cher Ami is credited with saving 200 lives during the Battle of the Argonne in World War I. The brave one-legged little birdie, one of his wings shot through, carried a message dangling from his remaining ligament. The blood-smeared little ball of feathers arrived just in time to warn that the Germans were about to bomb the city.

Stumpy Joe, another plucky pigeon, had such a heroic battle-scarred career that his fans stuffed him, mounted him, and put him on display in the National Air Force Museum in Dayton, Ohio. And millions of other brave birds have brought joyful messages to racing-pigeon enthusiasts around the world. In that fine tradition, I present the complimenting technique I call *Carrier Pigeon Kudos.*

Whenever you hear a laudatory comment about someone, don't let it end there. You don't need to write it, roll it up in a capsule, strap it to your leg like Stumpy Joe, and fly it to the recipient. Nevertheless, you can remember the kudo and verbally carry it to the person who will get the most pleasure—the person who was complimented.

Keep your ears open for good things people say about each other. If your colleague Carl says something nice about another colleague, Sam, pass it on. "You know, Sam, Carl said the nicest thing about you the other day."

Your sister tells you your first cousin is a dynamite relative. Go ahead and call Cuz'.

Your mother tells you she thinks Manny did a great job mowing the lawn. Pass it on to him. Hey, we all like a little appreciation, even from Mom.

Here's where it benefits you. Everyone loves the bearer of glad tidings. When you bring someone third-party kudos, they appreciate you as much as the complimenter. Call it gossip if you like. This is the good kind.

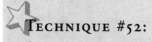

TECHNIQUE #52:
CARRIER PIGEON KUDOS

People immediately grow a beak and metamorphosize themselves into carrier pigeons when there's bad news. (It's called gossip.) Instead, become a carrier of good news and kudos. Whenever you hear something complimentary about someone, fly to them with the compliment. Your fans may not posthumously stuff you and put you on display in a museum like Stumpy Joe. But everyone loves the *Carrier Pigeon* of kind thoughts.

Carry More Cargo than Compliments

Another way to warm hearts and win friends is to become a carrier pigeon of news items that might interest the recipient. Call, mail, or e-mail people with information they might find interesting. If your friend Ned is a furniture designer in North Carolina and you see a big article in the *Los Angeles Times* about furniture trends, fax it to him. If your client Sally is a sculptor in Seattle and you see her work in someone's home in New York, sent her a note.

I have a friend, Dan, in San Francisco who, whenever he runs across anything in the paper on communications, clips it and sends it to me. No note, just "FYI—Regards, Dan" in the corner. He's like my own private West Coast clipping service.

Try it. Think of the money you'll save on greeting cards. A relevant clipping is the Big Winner's way of saying, "I'm thinking of you and your interests."

⭐ 53 ⭐ Implied Magnificence

"My Exalted Opinion of You Just Slipped Out"

Here's yet another caress for someone's ego. Don't give a blatant compliment. Merely *imply* something magnificent about your Conversation Partner. Several months ago, I was visiting an old friend in Denver whom I hadn't seen in a long time. When he came to my hotel to pick me up, he said, "Hello, Leil, how are you?" Then he paused, looked at me, and said, "You've obviously been well." Wow, I felt terrific. He *implied* I looked good and that made my evening.

Guess the Good Lord decided I shouldn't have too swollen a head, however, because later that evening, after my friend dropped me off, I got into the hotel elevator. A maintenance man entered at the third floor. He smiled at me. I smiled back. He looked at me again and said, "Gosh, ma'am, was you a model?" (Oh, man, was I feeling on top of the world now!) "... *when you was young?*" he continued.

CRASH! Why couldn't he have zipped his lip before the zinger? I loved the implication in the first part of his comment. But the second implied I was now an old lady. Ruined my next day. Heck, his unintentional low blow ruined my week. In fact I *still* feel wretched about it.

You have to be careful of unintentional bad implications. If, visiting a new city, you stop someone on the street and say, "Excuse me, could you tell me if there are any fine dining restaurants nearby?" you are implying the passerby is a person of taste. If, however, you ask that same passerby, "Hey, know any down and dirty bars in this burg?" your implication is entirely different. Find a way to *imply* magnificent qualities of those you wish to indirectly compliment.

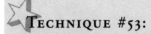

TECHNIQUE #53:
IMPLIED MAGNIFICENCE

Throw a few comments into your conversation that presuppose something positive about the person you're talking with. But be careful. Don't blow it like the well-intentioned maintenance man. Or the southern boy who, at the prom, thought he was flattering his date when he told her, "Gosh, MaryLou, for a fat gal you dance real good."

54 Accidental Adulation

Be an Undercover Complimenter

Next in our agglomeration of joy spreaders is a technique I call *Accidental Adulation.* Once, at a small dinner party, the subject turned to space travel. The gentleman seated to my right said, "Leil, you're much too young to remember this, but when Apollo 11 landed on the moon . . ."

If my life depended on it, I couldn't tell you what the chap said next. I simply remember smiling to myself and stretching to get a glimpse of my youthful self in the dining-room mirror. Of *course* I remember July 1969. Like the rest of the world, I was glued to the television watching Neil Armstrong's size 9½ B boot hit the moon. However, I certainly was not thinking of moon travel at that dinner party. I was too busy reveling in the fact that this lovely man didn't think I was old enough to remember 1969. I assumed his opinion of my youthfulness just slipped out. Therefore it *must* be sincere.

Sure! Now that I think about it, he probably knew darn well I was old enough to remember the moon landing. I bet he was using the maneuver I call *Accidental Adulation.* But it doesn't matter. My warm memories of him remain. *Accidental Adulation* is slipping praise into the secondary part of your point, putting it in verbal parentheses.

Try It. You'll Like It. *They'll* Love It.

Try *Accidental Adulation* and see smiles break out on the faces of the recipients. Tell your sixty-five-year-old uncle: "Anyone as fit as you would have zipped right up those steps, but boy, was I out of breath." Tell a colleague: "Because you're so knowledgeable in contract law, you would have read between the lines, but stupidly, I signed it."

You run the danger, of course, that you will please the recipient so profoundly with your parenthetical praise, he or she won't hear your main point.

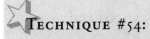

TECHNIQUE #54:

ACCIDENTAL ADULATION

Become an undercover complimenter. Stealthily sneak praise into the parenthetical part of your sentence.

Just don't try to quiz anyone later on your main point. The joyful jolt of your accidental adulation strikes them temporarily deaf to anything that follows.

So far we have explored four covert compliments: *Grapevine Glory, Carrier Pigeon Kudos, Implied Magnificence,* and *Accidental Adulation.* There are times, of course, when blatant praise does work. The next techniques will hone your skills in this precarious but rewarding venture.

⭐ 55 The Killer Compliment

Knock 'Em Out in the First Round

Would you like to have a little trick up your sleeve potent enough to kick start commerce, ignite a friendship or even a love affair? I'll give you one, but *only* if you heed its warning label. You must register your tongue as a lethal weapon once you've mastered the following technique. It's called the *Killer Compliment.*

It was born one night some years ago after my then-roommate Christine and I had just returned home from a holiday party. As we were taking off our coats, she had a silly smile on her face and a faraway look in her eye.

"Christine, are you OK?" I asked.

"Oh yes," she purred. "I'm going to go out with that man."

"Man? What man?"

"Oh, you know," she said, chastising me for not knowing, "the one who told me I had beautiful teeth."

Teeth!

That night I happened to walk by the bathroom door as Christine was getting ready for bed. I saw her grinning at herself in the mirror, tilting her head from side to side, and brushing each individual tooth. All the while she kept her eyes glued to the mirror inspecting each one for the beauty her new admirer commented on. I realized the fellow who had given Christine the unusual compliment had made her day—and had made a killer impression on her. Thus the *Killer Compliment* came into being.

What is the *Killer Compliment?* It is commenting on some very personal and specific quality you spot in someone. A *Killer Compliment* is not "I like your tie" or "You're a very nice person." (The first is not personal enough and the second is not specific enough.) A *Killer Compliment* is more like "What exquisite eyes you have," (very specific) or "You have a wonderful air of honesty about you" (very personal).

Because delivering your first *Killer Compliment* is difficult, I trick my seminar participants into pulling it off. About midway through the program, I'll ask them to close their eyes and think about a partner they had in an earlier exercise. Then I say, "Now recall one attractive physical quality or personality trait you observed in your partner. Not one you would necessarily comment on," I caution. "Perhaps your partner had a lovely smile or a twinkle in her eye. Perhaps he exuded a sense of calm or credibility. Got it in your mind?"

Then the thunderbolt: "OK, now go find your partner and tell them the nice quality you noticed. *"What? Tell them?"* The thought paralyzes them. One by one, however, they courageously seek their partners and deliver their *Killer Compliments.* As people hear a stranger tell them they have beautiful hands or pene-

TECHNIQUE #55:
THE KILLER COMPLIMENT

Whenever you are talking with a stranger you'd like to make part of your professional or personal future, search for one attractive, specific, and unique quality he or she has.

At the end of the conversation, look them right in the eye. Say their name and proceed to curl their toes with the *Killer Compliment.*

trating brown eyes, joy fills the room. Laughter explodes in every corner. I am now looking out at a sea of smiles and happy blushes. Everyone loves receiving his or her personal *Killer Compliment*. And everyone develops friendly feelings toward the giver.

The Killer Compliment User's Manual

Just like a cannon, if you don't use the *Killer Compliment* correctly, it can backfire. Here's the user's manual that comes with the mighty missile.

Rule #1: Deliver your *Killer Compliment* to the recipient in private. If you are standing with a group of four or five people and you praise one woman for being fit, every other woman feels like a barrel of lard. If you tell one man he has wonderful carriage, every other feels like a hunchback. You also make the blushing recipient uncomfortable.

Rule #2: Make your *Killer Compliment* credible. For example, I'm tone-deaf. If I'm forced to sing even a simple song like "Happy Birthday," I sound like a sick pig. If anyone in earshot were foolish enough to tell me they liked my voice, I'd know it was hogwash.

Rule #3: Confer only one *Killer Compliment* per half year on each recipient. Otherwise you come across as insincere, groveling, obsequious, pandering, and a thoroughly manipulative person. Not cool.

With careful aim, the *Killer Compliment* captures everyone. It works best, however, when you use it judiciously on new acquaintances. If you want to praise friends every day, employ the next technique.

56 Little Strokes

Itty-Bitty Boosters

In contrast to the big guns of *Killer Compliments* for strangers, and the *Tombstone Game* for loved ones, which we will learn shortly, here's a little peashooter you can pop off at anyone, anytime. I call it *Little Strokes*.

Little Strokes are short, quick kudos you drop into your casual conversation. Make liberal use of *Little Strokes* with your colleagues in the office:

"Nice job, John!"
"Well done, Kyoto!"
"Hey, not bad, Billy!"

I have one friend who uses a lovely *Little Stroke*. If I do something he likes, he says, "Not too shabby, Leil."

You can also use *Little Strokes* on the everyday achievements of your loved ones. If your spouse just cooked a great meal," "Wow, you're the best chef in town." Just before going out together, "Gee, honey, you look great." After a long drive, "You did it! It must have been tiring." With your kids, "Hey, gang, great job cleaning up your room."

I once read a poignant *Reader's Digest* article about a little girl who often misbehaved. Her mother had to continually reprimand her. However, one day, the little girl had been especially good and hadn't done a single thing that called for a reprimand. The mother said, "That night after I tucked her in bed and started downstairs, I heard a muffled noise. Running back up, I found her head buried in the pillow. She was sobbing. Between the sobs she asked, 'Mommy haven't I been a *pretty* good girl today?'"

The question, the mother said, went through her like a knife. "I had been quick to correct her," she said, "when she was wrong. But when she tried to behave, I hadn't noticed it and I put her to bed without one word of appreciation."

Adults are all grown-up little girls and little boys. We may not go to bed sobbing if the people in our lives don't notice when we are good. Nevertheless, a trace of those tears lingers.

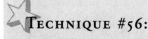

Technique #56:
Little Strokes

Don't make your colleagues, your friends, your loved ones look at you and silently say, "Haven't I been pretty good today?" Let them know how much you appreciate them by caressing them with verbal *Little Strokes* like "Nice job!" "Well done!" "Cool!"

Little Things Mean a Lot

Little Strokes are indeed, little. But as every woman knows, they mean a lot. I've yet to meet a woman who wouldn't agree with these lyrics from an old song sung by Kitty Kallen:

> Blow me a kiss from across the room.
> Say I look nice when I'm not.
> Touch my hair as you pass my chair.
> Little things mean a lot.

Send me the warmth of a secret smile
To show me you haven't forgot.
For always and ever, now and forever,
Little things mean a lot.

To further complicate the art of the compliment, one must consider timing. Blatant, barefaced, brazen flattery turns all but the blindest egomaniacs off. But the human animal never fails to amaze observers. There are moments when, if you *don't* give a blatant, barefaced, brazen compliment—even to a bright individual—you lose. The following technique defines those moments.

57 ⭐ The Knee-Jerk "Wow!"

Too Little, Too Late

I'll never forget the first time I gave a luncheon speech in front of strangers. I'd practiced for the stuffed animals on my bed and my roommate Christine, but this was my debut in front of a *real* audience.

As I shakily got to my feet, I looked out at seventeen smiling Rotarians waiting for my words of wit and wisdom. My tongue was dry as chalk dust, my palms as wet as a fish. The audience might as well have been seventeen *thousand* judges waiting to sentence me to eternal humiliation if I didn't inform and entertain each. I gave a last panic-stricken glance at Christine, who had driven me to the club, and began, "Good afternoon. It gives me great pleasure . . . "

Thirty minutes later, amidst scattered applause which I feared was obligatory, I crawled back to my seat next to Christine. I looked expectantly at her. She smiled and said, "You know this dessert isn't bad. Have some."

Dessert? "Dessert! Dammit, Christine, how did *I* do?" I silently screamed at her. A few minutes later Christine told me how much she and, she assumed, everyone else enjoyed my talk.

Nevertheless, by then it was too late. The crucial compliment-craving moment had passed.

Quick as a Hiccup, You Must Compliment NOW

When the doctor sadistically smacks your knee with that nasty little rubber hammer, you instantly give a knee jerk. And when people make a coup, you must instantly hit them with a knee-jerk "Wow, you were great!"

Say they've just successfully negotiated a deal, cooked a terrific Thanksgiving turkey, or sung a solo song at the birthday party. No matter whether their accomplishment is trivial or triumphant, you must praise it immediately—not ten minutes later, not two minutes later—*immediately.* The moment the winner walks out of the boardroom, the kitchen, the spotlight, there's only one sound the victor wants to hear: "WOW!"

> ## TECHNIQUE #57:
> ## THE KNEE-JERK "WOW!"
>
> Quick as a blink, you must praise people the moment they a finish a feat. In a wink, like a knee-jerk reaction say, "You were terrific!"
>
> Don't worry that they won't believe you. The euphoria of the moment has a strangely numbing effect on the achiever's objective judgment.

But What if They *Really* Bombed?

"Are you asking me to lie?" you ask. Yes. Absolutely, positively, resoundingly, YES. This is one of the few moments in life where a lie is condoned by the most ethical individuals. Big Winners realize that sensitivity to an insecure performer's ego takes momentary precedence over their deep commitment to the truth. They also know, when sanity returns to the recipient and they suspect they screwed up, it won't matter. He or she will retroactively appreciate your sensitivity and forgive your compassionate falsehood.

We've talked a lot about giving compliments, both covert and overt. Now let's talk about a skill that, for many, is even harder—*receiving* them.

Boomeranging

A National Weakness

I would like to dedicate the following technique to my French friends who contend the French are better at *everything*. Well, I concede one point. The French are, indeed, better at receiving compliments. I'll explain how shortly.

Americans, unfortunately, are beastly at accepting adulation. If someone compliments you and you react clumsily out of embarrassment, you unwittingly start a vicious cycle. A friend ventures a compliment:

He: (smiling) "Hey, that's a nice dress you're wearing."
She: (frowning) "Oh, this old thing?"
He: (thinking) "Whoops, she didn't seem to like hearing that. She thinks I have terrible taste to like that dress. I'd better keep my mouth shut."
Three weeks later . . .
She: (thinking grumpily) "He doesn't ever give me compliments anymore. What a boor!"
He: (thinking gloomily) "What's *her* problem?"

"Girls Don't Like *What*?"

Several months ago in one of my seminars, the group was discussing compliments. One fellow insisted that "Girls don't like compliments."

"Girls don't like *what*?" I asked incredulously.

He explained, "I once told a woman she had beautiful eyes. And she said, 'Boy, are you blind.'" The poor chap was so wounded by her reaction, he became gun-shy and had not aimed a compliment at a female since. What a shame for womankind and what a blight on his social skills.

Upon receiving a compliment, many people demur or proffer an embarrassed little "Thank you." Worse, they protest, "Well, not really but thanks anyway." Some people toss it off with, "just luck." When you react this way, you visit a grave injustice on the complimenter. You insult a well-meaning person's powers of perception.

"Vous Êtes Gentil"

Leave it to French folks to come up with a congenial catchall phrase. Upon receiving a compliment, they say, *"Vous êtes gentil."* Loosely translated, that is "How kind of you."

An American saying "How kind of you" could sound stilted—like the little flower girl in *My Fair Lady* trying to be cultured. Nevertheless, we Yanks can express the French *gentil* sentiment with a technique I call *Boomeranging*.

When you toss a boomerang, it makes an almost 180-degree swerve in midair, and soars back to land at the feet of the thrower. Likewise, when someone tosses a compliment your way, let the good feelings soar back to the tosser. Don't just say "Thanks." (Or worse, "Oh it's nothing.") Let them know of your gratitude and find a way to compliment them for their compliment. A few examples:

She says, "I like those shoes." You say, "Oh I'm so happy you told me. I just got them."

He says, "You really did a good job on this project." You say, "Oh, that's so nice of you to tell me. I appreciate your positive feedback."

You can also *Boomerang* the good feelings back when people ask you a question about your family, a project, an event, or anything that shows they are interested in you.

Your colleague asks, "How was your vacation in Hawaii?" You answer, "Oh, you remembered I went to Hawaii! It was great, thanks."

Your boss asks, "Are you over your cold now?" You answer, "I appreciate your concern. I feel much better now."

Whenever someone shines a little sunshine on your life in the form of a compliment or concerned question, reflect it back on the shiner.

TECHNIQUE #58:
BOOMERANGING

Just as a boomerang flies right back to the thrower, let compliments boomerang right back to the giver. Like the French, quickly murmur something that expresses "That's very kind of you."

Incidently, in that seminar, I decided to do womankind a favor by setting malekind straight on compliments once and for all. I asked the fellow who swore women hated praise to give three women sitting near him a sincere compliment. He chose the woman with "the beautiful silver hair sitting behind him," the girl with the "hands like a pianist" to his left, and the lady with "the lovely deep-blue eyes" on his right. He told them all.

Three women waltzed out of the room that night feeling a

little better about themselves than when they walked in. And, I hope, for all the women he would yet meet in his life, one man left with a changed attitude about compliments.

As we come to the end of our exploration of praise, I want to make sure you're aiming dead center for people's hearts. Whether you're giving little *Carrier Pigeon Kudos* or laying a *Killer Compliment* on your Conversation Partner, this next technique keeps you on target.

59 The Tombstone Game

The Ultimate Praise for Someone Near and Dear

Do you remember when you were a kid the hundreds of times Mommy's and Daddy's friends asked, "And what do you want to be when you grow up?" That was our cue to regale our adoring audience with dreams of being a ballerina, a firefighter, a nurse, a cowboy, or a movie star. Well, most of our lives wound up being a little closer to butcher, baker, or candlestick maker. Nevertheless, we all still have fantasies of our own greatness.

Even though most of us cashed in our childhood dreams of being the star we thought we'd be (so we could make some money), we all know that deep down we are very, very, *very* special. We say to ourselves, "Maybe the world will little note nor long remember how brilliant, how wonderful, how witty, how creative or caring I really am. However, those who *truly* know and love me—they will recognize my greatness, my magic, my specialness over all other ordinary mortals." When we find people with the supernatural powers of perception to recognize our remarkableness, we become addicted to the heady drug of their appreciation.

Praising someone you know and love requires a different set of skills from complimenting a stranger. The formula to bring someone even closer to you personally or professionally follows. I call it the *Tombstone Game*. It requires a little setup.

Step One: In a quiet moment chatting with your friend, your loved one, or your business partner, tell him or her you were reading something the other day about, of all things, tombstones! "The piece was about," you say, "what people fantasize inscribed above their grave after they die." You learned that people want the quality they are most proud of in life etched in stone. Then say, "The variety is surprising. Everyone has a different self-image, a different deep source of pride." Examples:

Here lies John Doe. He was a brilliant scientist.
Here lies Diane Smith. She was a caring woman.
Here lies Billy Bucks. By golly, he could make people laugh.
Here lies Jane Wilson. She spread joy wherever she went.
Here lies Harry Jones. He lived life *his* way.

Step Two: Reveal to your partner what you would like carved on your tombstone. Be serious about your revelation to encourage him or her to do likewise.

Step Three: Now, you pop the question, "You know, Joe, when all is said and done, what are you most proud of? What would you like the world to most remember about you? What would you want the world to see carved on your tombstone?"

Perhaps your business partner Joe says, "Well, I guess I'd sort of like people to know that I'm a man of my word." Listen carefully. If he expounds on it, take note of every nuance. Then file it away in your heart and don't say a word about it again. Joe will forget you ever played the tombstone game with him.

Step Four: Let at least three weeks pass. Then, whenever you want to improve the relationship, feed the information back to your partner in the form of a compliment. Say "Joe, you know the reason I really appreciate being in business with you is because you're a man of your word."

WOW, that hits Joe like a 747 out of the sky. "Finally," he says to himself, "someone who appreciates me for who I really am." Telling him you admire him for the same reason he admires himself has an impact on Joe like no other compliment in the world.

Now, suppose your friend is Billy Bucks, the one who wanted his wit carved on his tombstone. You'd say, "Billy, ol' buddy, you're terrific. I loves ya 'cause you can really make people laugh."

"I Love You Because . . . (*You* Fill in the Blank)"

Suppose your significant other is Jane Wilson in the preceding example. Tell your beloved, "Jane, I love you because you spread joy wherever you go."

Suppose your life partner is Harry Jones. You take his hand and say, "Harry, I love you because you live life *your* way." BLAM! You have found that tender spot where the heart and the ego blend.

TECHNIQUE #59:
THE TOMBSTONE GAME

Ask the important people in your life what they would like engraved on their tombstone. Chisel it into your memory but don't mention it again. Then, when the moment is right to say "I appreciate you" or "I love you," fill the blanks with the very words they gave you weeks earlier.

You take people's breath away when you feed their deepest self-image to them in a compliment. "At last," they say to themselves, "someone who loves me for who I truly am."

Tombstone Game compliments are *not* interchangeable. Billy Bucks might not appreciate your calling him a man of his word. Billy's thing is humor. Jane might not value your thinking she lives life her way. Her source of pride is spreading joy wherever she goes.

It's wonderful to tell people you appreciate or love them. When it matches what they appreciate or love about *themselves,* the effect is overpowering.

PART SEVEN

DIRECT DIAL
THEIR HEARTS

How to Be a Hit in Another Show

Hundreds of people have formed impressions of you through that little device on your desk, your bed table, your kitchen wall. And they've never actually met you. They've never seen your smiles, felt your frowns. They've never grasped your hand or enjoyed your hugs. They've never read your body language or seen how you dress. *Everything* they know about you came through tiny filaments, sometimes from hundreds of miles away. But they feel they know you just from the sound of your voice. That's how powerful the telephone is.

Powerful, yes, but not always accurate. For years I dealt with my travel agent only by phone. Rani, my faceless agent whom I'd never met in person, got me rock-bottom prices on airfares, cars, and hotels. But her snippy phone personality really ticked me off. A dozen times I vowed to find another agent.

One Monday morning several years ago, I received bad news and had to book an immediate flight home for a family emergency. There was no time to wait in line at the airport. So I jumped in a cab and asked the driver to wait in front of the travel agency while I grabbed tickets and a boarding pass.

Like a lit fuse, I zipped into Rani's agency for the first time. The woman sitting at the front desk, seeing my frenzied rush, sympathetically jumped up. She gave me a reassuring smile and asked how she could help me. As I blithered on about my need for an emergency ticket, she smiled, nodded, and lunged immediately into action. "What a terrific lady!" I thought as she printed out the tickets.

Moments later, darting out gratefully grasping the tickets in my fist, I called out over my shoulder, "By the way, what's your name?"

"Leil, I'm Rani," she said. I whirled around and saw a thoroughly congenial woman with a big smile on her face waving to wish me a safe trip. I was dumbfounded! Why had I previously thought she was so snippy? Rani was, well, so *nice*.

Sitting back in the cab on the way to the airport, I figured it all out. Rani's friendliness—her warm smile, her nods, her good eye contact, her body language, her "I'm here for you" attitude— were all *silent* signals that didn't travel through wires. I closed my eyes and tried to remember the voice I had heard moments ago. Yes, it was Rani's same crisp, curt pronunciation. But her friendly body language made her seem like a different person from the brusque agent I'd dealt with on the phone. Rani's phone personality and her demeanor in person were completely different shows.

I realized it's the same with all of us. Your personality, mine, and everyone's could be likened to a show, a theatrical performance. You want to make sure yours is a box-office smash, not a flop. The following ten techniques will get your phone personality rave reviews.

60 Talking Gestures

Make Your Manner Fit the Medium

I have a friend, Tina, who designed costumes for an off-off-Broadway show that became a smash hit last year. The tiny show was such a critical success, it won the heart of an angel—a backer—and it went to Broadway. There the show laid a big fat egg.

When I read the bad news, I called Tina. "Tina, why did the show get such bad reviews on Broadway?" Tina told me that, sadly, the director didn't insist the actors and actresses change their performances to adapt to the new surroundings. The actors' understated movements, which moved small audiences alternately to laughter and tears, were lost in the big Broadway house. Audiences couldn't see their subtle gestures and poignant facial expressions. Tina told me the performers neglected to make their movements much bigger to fit the new medium.

That excellent advice is not just for actors. Whenever you are talking, you must consider your medium. If your face were on a big movie screen, you might get your message across with a wink or an eyebrow raise. On radio, however, that would be meaningless. Because listeners couldn't see your wink, you'd have to *say* something like "Hi, Cutie." Because listeners couldn't see your raised eyebrows, you'd have to *say*, "Wow, I'm surprised!"

Your body language and facial expressions comprise more than half your personality. When people don't see you, they can get an entirely wrong impression as I did with Rani. To get your personality across on the phone, you must translate your emotions into sound. In fact, you have to exaggerate the sound because studies have shown people lose 30 percent of the energy level in their voices on the phone.

Say you meet an important new contact tomorrow. When you're introduced, you shake her hand, you fully face her. You make good, strong eye contact and let a sincere smile flood over your face. You even nod and smile, listening intently as she speaks. She likes you a lot.

But how good an impression could you make on that VIP if both you and she were blindfolded and the two of you had your hands tied behind your backs? That's the handicap you suffer on the phone.

If she couldn't see you, you'd have to substitute words to let her know you're agreeing or listening. You'd have to somehow verbalize that you're smiling and use her name more to replace the eye contact. You'd be using the technique I call *Talking Gestures*.

To make up for your missing eye contact, punctuate your phone conversations with "Uh huh" or "I hear you." So your listener knows you're nodding in approval, verbalize "I see," "Oh that's great," "No kidding," "Interesting," and "Tell me more!"

She didn't see you hitting your head in surprise? Better say "What a surprise!" or "You don't say!"

He just said something impressive and he can't see your look of admiration? Try "That was wise of you" or "You're no dummy!"

Of course, you need a big verbal smile in your repertoire. Try "Oh, wow, that's funny!" Obviously you're going to choose phrases that match your personality and the situation. Just make sure your phone listeners *hear* your emotions.

TECHNIQUE #60:
TALKING GESTURES

Think of yourself as the star of a personal radio drama every time you pick up the phone. If you want to come across as engaging as you are, you must turn your smiles into sound, your nods into noise, and all your gestures into something your listener can hear. You must replace your gestures with talk. *Then punch up the whole act 30 percent!*

61 Name Shower

A Verbal Caress

When you're not sitting across from each other resting your elbows on the same desk, your forks on the same table, or your heads on the same pillow, you need a substitute for intimacy. How can you create closeness when the two of you are hundreds of miles apart? How can you make the person you're talking to on the phone feel special when you can't pat their back, or give them a little hug?

The answer is simple. Just use your caller's name far more often than you would in person. In fact, shower your conversations with his or her name. When your listener hears it, it's like receiving a verbal caress:

"Thanks, Sam."
"Let's do it, Betty."
"Hey, Demetri, why not?"
"It's really been good talking to you, Kathi."

Saying a person's name too often in face-to-face conversation sounds manipulative. However, on the phone the effect is dramatically different. If you heard someone say your name, even if you were being jostled around in a big noisy crowd, you'd perk up and listen. Likewise, when your phone partner hears his or her own name coming through the receiver, it commands attention and re-creates the familiarity the phone robs from you.

If your listener is drifting, it brings him right back. If she's opening mail, she stops. If he's picking his teeth, he pulls the pick out. When you say someone's name on the phone, it's like yanking the person into the room with you.

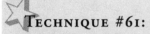

TECHNIQUE #61:

NAME SHOWER

People perk up when they hear their own name. Use it more often on the phone than you would in person to keep their attention. Your caller's name re-creates the eye contact, the caress, you might give in person.

Saying someone's name repeatedly when face-to-face sounds pandering. But because there is physical distance between you on the phone—sometimes you're a continent apart—you can spray your conversation with it.

62 Oh Wow, It's You!

Who Wants to Be a Cheshire Cat?

Brr-ing! No matter whether you hear the ring in the boardroom, the bedroom, or the bathroom, self-styled telephone experts tell you, "Smile before answering." Some pros even suggest you perch a mirror right next to your phone to monitor your grin.

Been there, done that, doesn't work. One evening, in the middle of my weekly mud-pack facial, the phone rang. The horror of seeing myself in the phone mirror made my voice as hideous as my face. I immediately trashed the pro's advice along with the mirror. Who wants to sound like a dizzy Pollyanna? A no-brain Cheshire cat? A lonely recluse whose life is so dull that the big thrill of the day is a phone call? *Any* phone call? From *anybody*!

Big Winners don't smile *before* answering. They put a smile in their voices *after* they hear who is on the line. That's when it counts. Answer the phone unemotionally, professionally. Say your name or the name of your company. Then when you hear who is on the line, the little trick is to let a big smile flood over your face.

"Oh *Joe*, (smile) how nice to hear from you!" "*Sally*, (smile) how are you?" "Bill, (smile) I was hoping it would be you."

I have a friend, Steve, in Washington, D.C., who heads a major trade association that lobbies on Capitol Hill. Whenever I call Steve, I never know which of his dozens of assistants is going to answer. Nevertheless, *whoever* answers gives me the same warm response.

First they say, "Cable Telecommunications Association," their name, and "How may I direct your call?" No fake friendliness. No prefab smiles in their voices. I am *sure* they're not beaming back at themselves in any mirror.

When I say "Is Mr. Effros available? This is Leil Lowndes calling," *that's* when they become superfriendly. "Oh yes, Ms. Lowndes," they purr. "Definitely! Let me put you right through."

Wow, does that make me feel special! As I'm waiting for Steve to come to the phone, I fantasize him sitting at the head of a long mahogany table in his weekly staff meeting. I can just hear him instructing his staff, "Now if the president or some higher-ups in the White House call, put them right through. Oh, and of course, if that important woman Leil Lowndes calls, put her right through, too."

While visiting Washington last year, I had lunch with Steve. I took the opportunity to tell him what a pleasure it was to call his office and how I appreciated his staff's warm phone reception. I thanked him for familiarizing each with my name and mentioning I might be calling from time to time. Steve looked across the table at me and blinked. "Leil," he said, "you teach telephone skills. Haven't you caught on?"

"Huh?"

"Forgive me if I'm bursting a bubble," Steve said, "but *everyone* gets that reception, no matter who's calling."

"Oh!"

When a Pain in the Neck Calls

"But Steve," I protested when I'd recuperated from the initial disappointment that I was a victim of a *technique* and not a VIP, "what if the caller is unknown, a complete stranger? Surely your staffers shouldn't fake they know the caller."

"Of course not, Leil. In that case, I instruct them to show energy and enthusiasm over the *reason* they're calling. For example, suppose the caller is a cable operator wanting to join our association. The caller would get a smile and a sincere, 'Oh yes, Mr. Smith, I'll put you right through.'"

"Yeah, but suppose the caller is selling office furniture?" I challenged.

"Doesn't matter," Steve said. "The salesperson gets the same reception after the staffer hears *why* he's calling. If my staffer says warmly, 'Oh, office furniture!' the caller feels good. And I find the salesperson is a lot easier to deal with later."

I told him, "OK, Steve, starting tomorrow morning, I'm going to put that 'Oh wow, I'm so happy you called for that reason' attitude in my voice."

The next morning, the first call was my dentist's office. "Ms. Lowndes, this call is to remind you you're overdue for your six-month checkup."

"Oh, of course, you're so right," I cooed. "I'm so glad you called." The receptionist sounded surprised but very pleased at my reaction. "I can't book an appointment right now," I continued, "but I'll call you as soon as my schedule frees up." She didn't hassle me with her usual "Well, when do you expect that to be?" She just hung up satisfied. (And I got what I wanted—no call from my dentist's office for at least another six months.)

The second time the phone rang, it was a man who had ordered my tape set calling to complain that one of the tapes broke. "Oh my goodness, I'm so glad you told me about that," I said with the enthusiasm of having won the lottery. The caller sounded a little shocked, but obviously pleased at my reaction. "Of course, I'll get another set out to you and I hope you accept my apologies." Caller hung up satisfied. (And I got what I wanted—his good will and word of mouth in spite of my tape duplicator's blooper.)

The third call was tougher. This was from a vendor I had completely forgotten to pay. "Oh, I'm so glad you reminded me of that bill," I lied. Again, shocked pleasure was the caller's reaction. (I was probably the first creditor in history who ever sounded *happy* she'd called.) "In the back of my mind I felt there was one bill I had overlooked. I'm writing the check as we speak."

Then I got my reward. The dunner said, "By the way, don't worry about the 2 percent per month late-payment charge. As long as we get your check by the end of the week, it will be OK." She hung up happy. (And I got a present—no finance charges in spite of my oversight.)

And so it went throughout the rest of the day, the rest of the week, and ever since. Try it. You'll find you get a lot more from anyone when you smile, after you find out who it is or why they're calling. Use the "*Oh Wow, It's You*" technique on almost every call.

TECHNIQUE #62:
"OH WOW, IT'S YOU!"

Don't answer the phone with an "I'm just sooo happy all the time" attitude. Answer warmly, crisply, professionally. Then, *after* you hear who is calling, let a huge smile of happiness engulf your entire face and spill over into your voice. You make your caller feel as though your giant warm fuzzy smile is reserved for him or her.

63 The Sneaky Screen

"No, No, Aaaaaagh, Not the *Screen*!"

Picture a torture device called The Screen. The mad scientist, laughing maniacally, forces the victim into a giant meat grinder that mashes him through a heavy-metal screen. It slices his body into a million molecules before he's reconstituted on the other side. Being screened when you call someone's office is the emotional version of that ordeal.

You place your cold call. "May I speak to Mr. Jones?" you pleasantly ask.

"Who's calling?" a haughty voice responds. Of course, your name is not prestigious enough for the screener to grant you the exalted status of speaking to Jones.

Her ruthless interrogation continues, "And what company are you with?" You submit your company's name, praying it will score with her. And then to top it off, she has the pluck to ask, "And what's this in reference to?" Aaaaaagh!

Several weeks after my luncheon with Steve, I had the occasion to call him again. "Is Steve Effros available? This is Leil Lowndes calling."

"Oh yes, Ms. Lowndes, definitely. Let me put you right through." I start humming happily as I wait for Steve to come to the line.

A moment later his assistant came back and said sympathetically, "I'm so sorry Ms. Lowndes. Steve just stepped out to lunch. I know he'll be sorry he missed your call." Meanwhile, I'm still smiling. Do I suspect that Steve didn't "just step out to lunch"? Do I suspect he's sitting right there? Do I ever, in my wildest paranoid dreams, think he doesn't have the time or inclination to talk to me? Do I feel *screened*? No way! I'm as happy as a carefree kitten as I leave my number for a callback. You see, I have probably fallen for the *Sneaky Screen*.

Technique #63:
The Sneaky Screen

If you must screen your calls, instruct your staff to first say cheerfully, "Oh yes, I'll put you *right* through. May I tell her who's calling?" If the party has already identified himself, it's "Oh of course, Mr. Whoozit. I'll put you right through."

When the secretary comes back with the bad news that Mr. or Ms. Bigwig is unavailable, callers don't take it personally and *never* feel screened. They fall for it every time. Just like I did.

64 Salute the Spouse

The Power *Behind* the Phone

I know a secret about a Big Cat who owns an international hotel chain with properties in six countries. He hires and fires thousands, awards or pulls immense contracts, borrows from major financial institutions, and makes lavish contributions to charities. Mr. Big Cat (we'll call him "Ed") has a respected and immediately recognizable name in his industry. And here's the secret: *Mrs. Big Cat is the real brains behind the operation.*

I became friends with Mrs. Big Cat (we'll call her "Sylvia") when I did some consulting for her husband's organization. Sylvia invited me to tea one afternoon. She sweetly apologized that this was "maid's day off" so we'd have to fend for ourselves. As we happily perched on the patio and were about to dive into our tea and crumpets, the phone rang. She excused herself to answer it.

I heard Mrs. Big Cat say, "No, I'm sorry, he's not in. Shall I tell him who called? . . . No, I don't know when he is planning on returning, but if you give me your name and . . . No, I said I don't know what time he'll be back . . . Yes, I'll tell him you called."

As Sylvia returned to the patio, I could she was annoyed by the call. Always on the lookout for a good phone story, I ventured a questioning look.

Picking up on my curiosity, she said, "That fool thinks he's going to get a contribution from Ed. Ha!" she laughed wryly. Her candor emboldened me to ask her more. It turns out the caller, a Mr. Creighton, was a fund-raiser for a major charity Ed was considering contributing to. My hostess said Creighton had called twice in the past two weeks when Ed was out. "And not once did he greet me, ask how I was, or apologize for the disturbance." This did not please Mrs. Big Cat.

Was it a major irritation for Mrs. Big Cat? No, only minor. But did it mean a major loss for the little cat who called? It sure did. In Ed and Sylvia's Big Cat household, subtleties count. At the dinner table, Mrs. Big Cat could say to her husband, "A very nice man named Creighton called for you today, dear." Or she might say, "A rather irritating chap named Creighton called for you today." One comment or the other could mean millions won or lost by Creighton's charity. And all because little cat Creighton mildly ruffled Mrs. Big Cat's whiskers.

⭐ TECHNIQUE #64:
SALUTE THE SPOUSE

Whenever you are calling someone's home, always identify and greet the person who answers. Whenever you call someone's office more than once or twice, make friends with the secretary. Anybody who is close enough to answer the phone is close enough to sway the VIP's opinion of you.

Home advice: *Salute the Spouse*. Office advice: *Salute the Secretary.*

A surprising number of Big Cat spouses—and secretaries—have deep claws into important business decisions. When it comes hiring time, firing time, promoting time, or buying time, many spouses have a say. When it comes to whose calls get through, whose proposals get put on the top of the boss's desk, who gets luncheon appointments made, secretaries' opinions count!

Only foolish callers don't realize *all* spouses and secretaries have names. *All* spouses and secretaries have lives. *All* spouses and secretaries have feelings. *All* spouses and secretaries have influence. Deal accordingly.

65 What Color Is Your Time?

"Are You Red, Yellow, or Green?"

When Alexander Graham Bell invented the phone, he and his comrades had no use for such trite phrases as "Hi, how ya doin'?" Bell and his boys never just started spouting their ideas into their listener's ears. The first words out of their mouths in those times were "Can you talk?" Bell and his buddies were, of course, referring to technical capabilities.

Little did they know, more than a hundred years later, Big Winners would use a form of that same greeting. Today, of course, "Can you talk?" means "Is it *convenient* to talk?" Before launching into conversation, they always ask "Is this a good time to chat?" "Did I catch you at a good time?" "Do you have a minute to discuss the widget account?"

All folks have a Big Ben in their brain that determines how receptive they are going to be to you and your ideas. When you mess with their internal cuckoo clock, they won't listen to you. No matter how interesting your information, or how pleasant your call, bad timing means bad results for you.

It's not your fault. Whenever you call someone at home, you never know whether she was sleeping or whether there's a fire raging in the kitchen stove. Whenever you call someone at work, you never know whether he's got two hours to get a report in or whether the big boss is not-so-patiently sitting on his desk.

Whenever you place a call, always—not occasionally, not frequently—*always* ask about your timing. Make it a habit. Make it a rule. Make it a self-punishable crime if the first words out of your mouth don't concern the convenience of your timing:

"Hi, Joe, is this a good time to talk?"
"Hello, Susan. Have you got a minute?"
"Hi, Carl, did I catch you good or did I catch you bad?"
"Sam, do you have a second for me to tell you about what happened at the game last Saturday?"

There are many ways to say it, but it all boils down to "Is this a good time to talk?"

My friend Barry, a broadcaster, accomplishes more in a day than most people do in a week. He came up with a clever conversational device that assures he'll never shatter anyone's emotional sundial. He calls it *What Color Is Your Time?* Barry introduces the device by telling people he's calling he has great respect for their time. He then asks permission to start his future conversations with a question that assures he'll never disturb them at an inopportune moment. Barry says he's going to ask what color their time is. They should honestly answer, "red," "yellow," or "green."

Red means "I'm really rushed."

Yellow means "I'm busy but what's on your mind? If it's quick, we can deal with it."

Green means "Sure, I've got time. Let's talk."

Red, like the stoplight at the corner, means stop. Yellow means hurry up, time is short, or stop and wait for the next green light. Green means go.

Busy people pick up quickly on his artful device and enjoy the game. Most especially, they enjoy Barry's sensitivity and respect for their time. In fact, he says, most of his callers play the same sensitive game when they call him. "Hi Barry, what color is your time? Are you green?"

Salesfolks, Wait for the Green Light

A note here for salespeople. If you ask a prospect if he or she has time to talk and the answer is "Not really, but tell me what's on your mind," *DON'T*! Do not make your sales pitch while they're red. Do not talk with them when they're yellow. Wait until they're green, very green. (If you ever want to see any green coming from them, that is.)

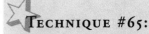

TECHNIQUE #65:
WHAT COLOR IS YOUR TIME?

No matter how urgent you think your call, always begin by asking the person about timing. Either use the *What Color Is Your Time?* device or simply ask, "Is this a convenient time for you to talk?"

When you ask about timing first, you'll never smash your footprints right in the middle of your telephone partner's sands of time. You'll never get a "No!" just because your timing wasn't right.

66 Constantly Changing Outgoing Message

Whoops, Your Paranoia Is Showing

You can tell a lot about people just from the outgoing messages they leave on their voice mail. "Hello," his machine answers. "I'm not in right now. But you probably don't want to talk to me anyway." Beep. Would you suspect this fellow has an inferiority complex?

"Hello," her machine answers. "The sound you hear is the barking of our killer Doberman pinscher, Wolf. Please leave a message after the tone." Beep. Would you suspect this woman is worried about break-ins? Most of us don't record our personal foibles so conspicuously for the world to hear. Nevertheless, people can hear a lot between the lines of what we say on our voice mail.

Last month I needed a graphic artist to do some work for one of my extremely conservative clients. I phoned Mark, an artist whose work I had seen and liked a lot. His answering machine blasted ear-splitting rock music through the receiver. Then his voice boomed over the electric guitar, "Hey there, dude, don't be crude. Jes' croon me an earful of sweeeeeeet sounds right at that lone tone. Yeah, yeah, yeah." Beep. I banged the receiver quickly back into the cradle to shut out horrible fantasies of how my client would react if he had to call Mark. His thirty-second talent show might have been an appropriate sample of a rock musician's talent. But a businessperson should opt for a more sedate outgoing message. The message you leave on your answering machine reflects your work. Keep yours friendly, neutral, and up-to-date.

And here's the secret: to give the impression you are really on top of your business, *change your message every day*. Studies show that callers perceive people to be brighter and more efficient when they hear an updated message each time they call. If appropriate, let callers know where you are and when you intend to be back. If you have customers who need to be attended to, this is crucial.

Try something like this on your office phone: "This is (name). It's Thursday, May 7th, and I'll be in a sales meeting until late this afternoon. Please leave your message and I'll get back to you as soon as I return." That way, if you don't call a client back until 4 P.M. he isn't steaming.

Also, keep it short. Some people change their message every day, but it's too long. I had a colleague, a public speaker named Dan, who in his finest mellifluous voice imposed his thought for the day on all unsuspecting callers.

Last year I was working on a project with Dan and had to call him three times in the same day to leave a progress report. Each time his machine answered:

> "Hello, this is Dan, and here's my daily motivator." He cleared his throat for his big recorded performance and then continued. "Did someone say something today that offended you? So what? That's their problem." He paused dramatically. "Did someone look at you the wrong way? So what? That's their problem." Again, a pause for the magnitude of that sentiment to sink in. "Replace your petty thoughts of anger, exasperation, and spite with thoughts of strength. Calm down. Rise above those little insignificant irritations in life. Focus your thoughts in the direction of fulfillment and accomplishment. Once again, this is Dan." I'm surprised he didn't also leave his agent's phone number here.

"Leave your message at the tone. And have a great peaceful day." Beep.

The first time I listened to Dan's "inspirational" message, the length mildly irritated me. The second time, I found myself hyperventilating while waiting for him to get through his unbearably long message. By the third call, his schmaltzy message seemed interminable. I was filled with those "petty thoughts of anger, exasperation, and spite" he warned against *because* of his darn message. I found it impossible to "rise above it" and "focus my thoughts in the direction of fulfillment and accomplishment." I wanted to punch him in the nose. Outgoing messages are *not* the venues to give inspirational messages *nor* to impress the world with one's accomplishments.

Another friend of mine, a writer, earned herself a few little cat stripes with this one on her machine:

> "Hello, this is Cheryl Smith. Cheryl is on her national book tour," (she paused so all callers could be appropriately impressed) "making appearances in twelve cities." (Another pause as though awaiting applause.) "She'll be returning on October 7." (What's this *she* bit? Cheryl herself is speaking.) "Please leave your message for her at the tone." Beep.

Yes, Cheryl, we know you're an important author. But your third-party reference to self, your narcissistic tone of voice, and topping it off with twelve cities would make any Big Cat snicker through his whiskers.

One last codicil: Avoid one particular message many businesspeople use these days—"I'm either away from my desk or on the other line." The subtext of this message is "I'm a slave chained to my desk and it is an amazing fact that I have escaped for the moment." One night I was working into the wee hours. At 4 A.M. I decided to leave a message on a colleague's business phone so she'd get it as soon as she came in at nine. "Hello," the message chirped. "This is Felicia. I'm either away from my desk or on the other line right now, but leave your message at the tone." Beep. Felicia, *of course* you're away from your desk—it's 4 A.M. on Sunday morning! "On the other line?" At this hour? I *hope* not!

You never know how your message is going to affect someone. Just keep yours neutral, friendly, constantly changing, short, and understated. No boasts, no bells, no whistles.

TECHNIQUE #66:
CONSTANTLY CHANGING OUTGOING MESSAGE

If you want to be perceived as conscientious and reliable, leave a short, professional, and friendly greeting as your outgoing message. No music. No jokes. No inspirational messages. No boasts, bells, or whistles. And here's the secret: *change it every day.* Your message doesn't have to be flawless. A little cough or stammer gives a lovely unpretentious reality to your message.

67 Your Ten-Second Audition

Neeexxxt!

Producers of big Broadway musicals can be brutal during auditions. An anxious wanna-be star, after rehearsing his audition song for weeks, steps onstage. He opens his mouth to sing. After a few notes, the heartless producer shouts, "Thank you. NEEEXXXT!" Dreams of stardom dashed in ten seconds!

Businesspeople's professional dreams can also be dashed in the first ten seconds of their "audition." Their audition is the message they leave on someone else's answering machine.

Competent businesspeople wouldn't dream of sending a messy handwritten business letter to a VIP on cheap yellow-stained paper and expect a response. They know the recipient would toss it in the trash. Nevertheless, some of these same folks will leave a lackluster message on a VIP's voice mail and expect a callback. No one ever told them that Big Winners scrutinize messages on their voice mail with the same consideration of a big Broadway producer. If you sound good, you've got a chance. If you don't, you are fast-forwarded out of their life.

Salespeople, suitors, candidates, and competitors who leave crisp, intelligent, upbeat messages on voice mail get called back. Losers with lackluster tones and uncrafted messages never hear from Mr. or Ms. Make It Happen. Make sure your message reflects three Cs: Confidence, Clarity, and Credibility. In addition, make it entice, entertain, or interest the listener. A flat "This is Joe, call me back" doesn't score with Big Winners.

Stay Tuned for . . .

Radio DJs use tricks to keep their listeners tuned in. Top salespeople have similar little tricks to entice prospects to call them back. Here's one called a *cliff-hanger*. To make sure listeners won't switch stations during the radio commercial, the broadcaster throws out a mini-mystery: "And right after the commercial we'll be back with the winning ticket . . . It could be yours . . . Stay tuned!" Whenever you leave a voice mail message for anyone, try to include a cliff-hanger: "Hi Harry, this is Andrew. I have the answer to that question you asked me last week." Or "Hi Diane, this is Betsy. I have some big news about that project we were discussing." Now Harry and Diane have a reason to call Andrew and Betsy back.

Pitch personality into your message, too. Picture the people listening to it. Say something to pique their curiosity or make them smile. The message you leave is your ten-second audition. Make it good.

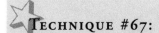

TECHNIQUE #67:

YOUR TEN-SECOND AUDITION

While dialing, clear your throat. If an answering machine picks up, pretend the beep is a big Broadway producer saying "Nexxxt." Now you're on. This is *Your Ten-Second Audition* to prove you are worthy of a quick callback.

Incidentally, if someone's voice mail *unexpectedly* comes on and you are unprepared, quickly hang up (before the beep so they don't get a hang-up message.) Take a moment to craft your entertaining, enticing, or interesting message. Rehearse it once with confidence, clarity, and charisma. Then redial to leave your great hot message.

A funny thing happens. If your party answers this time, you'll be disappointed.

68 The Ho-Hum Caper

Ho Hum, Business as Usual

The inspiration for this next telephone technique comes from personal experiences with mid-Manhattan toilets (a less-than-refined origin, to be sure). New York City, in spite of all its reputed sophistication, lags some of the shabbiest European cities in one respect. Manhattan has few public toilets. And none of those European-style, charming, and at times very much appreciated, freestanding structures on street corners.

In the days when I made sales calls around the busy city of New York, this presented a problem. Several times a day. I often found myself at the mercy of coffee-shop cashiers who jealously guarded their restroom facilities. Some shops even put menacingly scribbled signs in the window, "Bathrooms are for customers only."

I often found that if I played it straight—going up to the cashier and asking if I could use the amenities—I'd get shot down. So I used the following technique. Without casting a glance at the cashier, I'd strut confidently into the coffee shop. I'd march right past the bathroom bouncer and keep my gaze fixed on one of the booths. She'd assume I was coming for lunch or had simply returned to collect my forgotten gloves. Once past the gatekeeper of the loo, I'd wait for her to be busy ringing up the next check. Then, like greased lightning, I'd sprint into the john.

I dubbed this deception the *Ho-Hum Caper* after my feigned attitude of "Ho hum, business as usual. I come here every day with nothing on my mind but lunch."

Let us now translate that sneaky subterfuge into a seldom-fail phone technique. You can use the maneuver to sneak around secretaries and dodge their heartless screening. Instead of playing it straight and asking for your party by name, just say "Is *he* in?" or "Is *she* in?" Using the pronoun is verbally sprinting past the secretary with a business as usual, "Ho hum, I call every day" attitude.

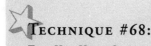

TECHNIQUE #68:
THE HO-HUM CAPER

Instead of using your party's name, casually let the pronoun *he* or *she* roll off your tongue. Forget "Uh, may I speak to Ms. Bigshot please?" Just announce, "Hi, Bob Smith here, is *she* in?" Tossing the familiar *she* off your tongue signals to the secretary that you and her boss are old buddies.

69 "I Hear Your Other Line"

"Do You Really Have to Take Care of That Fire in Your Kitchen?"

Whenever you're on the phone with someone, you hear a lot more than their voices. In the background you might hear dogs barking, babies crying, or a crackling sound. For all you know, the dog has his tail caught in the refrigerator, the baby has to be fed, or the house is on fire. When you acknowledge the sound by asking if they have to take care of it, you warm the hearts of your listeners.

When you are talking to someone at work, you often hear another phone ringing. Say immediately, "I hear your other line. Do you have to answer it?" Even if not, he or she will appreciate the gesture. If he does have to catch the other call, you can be sure he heard nothing you said after the first ring. He's only thinking "How can I interrupt this babbling person without being rude so I can answer my other phone?" In fact with every brr-ing, irritation sets in that you are holding him hostage from doing what he has to do.

Here is the technique guaranteed to save you from being in that uncomfortable position.

TECHNIQUE #69:
"I HEAR YOUR OTHER LINE"

When you hear a phone in the background, stop speaking—in midsentence if necessary—and say "I hear your other line" (or your dog barking, your baby crying, your spouse calling you). Ask whether she has to attend to it. Whether she does or not, she'll know you're a Top Communicator for asking.

The subtext, of course, is that you are sensitive to what's going on in your caller's world. If you're talking to someone far away or in another country, another way to show you're tops in the communications department is to translate time references into their time zone. When you leave a message, say "I can be reached between three and five *your* time."

And don't forget foreign holidays. Last July 1, I was on the phone with a client from Australia. I was impressed when he wished me "Happy Independence Day weekend." So impressed, in fact, I ran out to find a chart of international holidays. I made a note in my calendar next April 25 to wish my Aussie friend "Happy ANZAC Day"(after I figure out what it means). If you do business with people around the world, be sure to extend good wishes to them for their holidays. Forget about your own if they're not shared. I'm still mortified about the time last November when I was on a conference call with a Canadian client and seven of his salespeople. I wished them all "Happy Thanksgiving."

70 Instant Replay

It's Much Better the Second Time Around

The first time I saw *The Wizard of Oz*, the story bewitched me. The second time I saw *The Wizard of Oz*, the special effects amazed me. The third time I saw *The Wizard of Oz*, the photography dazzled me. Have you ever seen a movie twice, three times? You notice subtleties and hear sounds you completely missed the first time around.

It's the same on the phone. Because your business conversations are more consequential than movies, you should listen to them two, maybe three times. Often we have no clear idea of what *really* happened in our phone conversation until we hear it again. You'll find shadings more significant than the color of Toto's collar—and more scarecrows than you imagined who "haven't got a brain!"

How do you listen to your important business conversations again? Simply legally and ethically tape record them. I call the technique of recording and analyzing your business conversations for subtleties *Instant Replay*.

Having a tape recorder on her phone could have made a dramatic difference in the career of my friend Laura. Laura, a nutritionist, had developed an excellent health drink. It deserved to be marketed nationally.

I was in Laura's office one day discussing her plans and I said, "Laura, I've got just the contact for you. Several months earlier, I had met Fred, a man who owned a chain of supermarkets. Fred owed me a favor because, at his request, I'd given a pro bono talk for a social club he belonged to. Fred was a Big Banana in the supermarket world, and with one "yes" he could put my friend's health drink in his stores. That would launch Laura nationally.

I placed the call and, lo and behold, he was in. And, an even bigger lo and behold, Fred sounded interested in Laura's beverage.

"Put her on," Fred said.

I proudly handed Laura the phone and their conversation started out fine. "Oh sure, I'll send you a sample," Laura said. "What's the address?" Then I heard Laura say, "Uh, wait a minute, let me get something to write with." (I rapidly rolled a pen and pushed a pad in front of her nose.) "Uh, what's that again? Did you say 4201 or 4102?" (I moan inaudibly.) "And how do you spell the name of the street?" (My moan becomes audible.) "Whoops, this pen just ran out of ink. Leil, do you see another pen on my desk? (I did, and this time I felt like throwing it at her.) "Sorry, what's that again?"

Yikes, now I wanted to grab the phone out of Laura's hands. She shouldn't be bothering a busy Big Banana for details like repeating addresses. She could have called his secretary back later for clarification. But even that would have been unnecessary if she were recording the conversation with the technique I call *Instant Replay*. She could have merely mentioned that she was flipping on the recorder (most heavy hitters are comfortable with that concept) and she would have had it on tape.

Fred was nice to Laura that day. But my friend never heard back from him. And to this day, she wonders why. She'll never know the confused phone exchange nixed the deal.

Was Fred being unfair just because Laura was a little slow on the phone? Absolutely not. Fred figures, "If this woman is as insensitive about my time at the *beginning* of a possible business relationship, what's she going to be like down the pike?" Wise choice, Fred. I still like Laura. She's still my friend. But will I introduce her to any other Big Winners who might help her? I can't take the chance.

How to Set Up Your *Instant Replay*

Instant Replay is simple and cheap. Go to your local electronics store and ask for a recorder for your telephone. Slap it on your phone receiver, and plug the other end into a cassette recorder. Then turn the recorder on during your next important conversation. The device could earn you hundreds of dollars on your first call. In some states the law requires you inform the other party you are recording them. Make sure to check with the authorities about the legality in the state where you live. If it's one-party consent, don't worry. *You're* the one party. Obviously you must never ever use the tape for any other purpose than for your own second listening. Not only would that be unlawful, it would be unconscionable. For extra security, don't leave people's taped conversations lying around. Keep the same tape in your cassette machine and use it over and over to record important details.

With *Instant Replay*, you can catch balls your Conversation Partner throws out on the first bounce. You're on the phone with your boss. He rambles off four or five names in a law firm you're supposed to write to, then the address, then the nine-digit zip code. Realizing he's pitched you some pretty fast balls, he asks, "Shall I repeat that for you?" "No thanks, I got it," you proudly say, silently tapping your little tape recorder. Boss is impressed.

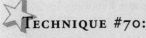

TECHNIQUE #70:

INSTANT REPLAY

Record all your business conversations and listen to them again. The second or third time, you pick up on significant subtleties you missed the first time. It's like football fans who often don't know if there was a fumble until they see it all over again in *Instant Replay*.

Yet another benefit of *Instant Replay*—it helps hide your ignorance. Recently I was on the phone with a cameraman negotiating a price on a videotape to use as a speaker's demo. Luckily I was recording the conversation because his flurry of *Hi-8*, *VHS*, *Super* VHS, *Beta SP*, and *three-quarter inch U-matic* had me wanting to crawl into a rodent hole in the wall. But I listened to the tape of our conversation afterward. I wrote down all the words I didn't understand and then asked a video friend what they meant. Now I was able to call the cameraman back and say, "I'd like a two-camera shoot on Beta SP. And can you give me a VHS dub so I can do some off-line editing?" Don't you think I got a much better price than if I'd asked, "Duh, what's a Beta SP?"

Forget What They *Said*, Hear What They *Meant*

Instant Replay also makes you sensitive to levels of communication far deeper than just your callers' words. You tune in to their real enthusiasm or hesitation about an idea.

When we want something, our minds play funny tricks on us. If we desperately crave "yes" from someone, we hear "yes." But "yes" isn't always what it seems. A client's forceful "YES" and her hesitant "yeee-sss" are different as heaven and hell. Last month I asked a woman who'd booked me for a speech if her office could reproduce my ten-page handout. She gave me the answer I wanted, which was "yes." Later, however, I re-listened to our conversation on tape. Her answer about the handouts had been a very hesitant, "Hmm, well, yes." I immediately called her back and said, "By the way, don't worry about those handouts."

"Oh, I'm *so* glad!" she purred. "Because we really don't have the budget for things like that." I gained much more in my client's goodwill than the value of reproducing a few sheets of paper.

Let us now return to your live, in-person show. We're going to talk not only about how to *be* a hit at a party, but how to smoothly *hit on* all the folks you want—just like a politician.

PART EIGHT

How to Work a Party Like a Politician Works a Room

The Politician's Six-Point Party Checklist

Most of us, when invited to a party, waft into a fluffy thought process. Our random reverie goes something like this: "Hmm, this could be fun . . . Wonder if they're going to serve food . . . Hope it's good . . . Might be some interesting people there . . . Wonder if my friend so 'n' so is coming . . . Golly, what should I wear?"

That's *not* the way a politician thinks about a party, however. While politicians, heavy-duty networkers, serious socializers, and Big Winners in the business world are staring at the invitation, they instinctively surf to a different channel. Before they RSVP with yes or no, their brains craft journalistic campaign questions. It's the *Six-Point Party Checklist*. Who? When? What? Why? Where? And How?

Let's take them one by one.

Who Is Going to Be at the Party?

More specifically, who will be there that I should meet? Serious networkers calculate "Who must I meet for business? Who should I meet for political or social reasons?" And, if single and searching, "Who do I want to meet for possible love?"

If they don't know who is going to be in attendance, they ask. Politicians unabashedly telephone the host or hostess of the party and ask, "Who's coming?" As the party giver chats casually about the guest list, politicians scribble the names of the people who interest them, then resolve to meet each.

When Should I Arrive?

Politicians do not leave arrival time to whenever they finish getting dressed. They don't ask themselves, "Hmm, should I be fashionably late?" They carefully calculate their estimated time of arrival and estimated time of departure.

If the party is bulging with contacts, Biggies get there early to start hitting their marks as each arrives. VIPs frequently come early to get their business done before party regulars who "hate to be the first one there" start arriving. They are never embarrassed to arrive early. After all, the only people who see them are other early arrivals who are often Heavy Hitters like themselves.

Nor will you find politicians prowling around, the last to slink out the door. Once they've accomplished what they set out to do, they're on their way to the next opportunity. If their agenda is more social, they try to leave their departure time open and their *après*-party schedule free. That way, if they make an important new contact, they can stay around and talk with him. Or drive her home. Or go somewhere else for coffee.

What Should I Take with Me?

A politician's checklist is not the usual, "Let's see, my comb, cologne, and breath mints." They pack more functional networking tools in their pockets or purses.

If Corporate Cats will be prowling the party, they pack a pocketful of business cards. If it's a gala where people are gadding about on the social ladder and they want to exude old-world elegance, they grab a handful of social cards containing only their name and possibly an address and phone number. (Some feel giving out a business card in a purely social setting can be gauche.) The most vital tool in their party pack is a small pad and pen to keep track of important contacts.

Why Is the Party Being Given?

The politician's perpetual philosophy of "penetrate the ostensible" enters here. (That's just a fancy way of saying "look under the rug.") They ask themselves, "What is the ostensible reason for the party?" A big industrialist is giving his daughter a graduation party? A newly divorced executive is throwing himself a birthday bash? A floundering business is celebrating its tenth year?

"Nice," politicians say to themselves, "that's the ostensible. But what's the *real* reason for the party?" Maybe the industrialist wants to get his daughter a good job so he's invited dozens of potential employers. The birthday boy is single again so the guest list is heavy with attractive and accomplished females. The business desperately needs good PR if it's going to stay around another ten years. So they've invited the press and community makers and shakers.

Politicians have expert under-rug vision to spot the host's real agenda. They will, of course, never discuss it at the party. However, the insight elevates them to a shared state of higher consciousness with other Heavy Hitters at the bash.

Their knowledge also makes them valuable agents for the party giver. A savvy politician introduces the job-seeking daughter to some executives at the party, or tells the most alluring women at the bash what a great guy birthday boy is. When chatting with reporters, he talks up the host's business that needs good PR. When people support the real *why* of the party, they become popular and sought-after guests for future events.

Where Is the Collective Mind?

Often people from one profession or one interest group will comprise most of the guest list. A politician never accepts any invitation without asking herself, "What kind of people will be at this party, and what will they be thinking about?" Perhaps there will be a drove of doctors. So she clicks on the latest medical headlines and rehearses a little doc-talk. If the guests are a nest of new-age voters, the politician gets up to speed on telepathic healing, Tantric toning, and trance dancing. Politicians can't afford to not be in the know.

How Am I Going to Follow Up on the Party?

Now, the big finale. I call it "contact cement." It's cementing the contacts the politician has made. After meeting a good contact and exchanging cards, practically everyone says, "It's been great talking to you. We'll stay in touch."

This good intention seldom happens without herculean effort. Politicians, however, make a science out of keeping up the contact. After the party, they sit at their desks and, like a game of solitaire, lay out the business cards of the people they've met. Using the *Business Card Dossier* technique described later in this section, they decide how, when, and if to deal with each. Does this person require a phone call? Should that one receive a handwritten note? Shall I e-mail or call the other one?

Use the *Six-Point Party Checklist*—the Who? When? Why? Where? What? and How? of a party as your general game plan. Now let's get down to specifics.

71 ⭐ Munching or Mingling

"How Come People Don't Approach Me?"

The average party goer, let's say Charlie, arrives at the bash. He makes a beeline for the refreshment table for munchies and a beverage. He then finds a few buddies and starts chatting away with them.

Chewing the nibbles on his plate and the fat with his friends, he occasionally looks around the room to see who might be new and fun to talk to. He's hoping several attractive and interesting people at the party will spot him and come over to talk.

What's wrong with Charlie's approach? *Everything* if Charlie wants to make the party productive. Let's start with the average party goer's first mistake—getting some refreshments and a drink right off the bat.

People mingling at a party make judgments, often subconscious, about whom they are going to approach. Have you ever lived on a farm? Or had a dog or a cat? Then you know you never disturb animals when they are eating. Likewise, when a human animal is eating, other human animals do not feel comfortable advancing. If party goers' eyes scan the crowd and see you with the feed bag on, they pass right over you. Subconsciously they're saying to themselves, "Let the hungry hound chow down and maybe we'll talk later." Later never comes because they wind up making friends with someone else whose mouth wasn't full.

Politicians always eat *before* they come to the party. They know they'd need a circus juggler's talent to shake hands, exchange business cards, hold a drink, and stuff crackers and cheese into their mouths—all with just two hands.

TECHNIQUE #71:
MUNCHING OR MINGLING

Politicians want to be eyeball-to-eyeball and belly-to-belly with their constituents. Like any Big Winner well versed in the science of proxemics and spatial relationships, they know any object except their belt buckles has the effect of a brick wall between two people. Therefore they never hold food or drink at a party.

Come to munch or come to mingle. But do not expect to do both. Like a good politician, chow down *before* you come.

72 Rubberneck the Room

How to Make an Unforgettable Entrance

Loretta Young makes television history when she appears at the head of her immense staircase and surveys the set. *Then* she swoops down to start the show.

The Pope steps out onto his balcony overlooking St. Peter's Square in Rome and surveys the crowd. *Then* he begins the benediction.

Bette Davis stops in the doorway and looks around. *Then* she mutters, "What a dump!"

And every late-night TV comic since "Heeeere's Johnny!" steps center stage and scrutinizes the applauding audience. *Then* he reveals the reason for the smirk on his face.

What do all these great entrances have in common? Each pauses momentarily and looks around *before* swooping into decisive action.

Movie directors love shots of THE DOORWAY where the camera pans, the music swells, and all eyes gravitate to the honcho or honchoette standing under the frame. Does the star skulk into the room like a frightened little kitten in a new owner's home? Or, like many of us do at a party, frantically gravitate to the first familiar face so people won't think he or she's unconnected? No, the star stops. Then, framed by the doorway, his or her notable presence is felt by all.

People who have mastered this trick have what envious theatrical wanna-bes call "stage presence." Stage groupies think some lucky stars are born with it. Think again, thespians. It's *cultivated.* Politicians don't just slink unnoticed into a roomful of people. Politicians make The Entrance.

With one simple technique, you too can make great entrances. I call it *Rubberneck the Room.* Before entering, stop dramatically in the doorway and survey the scene s-l-o-w-l-y with your eyes. It is significant that, while you're standing in the doorway, you're not thinking, "Look at me." The reason you're *Rubbernecking the Room* is not to show off. It is so you can diagnose the situation you're walking into. Take note of the lighting, the bar, and most important, the faces. Listen to the music, the buzz of the crowd, the clinking of glasses. See who is talking to whom. While rubbernecking, you'll also be using *Be the Chooser, Not the Choosee*, the next technique, which helps you select your first, second, and maybe third target. Now, like the Big Cat who rules the jungle, leap in to make your first move toward wiping up the room.

TECHNIQUE #72:
RUBBERNECK THE ROOM

When you arrive at the gathering, stop dramatically in the doorway. Then s-l-o-w-l-y survey the situation. Let your eyes travel back and forth like a SWAT team ready in a heartbeat to wipe out anything that moves.

In tandem with *Rubberneck the Room*, try using the following technique . . .

73 Be the Chooser, Not the Choosee

"Hmm, Any Interesting Strangers I Should Meet?"

Politicians don't wait for others to approach them. If the party host or their campaign manager has not supplied a "must meet" list, they choose their targets while *Rubbernecking the Room*. As their keen eyes scan the crowd, they're asking themselves "Who would I most enjoy talking to? Who looks like they could be most beneficial to my life? Who could I learn most from in this gang?"

How do they choose? They look at everyone the same way my friend, Bob, the caricature artist, looks at people. You can tell a whole lot more than you realize if you keep your gaze fixed on someone. Every twinkle in someone's eye and every line surrounding it tells a story—the story of the life he or she leads. Who was it who said, "At age thirty, everyone has the face he deserves"? Yet few of us consciously look into strangers' eyes. How foolish that, at a party or convention for making contacts, most people are embarrassed to make eye contact with people we don't know.

In my networking seminar, I prime participants to make intense visual contact by asking them to form a big circle, walk around the room, and silently stare at each other. "Gaze into each other's eyes," I tell them. "Examine each other's movements."

As they are walking, I say, "The most important business contact, the dearest friend, or the love of your life is probably not in this room. Nevertheless, sometime soon, you will be in a room where you will spot someone you sense could change your life. I want you to be prepared. I want you to have the courage to make the approach and not wait in vain for that special someone to approach you." While strolling and staring, I ask them to silently choose the four people they most want to talk to during the break.

"Only the Beautiful People Will Be Chosen"

When given this unfamiliar and uncomfortable assignment, the participants assume everyone will make a beeline for the most attractive people. It never happens. Something mystical occurs when people take the time to really look at each other. Everyone discovers a distinctive beauty in one or two other people that is very personal, very special, and speaks uniquely to the seeker.

The dearest friend in my life was a homely little fellow named Chip. He was only 5'2". Chip had a huge nose and funny little eyes peeping out through thick glasses. At a party, without using this technique, I probably would never have noticed Chip. However, my concentration was on him the day we met because he was giving a speech. When I gazed intently into his eyes and watched his lips moving, I saw such subjective beauty coming from his face. He became my best friend for twelve years until a tragic disease took his life. Nevertheless, Chip remained beautiful to me until the end because, no matter how twisted his body became with illness, the beauty shone through his spirit.

As the seminar participants explore each other's faces and movements, they discover the subjective beauty in their faces, in their spirits. No one can explain why one person chooses another as one of his or her special four. Yet practically everyone returns from the break having made a new good friend. Never is anyone left unchosen.

When you seek people's special qualities by exploring their

faces, you will find them. If you want to walk out of any gathering with your life enhanced, spend time with people *you* choose, not just those who choose you. Be *choosey* in who you pick. But don't wait to be the *choosee*.

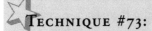

TECHNIQUE #73:
BE THE CHOOSER, NOT THE CHOOSEE

The lifelong friend, the love of your life, or the business contact who will transform your future may not be at the party. However, someday, somewhere, he or she will be. Make every party a rehearsal for the big event.

Do not stand around waiting for the moment when that special person approaches you. *You* make it happen by exploring every face in the room. No more "ships passing in the night." Capture whatever or whomever you want in your life.

"Sure, in a Seminar, It's Easy. But What About Real Life?"

Sometimes, after the break, a participant will say, "It was simple to go up to people I wanted to talk to this time because you gave it as an assignment. But what about at a real party?" Recently, one of my participants named Todd asked me this question in front of the group.

I asked, "Todd, how did you make the approach this time?"

"Well, I just went up and said, 'Hi, I'm Todd. I wanted to talk to you.'"

"Well?" I asked.

It dawned on him that he could use this opening phrase to meet *anyone* at *any* party. To smooth a potentially awkward moment, you quickly follow up with an innocuous question like

"How do you know the hostess?" or "Do you live in the area?"
Now, you're off and running just as though the host had introduced you.

Of course, other choosey people will be prowling around the
party. Some of them, after scrutinizing you, will decide you are
one of the special people they choose to talk to. The following is
a subliminal maneuver to make it easy for them come over to confirm they made a wise choice.

74 Come-Hither Hands

Your Body Can Beckon "Come on Over" or Growl "Go Away!"

Have you ever noticed how comfortable you feel sauntering into certain rooms? The chairs are arranged in a way that welcomes you as if saying, "Come right on in and sit on me." Conversely, you enter other rooms where you must navigate a circuitous route around tables and dressers before you finally find a free chair.

Likewise, some people arrange their body furniture, their arms and legs, to say, "Hey, come right on over and talk to me." Yet other people's body furniture shouts, "Keep out! Approach at your own risk." Shy people inadvertently say "stay away" when they fold their arms. They give off insecure signals by clutching a purse, clasping a drink, or smoking a cigarette.

Controlled studies show that party goers are more comfortable approaching people who stand with an open body—arms uncrossed and hanging at their sides, legs slightly separated, a slight smile on their faces. Any object between you and the crowd is a subliminal cutoff—even your purse. More people approach a woman who sports a shoulder bag than one squeezing a handbag. The shoulder bag hangs behind her back, thus leaving the path to talk to her open.

Give Them the Ol' Wrist Flash

Now, here's the *pièce de résistance*. Next to your face, your wrists and palms are one of the most expressive parts of your body. Palms up speak volumes of good sentiments.

The Pope's wrists and palms are up when he beckons "Come unto me my brethren." The burglar's wrists and palms are up when he says, "I give up, don't shoot." The innocent man's wrists and palms are up when he's saying, "I don't know who took the money." Vulnerable, open palms signify "I have nothing to hide."

They also signify acceptance. When you are listening to a business colleague to whom you want to signal acceptance, make sure your wrists and palms are up. Even if you're resting your head on your chin, turn your wrists forward. Whenever you are chatting with anyone, give yourself a constant hand check. Make sure you don't point your knuckles directly toward anyone. Let them have the pleasure of seeing the soft, tender "come hither" skin of your wrists and palms, not the wrinkled "go away" hide on your knuckles.

Romance on your mind? Ladies, let your hands do some talking for you. Women instinctively turn their wrists and palms upward when a man excites them. (In fact, the ol' wrist flash while talking with males subconsciously gives them a sexy jolt.)

TECHNIQUE #74:
COME-HITHER HANDS

Be a human magnet, not a human repellant. When standing at a gathering, arrange your body in an open position—especially your arms and hands. People instinctively gravitate toward open palms and wrists seductively arranged in the "come hither" position. They shy away from knuckles in the "get lost or I'll punch you" position. Use your wrists and palms to say "I have nothing to hide," "I accept you and what you're saying," or "I find you sexy."

Pave a Clear Path for People
Who Find *You* Special

Frightened little jungle cats crouch behind rocks and logs so no bigger animals will spot them. In the social jungle, shy people do the same. They instinctively seek out corners and sit in seats where they won't be seen.

Whereas lynxes and lions stroll confidently to the center of the jungle clearing, human Big Cats in the social jungle also stand confidently in a clearing so others can see them. Like a politician, position yourself near a doorway since everyone must pass your way at some point in the evening.

Now we come to a technique all politicians use. In fact, some political pundits have credited the election of both John Kennedy and Bill Clinton to their mastery of the technique I call *Tracking*.

 # Tracking

Make Them Feel Like
an Old-Time Movie Star

In the 1940s, movies were different. Before experimental films, cinema verité, and nouvelle vague, they had *stories*. Americans hopped in their Buicks—a foxtail tied to the radio antenna and baby boots suspended from the rearview mirror—drove to the movie house, and watched a *story* unfold before them.

Almost invariably, the hero and heroine on the silver screen would meet, fall in love, overcome seemingly impossible obstacles, get married, and (presumably) live happily after. Oh, the stories varied slightly. But there was *always* a leading man and maybe a leading woman. Then there was the rest of the world. The supporting characters could live or die without much brouhaha. But every minor event in the star's life was significant.

Well, movies may have changed. Human nature hasn't. Everyone feels like the star of a 1940s movie. Every trivial event in their lives is momentous. "There's ME. Then there's the rest of the world."

What someone had for breakfast, what shoes he chose to wear, and whether he took time to floss his teeth can be more important to that particular someone than the fall of faraway nations or the rise of global temperatures.

Husbands and wives sometimes share their spouse's minutia:

"What did you have for breakfast, Honey?"
"You didn't wear *those* shoes, did you?"
"Did you remember to floss?"

To create an interesting intimacy, Big Winners make a point to remember minute details of important contacts' lives. They obviously don't feign interest in what they had for breakfast, or whether they flossed or forgot. But to make someone feel like a big star, they remember details their contact does happen to share.

Take their lead. If a prospect mentions he had Rice Krispies for breakfast, allude to it later. If, in chatting, your boss tells you she wore uncomfortable shoes to work one day, find a way to refer to it on another. If your client mentions he's a resolute flosser, compliment him at a later date on his discipline. It hints he or she is a memorable star in the galaxy of people you've met. It's called *Tracking* their lives. When you track their minutia, you make them feel like 1940s movie stars, and that minor events in their lives are major concerns in yours.

Don't Leave It to Chance

Politicians make a science out of *Tracking*. They keep a little black box either on their desk, in their computer, or in their brain of the last concern, enthusiasm, or event discussed with everyone in their life. They keep track of where the people were, what they said, and what they were doing since the last conversation. Then the *first* words of the next phone call or meeting with that person relates to it that information:

"Hello, Joe. How was your trip to Jamaica?"
"Hey Sam, did your kid make the baseball team?"
"Hi, Sally. Have you heard back from your client yet?"

"Nice to hear from you, Bob. It means you survived that Szechuan restaurant you were going to last time we spoke."

When you invoke the last major or minor event in anyone's life, it confirms what they've known all along. They're the most important person in the world.

One of the most powerful forms of tracking is remembering anniversaries of people's personal achievements. Did your boss get promoted to her present position one year ago today? Did your client go public? How much more memorable than a birthday card to send a one-year congratulations note.

Remembering people's private passions is another. Several years ago, I wrote regularly for a magazine. My then editor, Carrie, was obsessed with her new kitten named Cookie. Recently I ran into Carrie at a writer's conference. In early conversation I said to her, "I guess Cookie's a full-grown cat by now. How is she?"

Carrie's astonished smile was my reward.

"Leil," she squealed, "I can't believe you remember Cookie. Yes, she's fine now and . . ." Carrie went on for another ten minutes about Cookie, the now full-grown cat.

TECHNIQUE #75:
TRACKING

Like an air-traffic controller, track the tiniest details of your Conversation Partners' lives. Refer to them in your conversation like a major news story. It creates a powerful sense of intimacy.

When you envoke the last major or minor event in anyone's life, it confirms the deep conviction that he or she is an old-style hero around whom the world revolves. And people love you for recognizing their stardom.

A week later I got a call from Carrie asking me if I'd do a big story for her magazine. Did she think of me because I used the *Tracking* technique and remembered Cookie? Nobody can say, but I have my suspicions. I've seen the *Tracking* technique work on too many people to assume the rewards are coincidental.

How do politicians remember so many facts to track about so many people? They use the following technique.

76 The Business Card Dossier

"How Did You Remember That?"

Several years ago, I attended a political fund-raising event in a Midwestern state. One guest intrigued me. Sometimes I'd see him in animated conversation with several people. Other times, he'd be standing alone scribbling something on a card in his hand. Then the next time I'd look up, he'd be chatting it up with someone else. The next minute, he'd be scribbling in his hand again. He repeated this pattern for over an hour. I became as curious as a nosy neighbor. Who was this fellow?

At one point during the evening, I was standing alone by the refreshment table. He came up to me with a big smile, a warm handshake, and introduced himself. "Hi, I'm Joe Smith." He asked me what I was drinking. I told him white wine and we started discussing preferences. I happened to mention my favorite white was Sancerre. While we talked, I had to bite my tongue to resist asking him what he'd been up to with the feverish note taking.

A few minutes later, I spotted a friend across the room and excused myself. He asked for my card and, as I walked away, I peeked over my shoulder. I knew it! There he was, scribbling on my card. That was my opening. I turned back and, trying to pass my inquiry off as a joke, said, "Hey, I didn't give you my measurements. What's that you're writing?"

He gave a hearty laugh at my tasteless joke and said, "You caught me!" He turned over my card and I saw one word written on it, "Sancerre." Then, to assuage my paranoia, he emptied his pocketful of people's business cards to show me scribbles on the back of each. I assumed it was just Joe's little system to help him remember people. It wasn't until months later that I saw the method to his madness.

One morning I went to my mailbox and found a personal postcard from Joe. He told me he was running for state senator. Then at the bottom of the card, he'd written, "Had any good Sancerre lately?" That won my heart. Had I lived in his state, a little touch like that might have swayed my vote to him.

TECHNIQUE #76:
THE BUSINESS CARD DOSSIER

Right after you've talked to someone at a party, take out your pen. On the back of his or her business card write notes to remind you of the conversation: his favorite restaurant, sport, movie, or drink; whom she admires, where she grew up, a high school honor; or maybe a joke he told.

In your next communication, toss off a reference to the favorite restaurant, sport, movie, drink, hometown, high school honor. Or reprieve the laugh over the great joke.

They may not jump up and down asking, "How did you remember that?" Nevertheless, they will remember *you*. No matter how important the VIP, he or she senses a special kinship with the person who refers to other than their usual well-known accomplishments.

Politicians are constantly selling themselves. (If you've ever wondered why America is called "The Land of Promise," just keep your ears open in election year.) But, of course, to know *what* to promise people, politicians use the next super sales technique called *Eyeball Selling*.

77 ➤ Eyeball Selling

Keep Your Eyes Open to See Every Word They Don't Say

The percentage of sales that Jimmi, a good friend of mine, makes is not to be believed. Even his sales manager doesn't know how he does it. But I do. Because he told me.

Jimmi says the fancy sales techniques he's learned over the years (*Benefits Selling, Partnering, Selling to Personality Types, Value-Added Concept, Rejection Proofing, Spin Selling*) all pale next to what he calls *Eyeball Selling*.

Eyeball Selling is not memorizing two dozen closing techniques. Nor is it verbally sparring with a customer to overcome objections. Jimmi says it's quite simply keeping his eyes open, watching his customer's reactions, and adjusting his sales pitch according to how his customer's body moves.

While Jimmi is giving his sales pitch, he's concentrating more on how his customer fidgets, twitches, and squirms than on what he's saying. He's scrutinizing his customer's involuntary head movements. He's studying her hand gestures, her body rotation, her facial expressions—even her eye fluctuations. Jimmi says when his customer is not saying a word, even if she's trying to give you a poker face, she cannot *not* communicate. She may not say in words how receptive she is to your pitch, but she's clearly telling you nonetheless. Jimmi says knowing what turns a prospect on, what turns her off, and what leaves her neutral from moment to moment can make or break the sale.

How Jimmi Finds Out Where the Buck Stops

The product Jimmi sells is expensive lighting equipment. Often he must make sales presentations to groups of ten, twenty, or more people. He says, "The first challenge in *Eyeball Selling* is discovering who the real decision maker is."

Jimmi meets his challenge in an unorthodox (not necessarily recommended) way. Right after "Good afternoon, gentlemen and ladies," he says something slightly confusing. Why? Because the surprised group doesn't know how to react. So their heads all twirl like weather vanes on a windy day to look at—guess who—the honcho, the heavyweight, the head man or woman. Now Jimmi's got his decision maker so he can continue *Eyeball Selling* to that person.

What to Do When You Get Your Cue

Some signals are obvious," Jimmi says. "People shrug their shoulders for indifference, tap their fingers for impatience, or loosen their collar when they feel uncomfortable. But there are hundreds of other unconscious gestures I keep my antennae tuned for.

"For example, I watch the exact angle of my prospect's head position. If it's fully facing me, especially if it's cocked at a cute little angle, it means they're interested. In that case, I keep right on talking. But if their head is slightly turning away, that's a bad sign. I take it as a cue to change the subject and maybe talk about a different benefit of my product."

Jimmi not only tailors what he's saying to his customers' reactions, he actively takes steps to change his prospect's body position if he feels it's not receptive. He says, "The body must be open before the mind can follow." For example, he continues, "If your customer has his arms crossed in front of his chest, hand him something to look at so he has to unfold them to take it from you." Jimmi always carries a briefcase full of props to break down the barriers. He has photos of his wife and kids to hand married prospects, snapshots of his Skye terrier for customers that have a dog, an antique watch to show antique lovers, and a pocket-size computer to show gadget fanatics. Jimmi says, "As long as I can get them to open their arms to reach for something, I have a shot at their minds."

Jimmi also paces the timing of his pitch to match his customers' covert reactions. When his client reaches for an object, he takes it as a cue to talk slower, or just be quiet. Reaching for a paper clip or fondling a folder on the desk says, "I'm thinking about it."

Of course, Jimmi is on constant lookout for sales-ready signals like picking up the contract, fondling the pen, or turning their palms up. At that point, he cuts quickly to the close.

Another cue to bring out the contract-signing pen is when your prospect's head starts bobbing up and down like a plastic duck. They're silently screaming, "Yes, I'll buy!" Unskilled salespeople just keep on talking until they finish the pitch they learned in training. Many keep talking so long, they *unsell* themselves. Conversely, when customers move their heads back and forth, no matter what they are saying, they mean "No!"

Eyeballing Is Not for Selling Only

Without a word, your friends and loved ones also show their wishes. When my friend Deborah became engaged to Tony, it seemed obvious to everyone—except Deborah—that it was not a marriage made in heaven. A few months before their wedding I said, "Deb, are you really sure Tony's the one for you?"

"Oh yes," she said, her head moving right and left, back and forth, "I love him very much." That marriage never took place. Her body recognized what her mind hadn't yet realized.

Like a politician, think of your social conversations as sales pitches. Even if you have no product, you want them to buy your ideas. If your listener turns away while you're talking, don't concentrate on how rude the person is. Like a sales pro, ask yourself, "How can I change the subject to turn this person on?" If their whole body starts to turn away, use the time-honored personal question ploy. Ask about their favorite topic. "George, how big did you say that bass you caught last week was?" Or use his name and ask a personal question. That's always a grabber. "Archibald, what did you say the name of your high school football team was?"

We've talked about only a few responses. Hints for reading someone's body language could fill a book. In fact, they have—many of them. I suggest a few of my favorites in the references.[21-26] Read up on body language and tune in to its visual channel whenever you're trying to sell to people, get their vote, or convince them you're the best candidate for the job or the role of life partner. Wouldn't it be super to have Jimmi's success rate with our listeners accepting whatever we say? We can if we just keep our eyes open.

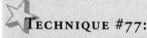

TECHNIQUE #77:
EYEBALL SELLING

The human body is a twenty-four-hour broadcasting station that transmits "You thrill me." "You bore me." "I love that aspect of your product." "That one puts my feet to sleep."

Set the hidden cameras behind your eyeballs to pick up on all your customers' and friends' signals. Then plan your pitch and your pace accordingly.

A Quick Review

That's all there is to it. You'll remember to eat before coming to the party (the *Munching or Mingling* technique) to leave your hands free for heavy networking. When you arrive, you'll stop in the doorway and *Rubberneck the Room* to get the lay of the land. While rubbernecking, you'll *Be the Chooser, Not the Choosee* and pick your prospects for the evening. When standing around, your hands will be relaxing in the inviting *Come Hither* position.

You haven't forgotten, of course, to use the meeting-people techniques from previous chapters. If you spot someone you want to talk to, check them out for a *Whatzit* you can comment on. Finding none, just ask the party giver, *Whoozat?* If the host or hostess is not in sight, simply stand near your target and resort to the *Eavesdrop In* technique.

While chatting with anyone you've previously met, you will, of course, use *Tracking* to win their vote or heart and all the techniques in Part Two to assure the conversation is interesting for your new acquaintance. Finally, you'll employ *Eyeball Selling* to make sure you're on target with every conversation. And don't forget, as you say "so long," to scribble material for your next contact on your *Business Card Dossier*.

It's a good feeling when you've done it all right. Continue using these techniques politicians use to work a room, and you'll suffer no more unimportant parties. And, following the advice throughout the book, you'll never strike anyone as an unimportant person.

Now we move on to the advanced section of *Talking the Winner's Way*. Some of the following techniques may make you scratch your head in confusion. Pay special attention to the ones that do because it means somewhere, sometime, you might find yourself scratching your head over something much more painful—like the bump from hitting a glass ceiling, or why the business deal, friendship, or love affair went sour. You might never know, unless you read it here, that it was your own communications fumble.

PART NINE

Little Tricks of Big Winners

The Most Treacherous Glass Ceiling of All

Every week, when I was a kid, my mother took me to the National Geographic Society to see a film. The one on tigers invades my nightmares these many years later. Sitting there in the darkened theater, I watched a mother give birth to three tiny cubs. One was born with a mangled leg. I witnessed how all the other tiger cubs excluded him. And right there in front of the cameras, he was tortured to death by the others. I remember crying and thinking how the healthy cubs were like a few of the kids in my school. Sometimes they could be very cruel.

My best friend in grade school was named Stella. Stella was a beautiful girl inside and out. But she had a speech defect, a cleft palate. And many of our classmates laughed at her behind her back and excluded her from their games.

Kids haven't changed much. When I give talks for colleges and young people's groups, the discussion often turns to popularity. Everyone wants to be liked. Occasionally students tell me stories about how some girl has a minor physical defect, say a crossed eye or a nervous twitch. They say some kids laugh and make fun of her. Or a boy has a limp so no one chooses him for their baseball team. Even if he can run just as fast as the other kids, some of his classmates don't like image of "a cripple" being on their side.

The years go by and kids become adults. Not too much changes. Adults are not as cruel, happily, about physical disabilities. But they can be brutal about social disabilities. Social disabilities are insidious because often we don't recognize them in ourselves. We can be blind to our social handicaps and deaf to our verbal deficiencies. But we're quick to recognize them in others.

How many times has one of your associates made a dumb, insensitive gaffe? How often have you written somebody off because of some stupid move? Do you think he knew what he was doing? Of course not. He had no idea he was crossing a line or stepping on your toes. Probably no one ever told him about the subtleties we're going to discuss in this final section of *Talking the Winner's Way*.

We've all heard about the glass ceiling some companies construct over women and minorities. People seldom discuss another kind of glass ceiling. This one is even more treacherous because you can't legislate against it and only Top Communicators recognize it. Yet it's a rock-hard shield. Many bright individuals hit their heads on the thick glass as they try to climb up the next rung of the ladder to join the Big Boys and Girls on top. The folks able to crash through are the ones who abide by the unspoken rules that follow.

Consider each of the following techniques. If you find any of them obvious, give yourself a pat on the back. It means you're already a tiger on that one. Be on the lookout for those communications sensitivities where you find yourself saying, "You gotta be kidding! What's wrong with that?"

Watch out! It means someday, somewhere, you might commit that particular insensitivity. Then, when a Big Winner responds coolly to your suggestion, doesn't return your phone call, doesn't give you the promotion, doesn't invite you to the party, doesn't accept your date, you'll never know what happened. Read each of the following techniques to assure you're not making any of these subtle mistakes, that let the Big Players lacerate you and keep you from getting what you want in life.

78 See No Bloopers, Hear No Bloopers

"Gesundheit!" "Whoops!" "Butterfingers!"

One remarkable reaction opened my eyes to yet another difference between Big Winners and little losers. Several years ago I was doing a project for a client. I had the pleasure of being taken to lunch by the four biggest fish in the firm. They wanted to familiarize me with communications problems their company was experiencing.

We went to a busy midtown restaurant at peak lunchtime. Every table was filled with a variety of corporate creatures. Upper- and middle-management types were lunching in their suits and ties or high-collar blouses. Workers and secretaries were munching in their blue shirts or short skirts. The restaurant was buzzing with conversation and conviviality.

Over the entrée, we were in deep discussion about the company's challenges. The CFO, Mr. Wilson, was talking about the financial outlook when suddenly, BLAM! Not six feet away, a waiter dropped a tray full of dishes. Glasses broke, silverware clattered against the marble floor, and a hot baked potato rolled under our table in a direct path for Wilson's feet.

Practically everyone in the restaurant turned toward the humiliated waiter. We heard a cacophony of "Uh-oh," "Butterfingers!" "Whoops, watch it!" "Boy, that's his last lunch here," and a variety of tittering and derisive laughter.

Wilson, however, didn't miss a word of his monologue. Not one Big Player at my table turned or blinked an eye. It was as though nothing had happened. The restaurant gradually quieted down around us as we continued our deliberations. (A few minutes later the baked potato shot back out from under our table. At that moment, I found myself wondering whether Wilson had been a soccer player in his youth.)

Over coffee, the director of marketing, Ms. Dawson, was discussing the company's planned expansion. Suddenly she made an expansive gesture with her arms that knocked over her coffee cup. Just as I was about to say, "Oh dear," I bit my tongue. Before I could grab my napkin to help, Dawson was dabbing the muddy puddle with hers, and not missing a syllable of her soliloquy. None of her cool colleagues at the table even seemed to notice the overturned cup.

At that instant, I realized Big Boys and Girls see no bloopers, hear no bloopers. They never say "Butterfingers." Or "Whoops." Or even "Uh-oh." They ignore their colleagues' boners. They simply don't notice their comrades' minor spills, slips, fumbles, and blunders. Thus, the technique *See No Bloopers, Hear No Bloopers* was born.

Let Me Suffer in *Your* Silence

I have one friend who every time I sneeze says, "Oh, are you coming down with a cold?" Every time I miss a step on a curb, it's "Be careful!" Every time he sees me after a long day's work he asks, "Are you tired?" Granted, this is small fry in the great bouillabaisse of bloopers. And the poor guy probably genuinely thinks he's being sensitive to my needs. But, darnit, coming down with a cold, missing the curb, and looking tired are less than cool. Let me suffer—in YOUR silence.

If you're having dinner with a friend and she makes a boner, be blind to her overturned glass. Be deaf to her sneeze, cough, or hiccups. No matter how well-meaning your "gesundheit," "whoops," or knowing smile, nobody likes to be reminded of their own human frailty.

"Fine," you say, "for small slips, but what should one do in extreme circumstances?" Say a rippling tide of Coca-Cola is flooding across the table in your direction and it will be impossible to ignore by the time it reaches your lap?

If possible, deftly flip your napkin to obstruct the current and keep talking. Try not to miss a syllable of the sentence you started before the oncoming tide. At this point, your companion might mutter incoherent apologies. Adroitly weave a parenthetical "It's nothing" into your current phrase and continue talking. On such small sands the castles of Big Cat camaraderie are built.

Technique #78:
See No Bloopers, Hear No Bloopers

Cool Communicators allow their friends, associates, acquaintances, and loved ones the pleasurable myth of being above commonplace bloopers and embarrassing biological functions. They simply don't notice their comrades' minor spills, slips, fumbles, and faux pas. They obviously ignore raspberries and all other signs of human frailty in their fellow mortals. Big Winners never gape at another's gaffes.

If people hate to be reminded of the moments when they're not shining, there is another event almost as disillusioning. It is when a talker *is* shining, and the spotlight abruptly pivots to a more urgent matter. The speaker is forgotten in the flurry.

Top Communicators put the glow back in the gloomy gabber's eyes with the technique that follows.

79 ⭐ Lend a Helping Tongue

"Now, Please Get Back to Your Story"

In ancient Japan, if you saved someone's life, it was their self-imposed task to spend the rest of their life serving you. Nowadays, if you rescue someone's story, a molecule of that ancient instinct still gushes through his or her veins.

It happens all the time. Someone in a group is telling a story and, just before their big point, BOOM! There's an interruption. Someone new joins the group, a catering person with a tray of crackers and cheese comes over, or a baby starts crying. Suddenly everyone's attention turns to the new arrival, the nibbles on the tray, or the "adorable" little tyke. Nobody is aware of the interruption—*except* the speaker. They forget all about the fact that the speaker hasn't made his or her point.

Or you're all sitting around the living room and someone is telling a joke. Suddenly, just before their big punch line, little Johnny drops a dish or the phone rings. After the crash, everyone talks about little Johnny's clumsiness. After the call, the subject turns to the impending marriage or medical operation of the caller. Nobody remembers the great punch line got aborted—*except* the joke teller. (When it's *you* regaling everyone at a restaurant, have you ever noticed how you can almost set your clock by the waiter coming to take everyone's order just before your hilarious punch line?)

Most joke and story tellers are too timid to say, after the invasion, "Now, as I was saying . . ." Instead, they'll spend the rest of the evening feeling miserable they didn't get to finish. Here's where you come in. Rescue them with the technique I call *Lend a Helping Tongue.*

Watch the gratitude in the storyteller's eyes as he stabilizes where his story sunk and he sails off again toward the center of attention. His expression and the recognition of your sensitivity by the rest of the group are often reward enough. You are even more fortunate if you can rescue the story of someone who can hire you, promote you, buy from you, or otherwise lift your life. Big Winners have elephantine memories. When you do them subtle favors like *Lend a Helping Tongue*, they find a way to pay you back.

Technique #79:
Lend a Helping Tongue

Whenever someone's story is aborted, let the interruption play itself out. Give everyone time to dote on the little darling, give their dinner order, or pick up the jagged pieces of china.

Then, when the group reassembles, simply say to the person who suffered story-interruptus, "Now please get back to your story." Or better yet, remember where they were and then ask, "So what happened after the . . .(and fill in the last few words.)"

Harvey Mackay, the world's most notable networker who rose from envelope salesman to corporate CEO and one of America's most sought-after business and motivational speakers, teaches us that the world goes 'round on favors. How right he is! The next three techniques reveal unspoken subtleties of this critical balance of power.

80 Bare the Buried WIIFM

"Look, Here's What's in It for Me—Here's What's in It for You"

Savvy businesspeople know everyone is constantly tuned to the same radio station—WIIFM. Whenever anyone says anything, the listener's instinctive reaction is *What's in It for Me?* Sales pros have elevated this constant query to the exalted status of acronym, WIIFM. They pay such strict attention to the WIIFM principle that they don't open their pitch with the features of their product or service. Top pros start by highlighting the benefits to the buyer.

Except for tactical reasons during sensitive negotiating, Big Winners lay both *What's in It for Me?* and *What's in It for You?* (WIIFY) right out on the table. This is so critical that, if one camouflages WIIFM or WIIFY, the concealer is relegated to the status of little loser.

I once invited a casual acquaintance to lunch. I had hoped to consult with Sam, the head of a marketing association, on my speaking business. I told him my desire and jokingly asked if an hour of his valuable time was available in return for lunch at a great restaurant. That was my way of saying, "Look Sam, I know there's no real benefit to you except a tasty lunch and the dubious pleasure of my company." (In other words, I was revealing

WIIFY.) To make the meeting even more convenient for him, I said, "Sam, choose the date and the best restaurant in your neighborhood."

The day of our lunch consultation lunch rolled around and I traveled forty-five minutes across town to his chosen restaurant. As I entered, I was surprised to see an assortment of people arranged around the largest table in the room with Sam as the smiling centerpiece. Obviously, this was not the setting in which I could consult with him. Unfortunately, Sam had already spotted me by the coat check. I was trapped.

It wasn't until after-lunch coffee arrived that I realized why Sam had assembled the group. He wanted each to donate presentations on their particular expertise to his organization. The sly fox hadn't revealed his own *What's in It for Me?*

Had Sam been a straight shooter and Big Player, he would have told me on the phone, "Leil, I'm getting a group of speakers who might be helpful to my organization together for a Dutch-treat lunch. I will, of course, try to answer your questions about your speaking business, but we will be a group of ten. Would you like to join us, or shall we choose another date when we can have more privacy?"

I would gladly have spoken pro bono for Sam's group had he been up-front about it. Instead, by not revealing WIIFM, we both lost. I lost a half day and, because of his trickiness, he lost my free speech for his group.

Don't Deny Them the Pleasure of Helping You

Big Winners also lay their cards on the table when asking someone for a favor. Many well-meaning folks are embarrassed to say how important the favor is to them. So they ask as though it's a casual inquiry when it's not.

A friend of mine named Stefan once asked me if I knew any bands his organization could hire for their annual event. I told him "No, I'm sorry. I really don't." But Stefan didn't let it go at that. He pressed, "Leil, didn't you once work with bands on ships?"

I told him "Yes, but I no longer have contact with them." I thought that was the end of it. But Stefan didn't. He grilled me further and I found myself getting confused and irritated. Finally I said, "Stefan, who's in charge of getting the band?"

He sheepishly said, "I am."

"Criminy jicketts, Stefan, why didn't you tell me it was your responsibility? In that case, let me do some research and see if I can find a good one for you." I was happy to do my friend a favor. But Stefan, by not telling me how important it was to him, risked not getting help. He also went down a notch or two in his friend's esteem by not revealing WIIFM.

When asking someone for a favor, let them know how much it means to you. You come across as a straight shooter, and the joy of helping you out is often reward enough. Don't deny them that pleasure!

⭐ TECHNIQUE #80:
BARE THE BURIED WIIFM (AND WIIFY)

Whenever you suggest a meeting or ask a favor, divulge the respective benefits. Reveal what's in it for you and what's in it for the other person—even if it's zip. If any hidden agenda comes up later, you get labeled a sly fox.

Asking or granting favors is a fabric that holds together only when woven with utmost sensitivity. Let us explore more ways to stitch this delicate cloth so your relationship doesn't rip.

81 Let 'Em Savor the Favor

Let the Sun Set—and Rise Again—Before You Make Your Move

Susan Evans, one of my clients, heads up a large real estate firm. Once, sitting in her office discussing an upcoming project, her secretary buzzed. "Excuse me, Ms. Evans, it's your brother-in-law Harry on the phone."

"Oh, of course," she smiled, "put him on." My client, making apologies for the interruption, picked up the phone. I left the room for a few moments to give her privacy.

When I returned, Susan was just hanging up, saying, "Sure, have him phone me." She told me the call was from her brother-in-law whose young cousin worked in a gas station but was interested in a career in real estate. "The young man is going to call me and I'll see if I can help him out." It was obvious she was happy to do her brother-in-law a favor. We picked up our discussion where we left off.

Not four minutes later, the secretary buzzed again. "Ms. Evans, a Sonny Laker is on the line. He says he's your brother-in-law Harry's cousin and he's supposed to call you." My client was taken aback. I could tell from her expression she was saying to herself, "Boy, my overanxious brother-in-law didn't waste any time, did he?" It seemed obvious to both of us what had happened. Like greased lightning, Harry must have hot-breathedly called Cousin Sonny to give him the big headline: Evans Would See Him! Then, by dialing Ms. Evans immediately, Sonny made it seem the big-deal interview was the most important event in his otherwise dull and dismal life.

True or not, one verity remained—Little Cousin was insensitive to an unspoken rule Big Winners always obey: *don't jump immediately when someone is doing you a favor.* Allow the person granting the favor time to savor the pleasure of agreeing to it, before having to pay up.

Both brother-in-law and potential employee slipped in Evans's estimate, and all because of timing. To ensure the kid wouldn't call his real-estate-mogul sister-in-law too quickly, Harry should have waited a day before telling his cousin the good news. Also, young Sonny should have asked Cousin Harry about Evans's schedule. Sometimes an immediate call is advantageous, but *not* when someone is granting you a favor.

TECHNIQUE #81:
LET 'EM SAVOR THE FAVOR

Whenever a friend agrees to a favor, allow your generous buddy time to relish the joy of his or her beneficence before you make them pay the piper.
How long? At least twenty-four hours.

One might think Evans was unfair judging Sonny harshly just because he didn't let her *Savor the Favor.* It runs deeper than that. Evans's subconscious thought process goes something like this: "If this kid is insensitive to the subtleties of timing when getting a job, how sensitive is he going to be when negotiating the sale of a house?" One agent's overanxious call to an owner can mean thousands lost in commissions for the firm.

Big Winners have supernatural vision into your future. They see every communications blunder you make as a visible blotch on your x-ray. It dims your prognosis for being successful in life.

Let's look at yet another tenuous thread between favor asker and favor grantor that must not be severed lest the relationship unravel.

82 Tit for (Wait . . . Wait) Tat

"I Did It Just Because I Like You"

I once asked a well-connected friend who works in a top Los Angeles talent agency if she knew any celebrities I could contact for a project I was working on. Tania flipped though her Rolodex and came up with just the names I needed. It was obvious to both of us, I owed her big time.

When I thanked her profusely on the phone, Tania said, "Oh I'm sure you'll find a way to pay me back."

"Well, of course I will," I said. "That goes without saying." And well it *should* have gone without saying. She was reminding me the favor wasn't out of friendship, but because she expected something in return.

Two days later, Tania called and said she was coming to New York in a few months. She was just checking now if I could put her up then. Naturally I could, but blatantly cashing in on the return favor so quickly was not a smooth move. When someone does something nice for you, you find yourself with an elephant's memory. In fact, you consciously look for ways to return the favor. Had Tania called, even years later, of course I would have remembered "I owed her one." Frankly, I was glad it came up so quickly so I could even the score. Nevertheless, I do wish the whole barter aspect had been left unspoken. It tarnished what should have been a generous sharing on both sides. Tarnish always wears off on the tarnisher.

When you do someone a favor and they obviously "owe you one," wait a few weeks. Don't make it look like tit for tat. Allow the favor asker the pleasurable myth that you joyfully did the favor with *no* thought of what you're going to get in return. *They* know that's not true. *You* know that's not true. But only little losers make it obvious.

Technique #82:

Tit for (Wait . . . Wait) Tat

When people do you favors and it's obvious "they owe you one," wait a suitable amount of time before asking them to "pay." Let them enjoy the fact (or fiction) that you did it out of friendship. Don't call in your tit for their tat too swiftly.

The next three techniques also involve timing, not of favors, but of important discussions.

83 Parties Are for Pratter

The First of Three Safe Havens

When police were hot on the tail of a thief in ancient times, he'd frantically seek a church to duck into. The crook knew if he could get to an altar, the frustrated posse could not arrest him until he came out.

When a pack of wolves in the jungle is in hot pursuit of a jackrabbit, the frightened bunny's eyes seek a hollow log. He knows the wolves can't devour him until he emerges.

Likewise in the human jungle, Big Cats have certain safe havens. Although unspoken, they are as secure as the tenth-century altar or a hole in the log. There are clearly understood times and places where even the toughest tiger knows he must not attack.

I have a friend, Kirstin, the president of an advertising agency who each year invites me to her company's Christmas party. One year, the holiday spirit was in extra-high swing. Conviviality was high and champagne flowed freely. It was a terrific bash.

The evening wore on, more bubbly flowed, and the decibel level of the holiday revelers went up and up. So high, in fact, that Kirstin told me she was going to tiptoe out the back door and offered to drop me off at my place.

As we were making our way toward the exit, we heard a woozy voice in the crowd, "Oh Kirrr-stin, Kirrr-stin!" A mail-room worker, warped with too much seasonal spirit, wobbled up to her boss and said, "You know, thish ish a great party, a grr-reat party. But I been doin' some figuring. If half what it cost went into a child-care facility for the seven, count 'em, seven mothers with preschool children who work here . . ."

Kirstin, a Top Communicator, took Jane's hands in hers and gave her a big smile. She said, "Jane, you're obviously excellent at math. You're right, just about half of what this party cost would indeed pay for the opening of such a facility. Let's talk about it during business hours." We then made a swift departure.

On the way back to my place, she let out a big breath and said, "Whew, I'm glad that's over."

"Didn't you enjoy the party, Kirstin?" I asked.

"Well, sure," she said, "But you never know what's going to happen. For instance," she said, "that remark Jane made." She went on to explain management had already had several meet-ings about opening a child-care facility for employees. In fact, plans for turning an unused storage area into a beautiful nursery were already in the works. Naively, I asked Kirstin why she hadn't mentioned that to Jane.

"It wasn't the right time or place." Kirstin had handled the situation at the party the way any Big Winner would—no spoken confrontation now (but probable silent condemnation later).

Jane, unfortunately, had broken the first unspoken safe-haven rule, *Parties Are for Pratter*. Did Kirstin chastise Jane? Did she punish her inappropriate behavior? Not then, of course. Never-theless, Jane would probably feel the repercussions a few months down the pike when it came to promotion time. But by then poor Jane wouldn't even know why she was passed over.

Will it be because of a one-time overimbibing? Jane might grumble, "Yes." Jane is wrong. It's simply that Big Players can't take the chance that one of their key people will feel too much holiday spirit at another party, and next time confront an impor-tant client.

TECHNIQUE #83:
PARTIES ARE FOR PRATTER

There are three sacred safe havens in the human jungle where even the toughest tiger knows he must not attack. The first of these is parties.

Parties are for pleasantries and good fellowship, not for confrontations. Big Players, even when standing next to their enemies at the buffet table, smile and nod. They leave tough talk for tougher settings.

Let's move to the second safe haven where Big Cats can escape the claws of Bigger Cats and, they hope, the growls of lesser ones.

84 Dinner's for Dining

Tough Negotiating Can Kill Your Appetite

Did you ever wonder why business lunches between Big Bosses go on interminably long, sometimes well into the afternoon? Did you ever suspect it's just because they like to sit, drink, and massage each other on the company expense account? Perhaps there's an element of that. But the main reason is because the dining table is an even more sacred safe haven than a party. Big Boys and Girls realize, whether it's a business dinner, lunch, or breakfast, breaking bread together is a time when they must discuss no unpleasant aspects of the business.

Let's listen in on an average business lunch between Big Players. We hear the clanking of glasses as they consume drinks over convivial conversation. They are discussing golf, the weather, and making general observations about the state of the business. During the main course, the discourse turns to food, the arts, current affairs, and other nonthreatening subjects.

"Wasted time?" one might ask. Not at all! The Big Players are watching each other's moves very carefully, calculating each other's skills, knowledge, prowess. Like NFL scouts observing college football practice, they're determining who's got the right stuff. Big Players know how people handle themselves at a social occasion is an accurate barometer of their big-business muscle. As they are smiling and laughing at each other's jokes, they are all making silent critical judgments.

Finally, coffee arrives. At this point one or more of the biggies gently broaches the business at hand. Naturally, he or she does it with supposed reluctance, trying to repress the obvious relief that at last they can get down to significant stuff. He exudes, "What a shame such genial company should have to concern itself with mundane matters like making money."

Only after they have played out this crucial charade can they discuss business. But no dirty business. The Biggies can brainstorm over coffee. They can discuss proposals over dessert. They can toss around new ideas over cordials. They can explore the positive side of the merger, the acquisition, or the partnership while waiting for the check.

However, should any disagreement, misunderstanding, or controversial aspect arise, they must immediately relegate it to another table, the conference table.

TECHNIQUE #84:
DINNER'S FOR DINING

The most guarded safe haven respected by Big Winners is the dining table. Breaking bread together is a time when they bring up no unpleasant matters. While eating, they know it's OK to brainstorm and discuss the positive side of the business: their dreams, their desires, their designs. They can free associate and come up with new ideas. *But no tough business.*

This convention probably arose out of a prudent agreement not to inflict indigestion on each other. Tough negotiating is unpalatable and can ruin an otherwise perfectly mouthwatering veal chop.

Incidentally, the same rule applies in the social jungle. If one partner in a friendship or a love relationship has some heavy relationship issues to discuss, save them for after dessert. Even if you don't solve the problem, you want to enjoy the delicious chocolate soufflé.

Let's crawl into our third and final safe haven to explore it.

85 Chance Encounters Are for Chitchat

"Ahha, I've Got You Now!"

William, who sells widgets, has been trying to get Big Winner on the phone for weeks to see if B.W.'s company will buy his line of widgets. Big Winner is still considering Willie's widgets and plans eventually to return his call. However, at this point in our story, our little hero's phone has not rung.

It just so happens, one evening Willie finds himself standing behind Big Winner in the supermarket line.

"What good fortune!" thinks Willie.

"*Oh hell!*" thinks Big Winner. "I hope he's not going to hit me with talk of his widgets at this hour."

Those who appreciate safe havens know there are two very different endings to this story. The Willie who brings up widgets with an "Aha, I've got you now" gleam in his eye, *never* gets his call returned. Even if Big Winner preferred Willie's widgets above all others, he would find the supermarket entrapment sufficiently painful to punish the little loser.

However, the Willie who just says "Hello there, B.W. How good to see you," with nary a word of widgets, shows he's a Big Player, too. This Willie will most certainly get his call returned—

probably the next day—out of Big Winner's relief and gratitude for Willie's graciousness.

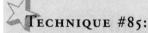

TECHNIQUE #85:
CHANCE ENCOUNTERS ARE FOR CHITCHAT

If you're selling, negotiating, or in any sensitive communication with someone, do NOT capitalize on a chance meeting. Keep the melody of your mistaken meeting sweet and light. Otherwise, it could turn into your swan song with Big Player.

Consistently create safe havens for people if you want them to elevate you to the status of Big Winner. You may find yourself dining with them, going to parties with them, getting big hellos in the hall, and closing deals much faster than during business hours. Who knows? If it's your desire, you even make yourself eligible for some heavy socializing at the top. Big Winners make it safe for each other to accept invitations to play golf, spend the weekend in their country homes, or relax by each other's pools. They know there will be no sharks swimming in the water, no razor blades buried in the shrimp cocktail.

86 Empty Their Tanks

"Tell Me About Your Cracked Skull Later. What's Your Insurance Number?"

Once night, several years ago on a New York City street, I caught a man trying to break into a car. I shouted for him to stop. Instead of being content escaping, the burly would-be burglar decided to retaliate. As he raced past me, he shoved me down onto the cement and I cracked my skull against the curb.

Dizzily, I wobbled into the emergency room of a nearby hospital. Holding an ice pack against my throbbing head, I was grilled by the emergency room triage nurse on my address, telephone, and social security numbers, insurance carrier, policy number, ad nauseam.

Don't bother me with that minutia! All I wanted to do was tell somebody, *anybody*, what happened to me. It wasn't until the very end of her ruthless and sadistic interrogation that she asked, "So what happened?"

I later told my sad story to a friend, Sue, a nurse who works in admitting in another emergency room. She said, "I know. I can't believe they print the forms that way. Injured people don't get to tell what happened to them until the *last* line of the form. Sue said getting crucial numerical details from people suffering in the

ER with broken bones and burns was a real challenge. *Until*, she said, she switched her questioning around. She'd *first* ask them what happened. They'd tell her all about it. She'd listen sympathetically. "Then," she said, "they were only too happy to give me the information I needed."

Good bosses understand this human need to talk. Robert, a colleague of mine who owns a small manufacturing firm, says whenever one of his employees complains about a problem, he never holds the griper's feet to the fire for facts first. He hears the employee out completely. He lets him carry on about the cantankerous customer, the uncooperative coworker. "Then, after he's gotten it off his chest," Robert says, "I get the facts a lot more clearly."

When *You* Have Important Information to Impart

Any kid working in a garage knows you can't pump more gas into a full tank. Too much topping it off, and it splashes onto the cement. Likewise, your listener's brain is always full of his or her own thoughts, worries, and enthusiasms. If you pump your ideas into your listener's brain, which is full of her own notions, you'll get a polluted mixture, then a spill. If you want your super-supreme ideas to flow into her tank unpolluted, drain her tank completely first.

TECHNIQUE #86:
EMPTY THEIR TANKS

If you need information, let people have their *entire* say first. Wait patiently until their needle is on empty and the last drop drips out and splashes on the cement. It's the only way to be sure their tank is empty enough of their own inner noise to start receiving your ideas.

Whenever you are discussing emotionally charged matters, let the speaker finish *completely* before you jump in. Count to ten if you must. It will seem like an eternity, but letting the flustered fellow finish is the only way he'll hear *you* when it's your turn.

"I'm Going to Make You Miserable Before You Can Enjoy Being My Customer"

Companies that run mail-order operations could take a hint from this technique. One reason I enjoy ordering from L.L. Bean, a mail-order clothing and sports-equipment outfit, is they let me ask questions about the wearable or widget I want first. They let me ramble on with my questions about the quality, the available colors, how it looks, how it feels, how it smells, and how it works. Then, when I'm all whacked up about receiving my four size-ten, red-and-chartreuse, soft, odorless widgets, they tastefully ask my credit card number.

Other companies have first grilled me on the number, the expiration date, my customer number (which I can never find on the back of the catalogue), and how often I've ordered from them in the past *before* I even get to fantasize about the wonderful widget I might want to buy from them. Takes all the joy out of the purchase and sometimes kills the sale.

Top Communicators do more than just let you babble on. They use the next technique while you're in the process of dribbling down.

87 Echo the EMO

Hear the Facts, but Smear the EMO

EMO is a word invented by Helen Gurley Brown, the grand dame of *Cosmopolitan* magazine. EMO translated is "Give more emotion!" Once *Cosmopolitan* asked me to write an article on communicating sensitive matters (most specifically advising young women on how to make their boyfriends more passionate). I interviewed a passel of psychologists, communications experts, and sexologists. My draft came back from *Cosmo* all marked up with "MORE EMO" scribbled on every page.

I called my editor and asked what it meant. She said that was Helen's way of saying downplay all that factual stuff with the sex therapists and so-called experts. Write about the *emotion* the young woman feels when her boyfriend isn't passionate enough, the *emotion* the accused male feels when confronted, and the *emotion* the couple feels about discussing their quandary. Helen Gurley Brown, a certified Big Winner, liked to have it all and knew just how to get it. Helen recognized, when the time is right, reject the rational and empathize with the emotions. In other words, smear on the EMO.

"Oh, No! He Must Have Been Mortified!"

L. L. Bean recently smeared EMO all over me. Several months ago, my friend Phil wanted to buy some trousers and asked for a recommendation. I dragged him to my closet to show him the quality and construction of the L. L. Bean clothes. That convinced him, and Phil ordered a pair of navy-blue dress trousers.

Phil wore his brand new L. L. Bean pants for the first time on a big date with a new girlfriend at an elegant restaurant. While following the maitre d' to the cozy corner booth which he'd requested, his date happened to drop her evening bag. Phil promptly bent over to pick it up. Riiiiiip! Right down the middle seam.

Most of the diners facing Phil's derriere mercifully looked away. A few tittered. Phil, tugging the torn seams together to blanket his buns, backed his way into the booth. The cool upholstery on his bottom the rest of the evening reminded him of his humiliation.

When I heard of Phil's tribulations, I was furious at L. L. Bean. I immediately called one of their customer service agents. She sympathized as I told her of Phil's ordeal, but I was still simmering. She patiently listened and even asked me details of the disaster. When I finished the long sad story, the agent said, "Oh that's terrible. I understand, your friend must have felt *awful*."

"Yes, he did," I agreed.

"He must have been mortified!" she said.

"He definitely was," I said, surprised at her excellent grasp of the situation.

"And you, when you heard about it. You must have felt terrible, too, especially after you'd recommended our products so highly."

"Well, your products usually are excellent," I said, calming down a bit.

"I'm so sorry we caused you this pain and aggravation," she said.

"Oh," I interrupted. "It's not your fault." Now I was completely appeased. "It must have just been a fluke that this one pair of pants was . . . "

> ## TECHNIQUE #87:
> ### ECHO THE EMO
>
> Facts speak. Emotions shout. Whenever you need facts from people about an emotional situation, let them emote. Hear their facts but empathize like mad with their *emotions*. Smearing on the EMO is often the only way to calm their emotional storm.

There's more to this story, but let me pause here to interject the *Echo the EMO* technique.

The clever customer service rep not only *Emptied My Tanks* and softened me up with *Echo the EMO*. She completely dissolved me with the next technique.

88 My Goof, Your Gain

Make 'Em *Happy* You Messed Up

The next day, UPS delivered not only the replacement slacks, but tucked into the package was a handwritten apology and a hefty gift certificate. Would I order from that company again? You bet I would. Would I recommend their clothes to someone else? You bet I would. Top customer service folks welcome mistakes because they know it gives their firm a chance to shine. Whenever you mess up and someone suffers because of it, make sure they come out ahead, way ahead. I call the technique *My Goof, Your Gain.*

Visiting an important client's office, I once tripped on a rug and took a nose dive, making a three-point landing in a vase on her desk. My nose was spared but her vase shattered into smithereens. Two tubes of crazy glue and lots of "Where the heck does this piece go" later, the vase was back on her desk, and we agreed it looked pretty good. Nevertheless, the next day I had a messenger deliver a beautiful vase, ten times the value of the almost-totaled one, with a dozen roses in it.

Whenever we speak, my client tells me every time she looks at the new vase, she smiles. (A better "incentive gift" than a pen with your name on it, no?) The next time I visit her office, my client may hide some of her more valuable breakables. But, thanks to *My Goof, Your Gain*, there will be a next time.

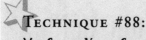

Technique #88:

My Goof, Your Gain

Whenever you make a boner, make sure your victim benefits. It's not enough to correct your mistake. Ask yourself, "What could I do for this suffering soul so he or she will be *delighted* I made the flub?" Then do it, fast! In that way, your goof will become your gain.

Now, suppose it's not your boo boo. It's theirs. How can you make *their* goof *your* gain? Read on.

89 Leave an Escape Hatch

A Genteel Way to Say, "Freeze, Punk, While I Frisk You"

In Japan, some citizens prefer to lose their lives than to lose face. In America, the same death wish exists, with one modification. The Yank dreams of the death of the mortal who *made* him lose face.

Why make enemies? Unless it is your obligation to catch cheaters or entrap liars, let them get away with it. Then immediately get them out of your life and the lives you're responsible for. Even when the case is open and shut against someone—when you've got the rat fink trapped—leave him an escape hatch.

The best example I heard of this high sensitivity was from one of my clients. She was invited to brunch at the home of a wealthy socialite known as "Lady Stephanie." Lady Stephanie's home was filled with beautiful objets d'art. Not the least among them was an exquisite collection of extremely valuable Fabergé eggs, which all the guests admired.

At the end of the elegant champagne brunch, my client told me she was walking out the door chatting with several other guests. Just then, Lady Stephanie sidled up to one woman leaving at the same time as my client. "Oh, I'm so happy you were admiring my Fabergé collection," Lady Stephanie said, sliding her hand into the pocket of the guest's mink coat and plucking out one of her priceless eggs. "You must have wanted to see this one in the sunlight. Come, let us look at it together. It does reflect the bright light beautifully."

The mink-clad thief gulped and furtively looked around to see who had witnessed her gentle entrapment. My client and everyone in the foyer saw what happened, but took Lady Stephanie's lead and pretended naïveté of the attempted heist.

Carrying the charade a step further, Lady Stephanie and the sticky-fingered guest "admired the egg in the sunlight." Then Lady Stephanie, with her Fabergé egg secured safely between her perfectly manicured fingers, marched home to put the treasure in its rightful place. The attempted egg snatcher crawled back to her car, from her *last* attendance at Lady Stephanie's coveted bashes. The hostess let the foiled filcher get away with a few slivered shreds of her ego left intact.

Why did Lady Stephanie come out ahead? Everyone who witnessed—and subsequently heard about—the thwarted burglary has renewed respect for Lady Stephanie. Snaring the thief, yet sparing her pride, helped Lady Stephanie keep her reputation of "hostess with the mostest."

Why do Big Winners let bad-news people get away with bummers? Because, like mothers confronting naughty children to correct them, confronting creeps is a way of saying "I care." By closing your mouth (and then the door forever), you are saying, "You are so beneath me I'm not going to even waste my words on you."

"Mea Culpa!"

Big Winners leave an escape hatch for the small foibles of friends they wish to keep by taking the blame themselves. If a friend gets lost and is an hour late arriving at your house, tell her "Those directions I gave you were terrible." He breaks your Limoges bowl? "Oh I shouldn't have left it in such a precarious position."

It's the old mea culpa routine that endears you to everyone, especially when they realize it wasn't your fault.

TECHNIQUE #89:
LEAVE AN ESCAPE HATCH

Whenever you catch someone lying, filching, exaggerating, distorting, or deceiving, don't confront the dirty duck directly. Unless it is your responsibility to catch or correct the culprit—or unless you are saving other innocent victims by doing so—let the transgressor out of your trap with his tricky puss in one piece. Then resolve *never* to gaze upon it again.

Residents of Toronto, Canada, have a well-earned reputation for grace. They demonstrated it last year in a downtown Toronto drugstore. A shopper attempted to stroll out through the security system with a purloined object in his pocket. Instead of a shrill alarm shattering all shoppers' eardrums, as in many American cities, a tasteful little chime sounded. A charming voice came across the public address. "Excuse us, *we* have failed to inactivate the inventory control system. Thank you for your patience while you wait for a customer care representative to come help you." Isn't that a nicer way of saying "Freeze, punk, while we come frisk you?"

Now let's move on to the next technique to keep people from messing up—and to help them give you their very best.

90 Buttercups for Their Boss

"You're Great! What's Your Boss's Name?"

A complimentary letter is called a *buttercup* because it butters up the recipient. Buttercups are nice. Even nicer are buttercups *about* someone to their boss.

I once needed a massive photocopying job. It was so immense that the assistant manager of Staples office-supply store didn't think it could be finished by the end of the week. Nevertheless, grudgingly, he grumbled, "I'll try." In my enthusiasm and hope he could, I gushed, "Wow, you're great! What's your boss's name? Your supervisor should get a letter of congratulations on hiring you. You really try harder for your customers." To my astonishment, not only was my printing job done two days early, but every time I walk into Staples, the assistant manager rolls out the red carpet.

"Hmm," I began to think. "I may be on to something." A premature letter of commendation for favors not yet received could be a clever tactic. I decided to check it out with a few Heavy Hitters on my consultation list.

One fellow I know, Tim, a top travel agent, is a real can-do guy. He gets anything his friends ask for in a finger snap. He's the fellow to call when you want hard-to-get theater tickets. He's the guy you call when your airline says the hotel is booked or the flight is oversold.

When I told him of my buttercup experience, Tim laughed and said, "Leil, of course. This is news to you? A complimentary letter to someone's boss—or the promise of one—is a great insurance policy. It's as good as a written rider that you will be well taken care of in the future."

Now I have a standard one in my computer. The buttercup reads as follows:

> Dear (name of supervisor),
>
> I know how important customer service is to an organization such as yours. This letter is to commend (name of employee). He/She is an example of an (employee title) who gives exceptional customer service. (Name of store or business) continues to have my business thanks in great part to the service given by (name of employee).
>
> Gratefully, (signature)

I've sent this letter to supervisors of parking lots, owners of insurance companies, and to managers of dozens of stores where I shop regularly. I'm sure that's why I never need to worry about getting a parking place when the lot is full, an immediate call-

Technique #90:
Buttercups for Their Boss

Do you have a store clerk, accountant, law firm junior partner, tailor, auto mechanic, maitre d', massage therapist, kid's teacher—or any other worker you want special attention from in the future? The surefire way to make them care enough to give you their very best is send a *Buttercup* to their boss.

back from my insurance agent, and attentive service at my regular shopping haunts.

But be careful! Don't just ask, "What's the name of your supervisor?" Hearing those words can make an employee as nervous as a turkey in November. Be sure to couch it in a compliment. Say something like, "Wow, you are terrific. What's your supervisor's name? I'd like to write him or her a letter." Then write it! You'll forever be a VIP in their book.

The next technique tells you how to stand out as a VIP when you're in a group.

91 Lead the Listeners

How to Tell a Leader from a Follower

During the McCarthy era, government spies infiltrated underground political rallies to determine who was "dangerous to national security." The agents were trained applause watchers. They photographed and investigated men who clapped first, shouted "Bravo" the loudest, and smiled the longest at the end of politically inflammatory speeches. The spies dubbed those the "dangerous ones." The infiltrators felt first responders were Confident Cats who had the power to persuade followers and the charisma to lead crowds.

In less politically sensitive gatherings, the same principle applies. People who respond *first* to a presentation or happening, without looking around to see how everyone else is reacting, are men and women of leadership caliber.

Cool Cats Clap First

You are sitting in an auditorium with hundreds of fellow employees listening to the president of your firm introduce a new concept. As you're slouching anonymously in the audience, you think your expression is invisible to the man or woman at the podium.

Not so! As a speaker, I guarantee you every one of my colleagues sees every smile, every frown, every light in every eye, and every emblem of extraordinary human intelligence flashing back at him or her.

Likewise, the company president making a presentation anxiously surveys his corporate jungle and, from the pusses peering back at him, senses which employees are sympathetic and which are not. He also knows which in the sea of faces floating in front of him has the potential to be a Heavy Hitter like himself. How?

Because Heavy Hitters, even when they do not agree with the speaker, support the podium pontificator. Why? *Because they know what it's like to be on.* They know, no matter how big or little the cat at the front of the room is, when giving a speech he's concerned about the crowd's acceptance.

When the company Big Shot delivers his last line, carefully contrived to bring the crowd to its feet or employees to acquiescence, do you think he's unaware of who starts the trickle, or the riptide, of acceptance? No way! Though his head is down while taking a bow, with the insight of a McCarthy-era spy, he perceives precisely *who* inaugurated the applause, precisely *how long* after the last words were uttered, and precisely *how enthusiastically!* Being the first to put your hands together, being the first to jump

TECHNIQUE #91:
Lead the Listeners

No matter how prominent the Big Cat behind the podium is, crouched inside is a little scaredy cat who is anxious about the crowd's acceptance.

Big Winners recognize you're a fellow Big Winner when they see you leading their listeners in a positive reaction. Be the *first* to applaud or publicly commend the man or woman you agree with (or want favors from).

to your feet, and, if appropriate, being the first to shout "Bravo," gets you Big Cat status with the tiger who was talking.

Be the first clapper no matter how small the crowd, no matter how informal the talk. Don't wait to see how everyone else is going to respond. Even if it's a small group of three or four people standing around, be the first to empathize with the speaker's ideas, the first to mutter "good idea." It's proof positive you're a person who trusts his or her own instincts.

92 ⭑ The Great Scorecard in the Sky

Bottom Dog Bows Lower, Barks Softer

Any minute, any second, football fans know the score. Even beer-guzzling Big George, dozing in front of the TV set on football Sunday knows. Poke his pudgy pot, and in a wink, he'll tell you who's winning, who's losing, and by precisely how many points.

Key Players in the game of life are like George. Even when you think they're dozing, they are constantly aware of the score between themselves and everyone in their life—friends and family included! They know who is winning, who is losing, and by how many points.

When two Japanese businessmen meet, it's obvious who is on top. You measure it in millimeters from how close to the floor their noses come when bowing. (Bottom man's nose dives lower.)

In America, we don't have carefully choreographed bows showing the score in a relationship. But Boys 'n' Girls in the business Big League know who is Top Dog and who is bottom dog *today*. (It can change tomorrow.)

Bottom dog must curtsy deeper. He or she must show deference. Bottom dog must offer to meet at Top Dog's office, pick up the restaurant tab when appropriate, and be respectful of Top Dog's time. If bottom dog fails to show the proper deference, he doesn't get his nose rubbed into the ground. He simply disqualifies himself to bark in the Big League.

That's what happened to my girlfriend Laura, who had developed the healthy milkshake. (Remember her from *Instant Replay?*) When we last left Laura, she was blowing her chances with Fred, the Top Banana of a supermarket chain, by grilling him for details of his mailing address, complaining her pen was out of ink, making him wait while she got another, writing numbers down wrong, ad nauseam.

I didn't tell you the worst part. After Fred was generous enough to invite Laura to send him samples of her health shake, she dropped another bomb by asking him which shipping service she should use. He must have said FedEx because I heard Laura say, "Well, my milkshake needs to stay refrigerated. Does FedEx have refrigerated trucks?"

At this point I knew she had strangled the deal by her own phone chord. She shouldn't nudge Supermarket Czar with dinky shipping details. In fact, Laura should be so grateful, she should personally deliver the drink the next day—rolling it all the way to his supermarket with her nose if need be. Laura was obviously not aware of the *Great Scorecard in the Sky*. That day the tally was "Fred everything, Laura nothing."

Big Winners—before putting pen to paper, fingers to keyboard, mouth to phone, or hand to someone else's to shake it—do a quick calculation. They ask themselves "Who has the most to benefit from this relationship? What has each of us done recently that demands deference from the other?" And what can I do to even the score?

Friends Keep Tabs Too

The *Great Scorecard in the Sky* is not just bobbing over businesspeople. If family members and friends look carefully over their loved ones' heads, they'll spot it. And, like an over-the-counter stock, it goes up or down every day. When you mess up, you have to even your score by doing more for the one who didn't. To keep love alive, keep your eye on the *Great Scorecard in the Sky*.

Several months ago, I met a nice chap named Charles at a convention. We started discussing our favorite foods. His was homemade linguine with pesto sauce. I liked Charles and I make a mean pesto sauce. The remarkable coincidence of these two elements emboldened me to invite him to dinner at my place. "Great," he said. We set it for seven-thirty the following Tuesday.

Tuesday afternoon, I begin preparations for the big date. The cuckoo clock on the wall monitored my progress. At five cuckoos, I run to the store to find pine nuts. By six cuckoos, I'm back home grinding basil and garlic. At seven cuckoos, I'm folding napkins, setting the table, pulling out fresh candles. Whoops, running late. I change clothes and spruce myself up. When seven-thirty strikes, I am all ready. The pesto and I await his arrival.

Eight o'clock rolls around and no friend. Well, I figure, I'll open the wine and let it breathe. Another hour passes and no Charles. The cuckoo calls me "cuckoo" nine times now. I begin to believe the bird. It is evident Charles isn't coming. I have been stood up.

The next day Charles called with halfhearted apologies and a semiplausible excuse. His car broke down. "Gee, I'm sorry," I said. (I *wanted* to say, "Did Martians capture you? Were you transported to another planet where there were no phones to call me?" I resisted the sarcasm.) However, he did sound contrite so I was almost willing to forget it. *Until his next question.*

He obviously wasn't aware of how he'd slipped in the *Great Scorecard in the Sky* because, instead of inviting me for linguine with pesto at a fine Italian restaurant to make up for his blooper, he asked, "When can we reschedule at your house?"

Never, Charlie.

TECHNIQUE #92:

THE GREAT SCORECARD IN THE SKY

Any two people have an invisible scorecard hovering above their heads. The numbers continually fluctuate, but one rule remains: player with lower score pays deference to player with higher score. The penalty for not keeping your eye on the *Great Scorecard in the Sky* is to be thrown out of the game. Permanently.

⭐ Your Destiny

WE'VE MET MANY PEOPLE in *Talking the Winner's Way*. A few of their names are changed, but each is very real. Recently, I decided to track down some of the folks with whom I'd crossed paths over the years. I wanted to see what they're up to now.

Laura, my old friend who dreamed of milkshake millions but ignored the Supermarket Czar's scorecard, is now back at her day job. Sam, who ruffled me by not revealing he wanted me to speak for his organization, no longer has one. Sonny, who hounded his brother-in-law's cousin by a too-quick call, is still pumping gas. Tania, who insisted on immediate tit for tat, no longer has that terrific job at the talent agency. Poor Jane, the mail-room clerk who confronted her boss at the Christmas party five years ago, is still wrapping packages. And Dan, who left the prolonged inspirational message on his phone, now has an unlisted number—not a good sign for an aspiring speaker.

Whereas Barry who asks everyone he calls, "*What Color Is Your Time?*" was recently chosen Broadcaster of the Year by the National Association of Talk Show Hosts. Joe, who keeps note of everyone on his *Business Card Dossier*, is now a state senator. Jimmi, the expert at *Eyeball Selling*, was recently written up in

Success magazine. Steve, whose staff insinuates *Oh Wow, It's You!* to every caller, is one of the most requested speakers on the cable circuit. Tim, the can-do guy who gets what he wants from workers in every industry by writing *Buttercups for Their Boss*, now owns the travel agency. And Gloria, my hairdresser who gives the great *Nutshell Resume*, recently opened a salon on New York's fashionable Fifth Avenue.

Does this mean to say that just because the first folks irked me and a few others they were exiled to a humdrum existence? And the latter group who made people smile would attain great heights? Of course not. Those isolated moments of their lives we examined were but one move of many they made each day.

But consider: if *you* had been who was ruffled by Laura, Sam, Sonny, Tania, Jane, or Dan and they called you, would you feel like extending yourself for them? Probably not. The memory of their ragged dealing would still smart.

Whereas if you heard from Barry, Joe, Jimmi, Steve, Tim, or Gloria, happy memories of your exchange would flood over you. You'd want to do whatever you could for them.

Multiply your response by many thousands. As we said in the introduction, nobody gets to the top alone. Over the years, the smooth moves of these Big Winners have captured the hearts and conquered the minds of hundreds of people who helped boost them rung by rung to the top of whatever ladder they chose.

How does one become an instinctive smooth mover rather than a ragged rider through life? The answer became blindingly clear one snowy day last winter. Lumbering along a neatly groomed track on cross-country skis, I spotted a Nordic skier swiftly striding toward me in the same trail. I didn't need to observe his high kick or his snazzy diagonal poling to let me know I was obstructing the path of a pro.

While mustering the energy to lug my throbbing legs out of the track so Super Skier could soar past, he deftly sidestepped out of the groove, leaving the groomed trail all for me. As he whizzed toward me, he slowed slightly, smiled, nodded, and said, "Good morning, beautiful day for skiing, isn't it?"

I appreciated his deference (and insinuation that we were equals on the snow!). I knew he was not thinking "Hey look at me. Here I am!" but "Ahh, there you are. Let me make room for you."

As I implied in the opening words of this book, the difference in the life success between those two types of thinkers is incalculable.

Why was Super Skier able to pull off his move so gracefully? Was he born with the skill? No. His was a deliberate move that grew out of practice.

Practice is also the fountainhead of all smooth communications moves. Excellence is not a single and solitary action. It is the outcome of many years of making small smooth moves, tiny ones like the 92 little tricks we've explored in *Talking the Winner's Way*. These moves create your destiny.

Remember, repeating an *action* makes a *habit*.

Your *habits* create your *character*.

And your *character* is your *destiny*.

May success be your destiny.

# Notes

1. Ekman, Paul. 1985. *Telling Lies: Clues to Deceit in the Marketplace, Politics, and Marriage*. New York: W. W. Norton Co., Inc.

2. Cheng, Sha, et al. 1990. "Effects of Personality Type on Stress Response." *Acta-Psychologica-Sinica* 22(2):197–204.

3. Carnegie, Dale. 1936. *How to Win Friends and Influence People*. New York: Simon & Schuster.

4. Goleman, Daniel. 1989. "Brain's Design Emerges as a Key to Emotions," quoting Dr. Joseph LeDoux, psychologist at Center for Neural Science at New York University. *New York Times*, August 15.

5. Kellerman, Joan, et al. 1989. "Looking and Loving: The Effects of Mutual Gaze on Feelings of Romantic Love." Conducted at the Agoraphobia Treatment & Research Center of New England. *Journal of Research in Personality* 23(2):145–161.

6. Argyle, Michael. 1967. *The Psychology of Interpersonal Behavior*. Baltimore: Pelican Publications.

7. Wellens, A. Rodney. 1987. "Heart-Rate Changes in Response to Shifts in Interpersonal Gaze from Liked and Disliked Others." *Perceptual and Motor Skills* 64(2):595–598.

8. *Ibid.*

9. Zig Ziglar, motivational teacher and author of the best-selling books *See You at the Top*, *Secrets of Closing the Sale*, *Over the Top*, and *Something to Smile About*.

10. Curtis, Rebecca C., and Miller, Kim. 1986. "Believing Another Likes or Dislikes You: Behaviors Making the Beliefs Come True." *Journal of Personality and Social Psychology* 51(2):284–290.

11. Hayakawa, S. I. 1941. *Language in Thought and Action.* New York: Harcourt Brace Jovanovich.

12. Aronson, E., et al. 1966. "The Effect of a Pratfall on Increasing Interpersonal Attractiveness." *Psychonomic Science* 4:227–228.

13. Carnegie Foundation for the Advancement of Teaching and Carnegie Institute of Technology studies in the 1930s showing that 85 percent of one's financial success, even in technical fields such as engineering, is due to communications skills.

14. U.S. Census Bureau of Hiring, Training, and Management Practices conducted a survey of 3,000 employers nationwide. The preferred qualities in job candidates were, rated in order of importance, attitude, communications skills, previous work experience, recommendations from current employer, recommendations from previous employer, industry-based credentials, years of schooling completed, score on interview tests, academic performance (grades), reputation of applicant's school, teacher recommendations.

15. Walsh, Debra G., and Hewitt, Jay. 1985. "Giving Men the Come-on: Effect of Eye Contact and Smiling in a Bar Environment." *Perceptual and Motor Skills* 61(3, Part 1): 873–874.

16. Walters, Lilly. 1995. *What to Say When You're Dying on the Platform*. New York: McGraw-Hill

17. Axtell, Roger. 1994. *Do's and Taboos Around the World*. New York: John Wiley & Sons, Inc.

18. Bosrock, Mary. 1997. *Put Your Best Foot Forward* series. Minneapolis: International Education Systems.

19. Nwanna, Gladson. 1998. *Do's and Don'ts Around the World* series. Baltimore: World Travel Institute.

20. Byrne, Donn, et al. 1970. "Continuity Between the Experimental Study of Attraction and Real-Life Computer Dating." *Journal of Personality and Social Psychology* 1:157–165.

21. Fast, Julius. 1970. *Body Language*. New York: Simon & Schuster.

22. Fast, Julius. 1991. *Subtext: Making Body Language Work in the Workplace*. New York: Viking.

23. Lewis, David. 1989. *The Secret Language of Success*. New York: Carroll & Graf Publishers Inc.

24. Nierenberg, Gerard, and Caliero, Henry. 1993. *How to Read a Person Like a Book*. New York: Barnes & Noble Books.

25. Pease, Allan. 1981. *Signals: How to Use Body Language for Power, Success and Love*. New York: Bantam Books.

26. Sannito, Thomas, and McGovern, Peter J., 1985. *Courtroom Psychology for Trial Lawyers*. New York: John Wiley & Sons, Inc.

 # Select Bibliography

Books

Alessandra, Tony, and Michael J. O'Connor. *The Platinum Rule*. New York: Warner Books, Inc., 1996.

Apte, Mahadev. *Humor and Laughter: An Anthropological Approach*. Ithaca, N.Y.: Cornell University Press, 1985.

Argyle, Michael. *The Psychology of Interpersonal Behavior*. Baltimore: Pelican Publications, 1967.

Bandler, Richard, and John Grinder. *Frogs into Princes: Neurolinguistic Programming*. Moab, Utah: Real People Press, 1979.

Bellack, L., and S. Baker. *Reading Faces*. New York: Holt, Rinehart and Winston, 1981.

Berscheid, E., and E. H. Walster. *Interpersonal Attraction*. 2nd ed. Reading, Mass.: Addison-Wesley, 1978.

Bolton, Robert. *People Skills*. New York: Simon & Schuster, Inc., 1979.

Booher, Dianna. *Communicate with Confidence!* New York: McGraw-Hill, 1994.

Brooks, Michael. *Instant Rapport*. New York: Warner Books, 1989.

Brown, Les. *It's Not Over Until You Win!* New York: Simon & Schuster, 1997.

Burg, Bob. *Endless Referrals*. New York: McGraw-Hill, 1994.

Carnegie, Dale. *How to Win Friends and Influence People*. New York: Simon and Schuster, 1936.

Cundiff, Merlyn. *Kinesics: The Power of Silent Command*. New York: Parker Publishing Co., 1972.

Ekman, Paul. *Telling Lies: Clues to Deceit in the Marketplace, Politics, and Marriage*. New York: W. W. Norton Co., 1985.

Erickson, M. H., et al. *Hypnotic Realities*. New York: John Wiley & Sons, Inc., 1976.

Evatt, Chris. *He & She: 60 Significant Differences Between Men and Women*. Berkeley, Calif.: Conari Press, 1992.

Farber, Barry. *Making People Talk*. New York: William Morrow and Co., Inc., 1987.

Fast, Julius. *Body Language*. New York: Simon & Schuster, 1970.

Fiedler, F. *A Theory of Leadership Effectiveness*. New York: McGraw-Hill, 1967.

Friedman, Nancy J. *Telephone Skills from A to Z*. Menlo Park, Calif.: Crisp Publications, 1995.

Gabor, Don. *How to Start a Conversation and Make Friends.* New York: Fireside, 1983.

Glass, Lillian. *He Says, She Says.* New York: G. P. Putnam's Sons, 1992.

Goffman, E. *The Presentation of Self in Everyday Life.* New York: Doubleday, 1959.

Gray, John. *Men Are from Mars, Women Are from Venus.* New York: Harper Collins Publishers, 1992.

Hayakawa, S. I. *Language in Thought and Action.* New York: Harcourt Brace Jovanovich, 1941.

Hess, Eckhard. *The Tell-Tale Eye.* New York: Van Nostrand Reinhold, 1975.

Lavington, Camille. *You've Only Got Three Seconds.* New York: Doubleday, 1997.

LeBoeuf, Michael. *How to Win Customers and Keep Them for Life.* New York: The Berkley Publishing Group, 1987.

Lewis, David. *The Secret Language of Success.* New York: Carroll & Graf Publishers, Inc., 1993.

Lowndes, Leil. *How to Make Anyone Fall in Love with You.* Chicago: Contemporary Books, 1996.

Lowndes, Leil. *How to Talk to Anybody About Anything.* New York: Citadel, 1993, revised 1996.

Lowndes, Leil. *Shopping the Insider's Way.* New York: Citadel, 1985.

Mackay, Harvey. *Dig Your Well Before You're Thirsty*. New York: Doubleday, 1997.

Mackay, Harvey. *Swim with the Sharks Without Being Eaten Alive*. New York: Fawcett Columbine, 1988.

Martinet, Jeanne. *The Art of Mingling*. New York: St. Martin's Press, 1992.

Mehrabian, A. *Nonverbal Communications*. Chicago: Aldine, 1972.

Meyer, Paul J. *The Art of Creative Listening*. Waco, Tex.: Paul J. Meyer, 1980.

Michael, Gary. *It Gives Me Great Pleasure*. New York: Citadel, 1996.

Morris, Desmond. *The Naked Ape*. New York: McGraw Hill, 1967.

Nierenberg, Gerard, and Henry Callero. *Meta-Talk: Guide to Hidden Meanings in Conversations*. New York: Trident Press, 1973.

O'Barr, W., and B. K. Atkins. "Women's Language or Powerless Language?" in *Women and Language in Literature and Society*. New York: Prager, 1981.

Pease, Allan. *Signals: How to Use Body Language for Power, Success and Love*. New York: Bantam Books, 1981.

Perper, Timothy. *Sex Signals: The Biology of Love*. Philadelphia: ISI Press, 1985.

Qubein, Nido. *How to Be a Great Communicator*. New York: John Wiley & Sons, Inc., 1996.

Rabin, Susan. *How to Attract Anyone, Anytime, Anyplace.* New York: Penguin Books, 1993.

Rackham, Neil. *Spin Selling.* New York: McGraw-Hill, 1988.

Richardson, Linda. *Stop Telling, Start Selling.* New York: McGraw-Hill, 1994.

Roane, Susan. *How to Work a Room.* New York: Warner Books, 1989.

Sannito, Thomas, and Peter J. McGovern. *Courtroom Psychology for Trial Lawyers.* New York: John Wiley & Sons, Inc., 1985.

Slutsky, Jeff, and Michael An. *The Toastmaster's International Guide to Successful Speaking.* Chicago: Dearborn, 1997.

Tannen, Deborah. *Conversational Style: Analyzing Talk Among Friends.* Norwood, N.J.: Ablex, 1984.

Tannen, Deborah. *You Just Don't Understand.* New York: William Morrow and Co., 1990.

Thibaut, J. W., and H. H. Kelley. *The Social Psychology of Groups.* New York: John Wiley & Sons, Inc., 1959.

Walters, Barbara. *How to Talk to Practically Anybody About Practically Anything.* New York: Doubleday, 1970.

Walters, Lilly. *What to Say When You're Dying on the Platform.* New York: McGraw-Hill, 1995.

Ziglar, Zig. *Ziglar on Selling.* New York: Ballantine Books, 1991.

Zimmerman, Don H., and Candace West. "Sex Roles, Interruptions and Silences in Conversation." *Language and Sex: Difference and Dominance*, 105–129. Edited by Barrie Thorne and Nancy Henley. Rowley, Mass.: Newbury House, 1975.

Studies, Papers, Commentary in Professional Journals

Adger, Carolyn. "Empowering Talk: African-American Teachers and Classroom Discourse." Paper presented at the 1993 annual meeting of the American Education Research Association, Atlanta, 1993.

Anderson, N. H. "Ratings of Likableness, Meaningfulness, and Likableness Variances for 555 Common Personality Traits Arranged in Order of Decreasing Likableness." *Journal of Personality and Social Psychology*, 1968, 9:272–279.

Aronson, E., et al. "The Effect of a Pratfall on Increasing Interpersonal Attractiveness," *Psychonomic Science*, 1966, 4:227–228.

Backman, C. W., and P. F. Secord. "The Effect of Perceived Liking on Interpersonal Attraction." *Human Relations*, 1959, 12:379–384.

Bem, D. J. "Self Perception Theory." *Advances in Experimental Social Psychology*, 1972, 6:1–62.

Bennett, Adrian. "Interruptions and the Interpretation of Conversation." *Discourse Processes*, 1981, 4/2:181–188.

Brown, Roger, and Albert Gilman. "The Pronouns of Power and Solidarity." *Style in Language*, 1960. Edited by Thomas Sebeok. Cambridge, Mass.: MIT Press.

Byrne, D., and D. Nelson. "Attraction as Linear Function of Proportion of Positive Reinforcements." *Journal of Personality and Social Psychology*, 1965, 1:659–663.

Cheng, Sha, et al. "Effects of Personality Type on Stress Response." *Acta-Psychologica-Sinica*, 1990, 22(2): 197–204.

Cook, Mark. "Gaze and Mutual Gaze in Social Encounters." *American Scientist*, 1977, 65:328–333.

Costanzo, F. S., et al. "Voice Quality Profile and Perceived Emotion." *Journal of Counseling Psychology*, 1969, 16:27–30.

Curtis, Rebecca C., and Kim Miller. "Believing Another Likes or Dislikes You: Behaviors Making the Beliefs Come True." *Journal of Personality and Social Psychology*, 1986, 51(2):284–290.

Day, M. E. "Eye Movement Phenomenon Relating to Attention, Thought, and Anxiety." *Perceptual and Motor Skills*, 1964, 19:443–446.

Dion, K., et al. "What Is Beautiful Is Good." *Journal of Personality and Social Psychology*, 1972, 24:285–290.

Eckman, P., and W. Freisen. "Detecting Deception from the Body or Face." *Journal of Personality and Social Psychology*, 1974, 29(3):294.

Eckman, P., and W. Freisen. "Nonverbal Leakage and Clues to Deceptions." *Psychiatry*, 1969, 32:99.

Efran, J. "Looking for Approval Effects on Visual Behavior of Approbation from Persons Differing in Importance." *Journal of Personality and Social Psychology*, 1968, 10:21–25.

Efran, M. G. "The Effect of Physical Appearance on the Judgment of Guilt, Interpersonal Attraction, and Severity of Recommended Punishment in a Simulated Jury Task." *Journal of Personality*, 1974, 8:45–54.

Goguen, J. A., and C. Linde. "Linguistic Methodology for the Analysis of Aviation Accidents." Report by the National Aeronautics and Space Administration Scientific and Technical Information Branch, 1983.

Griffitt, W., and R. Veitch. "Hot and Crowded: Influence of Population Density and Temperature on Interpersonal Affective Behavior." *Journal of Personality and Social Psychology*, 1971, 17:92–98.

Griffitt, W., and T. Jackson. "The Influence of Ability and Nonability Information on Personnel Selection Decisions." *Psychological Reports*, 1970, 27:959–962.

Haase, R.,and D. Tepper. "Nonverbal Components of Empathetic Communication." *Journal of Counseling Psychology*, 1972, 19:417–424.

Kellerman, Joan, et al. "Looking and Loving: The Effects of Mutual Gaze on Feelings of Romantic Love." Conducted at the Agoraphobia Treatment & Research Center of New England. *Journal of Research in Personality*, 1989, 23(2):145–161.

Kleinke, C., et al. "Effects of Gaze, Touch and Use of Name on Evaluations of Engaged Couples." *Journal of Research in Personality*, 1972, 7:368–373.

Major, Brenda, et al. "Physical Attractiveness and Self Esteem: Attributions for Praise from an Other Sex Evaluator." *Personality and Social Psychology Bulletin*, 1984, 10(1):43–50.

Maslow, A. H., and N. L. Mintz. "Effects of Aesthetic Surroundings." *Journal of Psychology*, 1956, 41:247–254.

Richards, J. Heuer, Jr. "Cognitive Factors in Deception and Counter Deception." *Strategic Military Deception*, 1982. Edited by Donald C. Daniel and Katherine L. Herbig. New York: Pergamon Press.

Secord, Paul F. "Facial Features and Inference Processes in Interpersonal Perception." *Personal Perception and Interpersonal Behavior*, 1958. Edited by R. Taguiri and L. Petrullo. Stanford: Stanford University Press.

Stodgill, R. "Personal Factors Associated with Leadership: A Survey of the Literature." *Journal of Psychology*, 1948, 25:35–71.

Walsh, Debra G., and Jay Hewitt. "Giving Men the Come-on: Effect of Eye Contact and Smiling in a Bar Environment." *Perceptual and Motor Skills*, 1985, 61(3, Part 1): 873–874.

Wellens, A. Rodney. "Heart-Rate Changes in Response to Shifts in Interpersonal Gaze from Liked and Disliked Others." *Perceptual and Motor Skills*, 1987, 64(2):595–598.

Articles, Audiotapes, and Newsletters

Bakin, P. "The Eyes Have It." *Psychology Today*, April 1971, 67.

Communication Briefings newsletter. Alexandria, Va.: Capitol Publications, Inc.

Eckman, P. "The Universal Smile, Face Muscles Talk Every Language." *Psychology Today*, September 1975.

Goleman, Daniel. "Brain's Design Emerges as a Key to Emotions," quoting Dr. Joseph LeDoux, psychologist at Center for Neural Science at New York University. *New York Times*, August 15, 1989.

Goleman, Daniel. "People Who Read People." *Psychology Today*, July 1979, 66–78.

Hess, Eckhard. "The Role of Pupil Size in Communication." *Scientific American*, 1965, 233:110–119.

Lowndes, Leil. *Conversation Confidence*. Audiocassettes. San Clemente, Calif.: Verbal Advantage, 1996.

Mackey, Terry W. "Jury Selection: Developing the Third Eye." *Trial*, October 1980, 22–25.

Sacks, Harvey, et al. "A Simplest Systematics for the Organization of Turntaking for Conversation." *Language*, 1974, 50/4:696–735.

Schulman, J., et al. "Recipe for a Jury." *Psychology Today*, 1963, 6:37–44.

Tracy, Brian. *The Psychology of Selling*. Audiotapes. Niles, Ill.: Nightingale-Conant Corporation.

Wetzel, Patricia. "Are Powerless Communications Strategies the Japanese Norm?" *Language in Society*, 1988, 17:555–564.

Zorn, E. "Here's Looking at You: Is Your Face a True Personality Profile?" *Chicago Tribune*, May 13, 1981, 18.

About the Author

LEIL LOWNDES IS an internationally acclaimed communications expert who coaches top executives of Fortune 500 companies as well as frontline employees to become more effective communicators. She has spoken in practically every major U.S. city and conducts communications seminars for the U.S. Peace Corps, foreign governments, and major corporations. In addition to engrossing audiences on hundreds of TV and radio shows, her work has been acclaimed by the *New York Times*, the *Chicago Tribune*, and *Time* magazine. Her articles have appeared in professional journals and popular publications such as *Redbook*, *New Woman*, *Psychology Today*, *Penthouse*, and *Cosmopolitan*. Based in New York City, she is the author of four books including the top-selling *How to Talk to Anybody About Anything* and *How to Make Anyone Fall in Love with You.*

If you come across any little tricks of Big Winners in your life, share them with Leil—so she can share them with others, credited in her next book, of course, to you.

Leil's mailing address is Applause, Inc., 127 Grand Street, New York, NY 10013.

Or e-mail her at leil@lowndes.com

Leil's website address is http://www.lowndes.com